No Child is Ineducable

SPECIAL EDUCATION — PROVISION AND TRENDS

The future of mentally handicapped children depends on the action of aroused and dedicated citizens. The only question will be, who offered hope and encouragement in their darkest hour, and who will be regarded as a stranger.

EUNICE K. SHRIVER   (1964)

Frontispiece. Help for the word-blind. A centre for dyslexic children provided by the Invalid Children's Aid Association.

No Child is Ineducable

SPECIAL EDUCATION — PROVISION AND TRENDS

BY

S. S. SEGAL

Headmaster, Franklin Delano Roosevelt School, London

PERGAMON PRESS

OXFORD · LONDON · EDINBURGH · NEW YORK
TORONTO · SYDNEY · PARIS · BRAUNSCHWEIG

Pergamon Press Ltd., Headington Hill Hall, Oxford
4 & 5 Fitzroy Square, London W.1

Pergamon Press (Scotland) Ltd., 2 & 3 Teviot Place, Edinburgh 1

Pergamon Press Inc., 44–01 21st Street, Long Island City, New York 11101

Pergamon of Canada, Ltd., 6 Adelaide Street East, Toronto, Ontario

Pergamon Press (Aust.) Pty. Ltd., 20–22 Margaret Street, Sydney,
New South Wales

Pergamon Press S.A.R.L., 24 rue des Écoles, Paris 5ᵉ

Vieweg & Sohn GmbH, Burgplatz 1, Braunschweig

Printed in Great Britain by A. Wheaton & Co. Ltd., Exeter and London

A000005710830

Contents

Acknowledgements

THE organizations and individuals to whom the author is most indebted will be apparent from the content. To all who readily helped to make this book as useful as possible I express the hope that they will feel that its publication has merited their assistance.

In particular I must express my deep appreciation of the assistance provided by Mrs. T. Appleby (Spastic Society), Dr. Gunnar Dybwad and Dr. Rosemary Dybwad, the Rev. D. H. Denney, the members of the Council of the Guild of Teachers of Backward Children, Mr. George Ball, Dr. A. Kushlick, Mr. J. Lumsden, Dr. N. O'Connor, Dr. M. K. Pringle, Professor J. Tizard, Dr. W. D. Wall, and Mr. F. H. Pedley.

The author is particularly indebted to Mrs. B. Vernon, J.P., who prompted the writing of the book.

The book owes a great deal to the Editor of *Educational Research* and other publications which have provided source material. It is hoped that many readers will want to consult the original books which are listed in the Bibliography (pp. 307).

Finally, The Inner London Education Authority accepts no responsibility for the author's opinions and conclusions.

Introduction

THE building of the welfare state was accompanied by a new humanity in our approach towards handicapped children. Not only the needs of the children but also the plight of their parents came under review. If there was as yet no question of *equality of opportunity* there was at least a move towards *equality of consideration*. And in 146 different local education authorities new experiments were begun, creating an uneven pattern of opportunities for physically, mentally, emotionally, and socially handicapped children.

What provision now exists? What are the trends? This book is an effort to provide an introduction to special educational developments in England and Wales.

To help provide a broader framework within which to assess trends and possibilities, references are made to some developments in other countries. Due to the overriding importance attached everywhere to learning handicaps, it has been necessary to describe in some detail some of the research on mental handicaps, the causes of the changing attitudes towards the intelligence quotient, and the efforts to provide forms of differential diagnosis which will help guide differential treatment.

Nevertheless, the author has throughout kept in mind as possible readers intelligent parents who seek educational advances, as well as students and colleagues professionally interested in this area from a medical, educational, social, vocational, or allied viewpoint.

It is because adults have proved capable of changing their attitudes that there is a greater awareness today that "no child is ineducable". Our local authorities reflect our changing attitudes —and in some cases have proved able to do far more than was foreseen by pre-war pioneers.

This book is intended not only as a tribute to those courageous parents, voluntary organizations, outstanding educationists, psychologists, psychiatrists, paediatricians, social workers, and allied colleagues whose work has helped to generate a new optimism about the educability of the entire population, but as a stimulus to further effort.

London, 1966   S. S. SEGAL

PART I

The Theory and Provision

CHAPTER 1

The 1944 Education Act

What a wise and good parent desires for his own child, we, as a state, should desire for all our children.

(TAWNEY.)

THE 1944 Education Act was shaped at a time when the whole nation was aware, more than ever before, of fundamental human values. A determination to provide children with equal educational opportunities helped to underline the inequalities occasioned by social, physical, and intellectual handicaps. Whilst the straitjacket of history constricted certain areas, hiding from the nation, for example, those children who were excluded from our schools, the handicapped children within the school system were given fresh consideration.

For the first time it became the direct responsibility of each of our local education authorities (at that time 146 in number) to ascertain which children over the age of 2 years required *special* educational treatment. Compared with the five categories of handicap recognized before the war, ten were now defined for whom the local authorities were required by law to make provision. These categories are given below as stated in the Handicapped Pupils' and Special Schools Regulations, 1959, and Amending Regulations, 1962. In addition to children with physical and sensory handicaps, the categories extend to children handicapped emotionally as well as to children who are educationally subnormal for whatever reason. Of all these important developments the concept of educational subnormality was the most significant and has relevance to all the kinds and degrees of handicap now recognized.

3

The form that special education was intended to take was flexible except that pupils with certain handicaps (e.g. those who were blind or deaf) had to be educated in special schools unless the Minister of Education* otherwise approved. For children with other handicaps, special educational treatment could be given in either special schools or ordinary schools. And implicit in the whole concept of special educational treatment were special facilities, suitable programmes, and specially selected and trained teachers able to make the best use of the new opportunities.

Categories

1. *Educationally subnormal pupils*

   "Pupils who by reason of limited ability or other conditions resulting in educational retardation, require some specialized form of education wholly or partly in substitution for the education normally given in ordinary schools."

2. *Maladjusted pupils*

   "Pupils who show evidence of emotional instability or psychological disturbance and require special educational treatment in order to effect their personal, social or educational readjustment."

3. *Epileptic pupils*

   "Pupils who by reason of epilepsy cannot be educated under the normal regime of ordinary schools without detriment to themselves or other pupils."

4. *Blind pupils*

   "Pupils who have no sight or whose sight is or is likely to become so defective that they require education by methods not involving the use of sight."

5. *Partially sighted pupils*

   "Pupils who by reason of defective vision cannot follow the normal regime of ordinary schools without detriment to their

* Now the Secretary of State for Education and Science.

sight or to their educational development, but can be educated by special methods involving the use of sight."

6. *Deaf pupils*
"Pupils with impaired hearing who require education by methods suitable for pupils with little or no naturally acquired speech or language."

7. *Partially hearing pupils*
"Pupils with impaired hearing whose development of speech and language even if retarded is following a normal pattern and who require for their education special arrangements or facilities though not necessarily all the educational methods used for deaf pupils."

8. *Physically handicapped pupils*
"Pupils not suffering solely from a defect of sight or hearing who by reason of disease or crippling defect cannot, without detriment to their health or educational development, be satisfactorily educated under the normal regime of ordinary schools."

9. *Delicate pupils*
"Pupils not falling under any other category in this regulation, who by reason of impaired physical condition need a change of environment or cannot, without risk to their health or educational development, be educated under the normal regime of ordinary schools."

10. *Pupils suffering from speech defects*
"Pupils who on account of stammering, aphasia, or defect of voice or articulation not due to deafness, require special educational treatment."

Excluded Children

If the 1944 Education Act failed to include "ineducable" children, the new climate gave desperate parents new energy.

Amongst these were a few who in 1952 founded the Spastics Society, countering the assumption that the majority of children suffering from cerebral palsy were mentally defective. And 6 years before this, one far-sighted mother—after working for 2 years with a pioneering voluntary organization, the National Association for Mental Health—called upon other mothers of mentally handicapped children to join her and founded a National Association of Parents of Backward Children (1946). Parents, and notably mothers, now at last had their own organization. It erupted into the light, giving inspiration and emotional release to thousands of unfortunate parents throughout the country.

Enlisting the support of interested specialists, this parents' organization was able to organize a significant national conference in 1950 at the Fountain Hospital, where the need for a Royal Commission on Mental Illness and Mental Defect was pressed.

Though it gestated until 1959, a widely approved Mental Health Act was finally slapped into life, and from a statutory point of view at least, mentally handicapped children and their parents were no longer stateless.

The concept "ineducable", long under critical review, was supplanted by "unsuitable for school". "Trainable" children were no longer to be ignored or left as a full-time responsibility to their hard-pressed parents. Local health authorities, if not yet duty-bound to build sufficient training centres, were given permissive powers to provide them. And instead of having to compete for the few available places in the former "occupation centres", attendance at training centres was on the way to becoming a right rather than a privilege.

The "Unsuitable for School"

But now the separation of the training centres from the education system was increasingly seen as an obstacle to progress. This was underlined when some modest proposals, which even if carried out in their entirety would still have left the centres far behind the schools, were viewed as unrealistic by some administrators and medical colleagues.

The Minister of Health's Standing Mental Health Advisory Committee (1959) appointed a sub-committee under the chairmanship of Dr. Scott (LCC, MOH), to consider "the training of staff in the centres and the numbers required". An attempt to shelve this report met widespread opposition. After some delay and controversy a compromise was reached. Voluntary efforts, along with some of the Scott Committee's major recommendations, began to influence important developments.

The major recommendations were:

(a) that 2-year courses for teachers of the mentally handicapped should be established (this at a time when only a small fraction of the staff of training centres had been given the opportunity for even a 1-year course of training);

(b) that university institutes of education should be encouraged to provide 1-year courses for Burnham teachers (i.e. for teachers recognized by the Ministry of Education as qualified teachers) who wished to enter this work;

(c) that a Central Training Council be established to supervise the training of teachers in this particular field on a national basis;

(d) that this Central Training Council should consider the introduction of a specially designed experimental course lasting 3 years for unqualified staff in a teacher-training college;

(e) that the minimum standards of entry to training courses should be at the GCE O-level with not less than three passes;

(f) that the ratio of teaching staff to pupils in junior centres should be of the order 1 to 10;

(g) that authorities and staff should be made aware of the need for educational and psychological research on mental subnormality.

Whilst local health authorities retained responsibility (or were squarely given responsibility) for mentally handicapped children, this responsibility was no longer felt to exclude educational experiments. The training centres not only increased in numbers at rapid rate, but perceptibly began to move closer to the school. Professional organizations of teachers, too, began to show interest in this area and in the staff of such centres.

Today "special education", for practical as well as theoretical reasons, cannot be discussed comprehensively without reference to the role of training centres and to the educability of children designated as *severely subnormal*.

Similarly, "throughout the whole range of categories of handicapped children", as the National Union of Teachers pointed out in 1960, "the basic educational problem is that of the slow learner, whether the slowness is of physical, mental or emotional origin or a combination of these factors".

Educational subnormality and mental subnormality accordingly occupy a major section of this book.

Modern Handicaps

With compulsory education, a range of sensory, physical, and mental defects were observed along with a new consequence or handicap, *scholastic backwardness*. With increasing demands upon the skills and intelligence of average citizens, new shades of disability or inefficiency were recognized if not created. Similarly, accompanying material and social developments, new shades or kinds of delinquency became apparent. Backwardness and delinquency seemed to be highly correlated. Special education was seen increasingly to have some bearing upon these areas, too. Those who, for various reasons, could not or would not ignore the problem, began to consider in greater detail the needs, care, and education of unsuccessful scholars in ordinary schools.

Today it may seem an academic exercise to unravel the dominant influences responsible for our current range of attitudes towards "the backward". Religion? Humanism? Democracy?

Economics? Concern for property and alarm at the increase in delinquent attitudes?

In an increasingly humane society, certain "traditional" attitudes conflict increasingly with stated religious beliefs, with declared humanism, with proclaimed concepts of democracy, and with economic interests. Change, or the need for change, is not everywhere acknowledged. Old prejudices or philosophies still rise up determinedly, like Victorian school buildings, to assert their presence beside the most modern of architecture. Yet this analogy carries with it a caution. An old Victorian building can house a living centre of education, just as a modern structure may veneer an outmoded practice or depressing institution. Every society is as complex as its members.

The Perspective of this Book

Future generations will see our weaknesses as keenly as we can see the weaknesses of preceding generations. Can we anticipate what they will seize upon? Our educators, administrators, and institutions reflect our aspirations—our differences as well as agreement. Our schools and our teachers are our responsibility as well as our creation. If they are not everywhere ahead of the times they are unquestionably a part of the times.

Do none of us lose sight of the concept "children" when we refer to some as "average", or "above average", or "below average"?

Need any of us express surprise that parents of mentally handicapped children were for a long time alone in advancing the claim "no child is ineducable"?

Our estimates for future provision vary as widely as the current provision we make, our scientific achievements, and our beliefs. "Special Education" is at one and the same time the child of today and the offspring of different philosophies. Current trends or controversies have made questions of the following kind typical and insistent—even to the point of being confused with each other. If these questions have relevance to all handicapped children within our school system, they usually show no awareness of "the severely subnormal" or of the children excluded from our schools.

1. Are special schools necessary?
2. Can we afford them?
3. All in all, is it worthwhile making such provision; are not we being a bit sentimental rather than practical?
4. Is it right to segregate children in special schools? (This question is sometimes blurred with—as though an extension of—5 below.)
5. Is streaming in our schools right or wrong?

For this book "to stream or not to stream" is not the question. Instead we begin with a "snap-shot" of the special provision made by one local education authority. We shall then consider how and why and even what special educational provision has arisen nationally; what it has displaced; what it has sought to do and how effective it has been.

With some grasp of the circumstances in which existing forms of provision arose, we may be able the better to understand and see in perspective and some depth (a) what is being done, (b) the facilities available, (c) the theories or assumptions guiding us, and (d) the changes that are necessary and possible. Here science may inspire as well as caution us.

In a world where different levels or stages of civilization exist side by side, it is worth recalling that what is progressive in one country or at one stage of development can be an obstacle to progress in another country or at a later stage.

If to guide a handicapped child intelligently we first make some kind of "case study", to understand "special education" developmentally a "case study", however limited, may assist.

But first it is helpful to look at the current range of provision within a good local authority.

CHAPTER 2

The Range of Provision

... The causes of educational retardation start early, sometimes before birth, sometimes at birth, anyway in the first year. Many parents of these children know perfectly well; so do many doctors and health visitors, and if they don't know they may suspect. My thesis is that we could do a lot more for these children if help started earlier, and that we could do a lot more for these and all children if we studied these children to learn more about the learning processes.

(DR. SIMON YUDKIN, 1964.)

WHAT is the current range of educational provision available for handicapped children in a good authority? Here some account must be taken of services provided by the health as well as the education authority. Account must also be taken of the range of pre-school provision, some under health and some under education. (See Fig. 1.)

In recent years the value of registers of all infants "at risk" has been underlined. The information for such registers has been provided by midwives, by hospitals, and by general practitioners. Children "at risk" were those who, because of the parents' medical history or other reasons, might be at risk of a handicap, or who were found to have acquired a handicap. It was the responsibility of the senior medical officer to ensure that the family of such handicapped infants not only received guidance in caring for the child but that the special needs for education and leisure were planned in advance and that the child was followed up through the health visiting service.

Dr. J. Edwards, Principal Medical Officer of the Inner London Education Authority, described a recent extension to London's

11

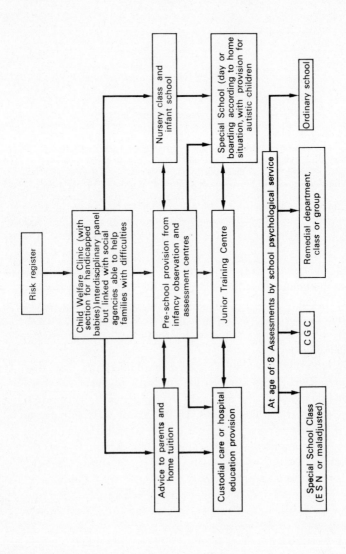

Note: Administration must make for ease of transfer at any stage

Fig. 1.

range of pre-school provision in this way (*Forward Trends*, 1965 Conference issue):

> When this particular problem was brought to the notice of the Council by the Parents' Association for the Mentally Handicapped, by Mental Welfare Officers, and others, it was decided to set up special clinics in certain Maternity and Child Welfare Premises, where children from birth to five years who were considered to be retarded could be seen by a medical officer specially experienced and interested in this type of child. A mental health social worker and a health visitor are available during the session to help. . . . Mothers of children who are obviously backward often refuse to attend ordinary sessions at Maternity and Child Welfare Clinics for reasons which can well be appreciated, but they are often pleased to attend these special sessions arranged for their special needs. . . .
>
> The first clinic was set up in Stepney in 1953, it quickly proved its need and others soon followed . . . so that now each Borough has its own clinic.

Plainly, where such clinics do not exist, handicapped infants are in danger of further retardation as a result of the failure of distressed or unhappy parents to brave the normal clinic.

Early provision today not only includes special clinics for backward babies, and special day nurseries (e.g. for infants with impaired hearing or who failed to acquire language because their parents were deaf), but screening tests for a recently discovered condition known as "phenylketonuria"—a condition easily detected and treated by diet, but if neglected carrying a risk of mental handicap.

The health authority, too, was responsible for the training centres provided for children excluded from the school system. Psychiatric care, after-care, and child guidance clinics, along with final placement in the community or in "special care" were also part of the health services.

But if we leave aside provision made by the health authority, and make no attempt at this stage to relate actual provision to required provision, what is there educationally and vocationally for physically, intellectually, or emotionally handicapped children?

The following sketch is drawn in the main from a document issued by the London County Council, an authority which ceased to exist in 1965 as a result of reorganization of boundaries.

This authority had exercised its responsibilities for handicapped children through a Special Education Subcommittee and a Special Services Branch of the Education Office. It provided, in addition, a team of educational psychologists who were available for advice, and encouraged a range of provision within ordinary schools. "Special Education is often thought of as something that is provided only in special schools. This is quite untrue. 'Special education' is simply education that is specially adapted to meet a child's needs. If these needs can be fully met within his ordinary primary or secondary school, so much the better." (Reports on Education No. 23, 1965.)

The Obligation

Section 34 of the Education Act, 1944, required local education authorities to ascertain which children in their area needed special educational treatment, and *to make appropriate provision for them.*

Different local education authorities interpreted the first part of this obligation differently, few actually testing an entire age range in either the infant or the junior stages. London's provision (which is paralleled by that of other, often the larger, education authorities) took the following forms. It built or used:

1. Its own special day and special boarding schools, adapting old school buildings, purchasing suitable properties, and designing new purpose-built schools.
2. Hospital special schools.
3. Special boarding schools maintained by other authorities.
4. Voluntary and independent special boarding schools.
5. Individual tuition at home or in hospital.

The Curriculum, Provision, and Services for Handicapped Children

Whilst the special needs of handicapped children (including medical care and treatment) were considered, this Education

Authority sought as far as it was able to provide a basic education similar to that available in the ordinary school. Cultural activities available to the education service as a whole were shared. The children were encouraged to disregard their handicap as much as possible. They took part in physical recreation, sports, swimming, camps, educational visits, and school journeys.

For day pupils who were physically handicapped, deaf, partially deaf, or partially sighted, there was a fleet of school buses (some specially designed) to carry them to and from school. This service extended to junior pupils in schools for the delicate and the educationally subnormal. In some cases "guides" were provided for junior pupils, a service which was occasionally extended to immature pupils at the secondary stage.

Boarding schools were viewed as

> a necessary part of the general provision for handicapped children for a number of reasons. Blind children, for instance, are few in number and their attendance at a boarding school prevents long and tiring journeys. Boarding schools provide long or short term care for children who need convalescence or special care because they are delicate. Some severely physically handicapped children whose parents are unable to look after them, or are overseas or have special difficulties such as poor housing conditions, also need residential care. Part of the treatment of maladjusted children may be removal from home. . . . Educationally subnormal children may show delinquent and disturbed behaviour which may only be contained and improved when they are away from home for a period. Others need to be placed in boarding schools because of poor home circumstances.

The Youth Employment Service, set up as a result of the Employment and Training Act, 1948, sought to place the handicapped school-leaver in suitable employment. Employers with good welfare services were selected, and medical and educational reports influenced the pupil's placement. Liaison was maintained with national and voluntary associations for the care of the handicapped, and "young people in most categories receive specialized after-care when they leave school".

Significantly, this Authority had found it necessary to review its original plans. The London School Plan, designed in 1947, had not anticipated the "considerable variations in the incidence

of handicap due mainly to social and medical advances". Views
had also changed on

> the desirability of educating in normal schools children with a moderate
> degree of handicap. Many children, it is now considered, are properly
> placed in schools for normal children provided that there are arrange-
> ments for special help. On the other hand some difficult and disturbed
> or retarded children make much better progress in small special schools,
> where previously they might have remained in schools for normal children.

The Principles Underlying Provision

Certain broad principles underlie all the special provision made
by London. Briefly, whatever the nature of the handicap or its
degree of severity, the child was first and foremost like all other
children in his or her need for security, personal affection, and
opportunity to develop capacities. The greater the disability, the
greater were the skill and determination needed to help the child.
"The results of success are seen in part in the very high percentage
of handicapped children today who obtain and keep work of
value to the community and of interest to themselves." The
Authority also noted that the quality of staff was "perhaps
the most important single element in making education a
success".

The Educationally Subnormal

Pupils who were ESN formed the largest of all the categories of
handicapped children. It was policy to educate the majority of
backward pupils in ordinary schools. But there was an estimated
"one per cent of the school population whose degree of backwardness is such that education in special schools is advisable".
Remedial departments and special classes in ordinary schools,
coupled with the growing interest taken by teachers in the
problems of backwardness, had helped "to blur the rigid distinction once made between work for very dull children in special
schools and remedial help in ordinary schools".

A number of purpose-built special schools were in use, each accepting pupils from the age of 5 and covering the entire age range to 16 and including both sexes. The number of pupils in each ranged from 160 to 200. The least able of these pupils, like the youngest, were usually placed in classes smaller than the prescribed maximum of 20.

Whilst the trend in the new schools was towards "all-age" special schools for both sexes, other patterns were included in the older buildings. Amongst these were separate secondary special schools for boys, separate secondary special schools for girls, and all-age schools from which boys were transferred on reaching secondary age.

Where children were "of doubtful educability" they were given "a trial period in a special school before the final decision was made". If found "unsuitable for school" they became the responsibility of the medical officer of health who had to provide them with "suitable training".

Within the schools, the youngest entrants were placed in a nursery class type of organization. They were encouraged to mix, to play, and to speak intelligibly. Guided, practical experiences introduced them to applied basic skills, and many of these pupils were able—on leaving school—to enjoy reading, show competence in some handicrafts, and prove ready for employment. "Opportunities for fun and enjoyment and for countless small successes", throughout their schooling, "markedly increased the will to learn." The children were also reported as growing and developing rapidly to weights and heights comparable to children in ordinary schools, although often smaller than normal children on entry to the schools.

The schools sought to prepare the pupils for employment by making the school work relevant, and visits, films, form-filling, mock interviews, etc., were organized. A decision as to whether the pupil required some form of after-care was made by the principal school medical officer. Youth employment officers and social workers in the Public Health Department maintained close co-operation.

The Education of the Maladjusted

It was not easy to diagnose maladjustment as such. In contrast with some handicaps, the size of this problem appeared to be "increasing rather than diminishing". Difficult children were referred to a "Problem Case Conference" which was organized in each division. The conference was attended by the district inspector, the divisional educational officer, the divisional medical officer, an educational psychologist, and the divisional school-care organizer who acted as secretary. (See reference to Care Committees on p. 27.)

Each problem case conference took place at least once a month and considered all children referred to it. If necessary the class or head teacher attended. Resulting action included reference to child guidance clinics or to social agencies, recommendations for recuperative holidays, or a request for a special examination by the principal school medical officer.

The child guidance clinic might recommend various forms of special placement, including residence in a special hostel.

A high proportion of the pupils in day schools for the maladjusted had a history of school refusal or had been excluded from school for behaviour detrimental to the welfare of other pupils.

> Thorough investigation . . . often reveals a failure of relationships within the child's home. In some cases the parents may be neglectful or incompetent. . . . In others, illness, divorce or the acquisition of step-parents produces an atmosphere of tension. In some apparently good homes the child may feel rejected and express his unhappiness by aggressive and withdrawn behaviour.

Sometimes the child guidance clinic provided regular treatment for a child who remained within the ordinary school. Some pupils remained on the roll of an ordinary school whilst attending "tutorial classes" for part of the week. Others required placement in special schools. Removal from home was a step taken "with reluctance as a result of the increasing knowledge of parent–child relationship". If the strains at home were so great as to necessitate removal, close contact would be maintained between the boarding school and the home, the child going home for holidays, the parents being encouraged to visit the school, and care committee workers or psychiatric social workers visiting the parents.

Fifty pupils were considered by London to be the maximum size for such a school. The entire atmosphere had to be therapeutic, with each pupil being accepted as he or she was, and with the aims being to effect "the personal, social and educational readjustment" of each pupil. A range of creative activities was provided to relieve tension and build up confidence. "As stability increases the discipline of heavy crafts and vocational skills such as typewriting have their place in giving a sense of purpose to the curriculum." A stimulating programme was viewed as essential because of the characteristic lack of interest and persistence, and because full recovery was not possible without "progress in the basic skills and the formation of some lasting interests".

The maximum size of classes for maladjusted children was 15, but this local authority restricted the number to 10 and provided extra staffing for specialist teaching. Sometimes individual psychotherapy was provided for children who required insight into their own difficulties. There were also special units for autistic and psychotic children.

In its efforts to meet the growing need, the Authority also made use of other special schools (non-maintained) and of some independent boarding schools for normal children which were prepared to accept a few problem pupils. Such outside schools were reported upon by the Council's inspectors.

When it came to employment, particularly sympathetic employers had to be sought. The youth employment officer, care committee, psychiatric social worker, and child guidance clinic maintained close touch.

The Education of Blind Children

With the recent decrease in the total numbers of blind children, the proportion of those with other handicaps such as limited intelligence, impaired hearing, or physical disability, has increased. These children require to be taught in exceptionally small groups, and special schools for dually handicapped children have been established by the Royal National Institute for the Blind.

Whilst nursery education from the age of 2 was available through the Royal National Institute for the Blind, "residential placing at this very early age is now rare". The local authority provided a purpose-built school which took children from the age of 5 to 16. Pupils entered this school from their homes or from the nursery school. The children were taught to read and write by means of the braille system. Embossed dots were decoded by touch. Whilst the dots could be reproduced by means of a stylus guided by a metal writing frame, "this laborious method is being superseded by the use of braille writing machines with some resemblance to typewriters". "Children of marked academic ability may proceed to selective schools providing education up to standards of university entrance. Others with a technical bent may take up, from the age of 16, training in commercial subjects, music, piano tuning, telephony, brush and basket making, or capstan lathe operating."

The Authority's own school was able to provide an extended course up to the age of 18, with preparation in some cases for external examinations. The education process was directed towards enabling blind children to take their place confidently in the seeing world without fear or embarrassment. They were no longer restricted to a narrow range of occupations although "sheltered employment is still available for those in whom the handicap of blindness is aggravated by other physical and mental disabilities".

The Partially Sighted

Blindness varies in degree from total inability to see to an ability to distinguish light and dark sufficiently to be able to move about with some confidence in a building. The line of demarcation between blindness and partial sight was not always an easy one to draw. Since the 1944 Act, a substantial change was reported in the attitude towards the partially sighted and in place of "sight-saving", individual sight difficulties were more fully studied and specific teaching methods were devised to cater for individual needs.

For the first time, special schools were introduced after the war for partially sighted children aged from 5 to 16. For this local authority, "early diagnosis and remedial care helped to prevent deterioration of existing sight and the new attitude to education fostered self-reliance and the ability to participate more fully in daily life".

Methods of instruction differed from that in ordinary schools, although, as with the blind, the normal curriculum was followed as far as possible. The younger children wrote with chalk on specially prepared, self-illuminating blackboards, or with thick black crayons on large sheets of white paper. Telescopic visual aids were available. Special furniture was designed. Whilst books with suitable large type were available for younger children, teachers had to devise their own for older pupils.

If sight deteriorated, the child might have to go to a school for the blind. If sight improved, the child could go to the normal range of schools. If boarding provision was essential, the Authority utilized non-maintained schools.

The Education of the Deaf

The Authority's special schools for the deaf each had a nursery department and accepted children from the age of 2 to 12. As with the blind, all the teachers were specially trained. Residual hearing was used. The aim was to develop communication, speech, and language, "using lip reading and making full use of hearing aids".

Classes never exceeded 8. Each child had a body-worn hearing aid, and all rooms used a loop induction system which magnified sounds passing through a microphone. A group hearing-aid system was provided in all rooms other than those used by the nursery groups. To train individual children, teachers were able

B

to use small, powerful mains amplifiers. The rooms were specially treated to minimize interference, and double-glazed windows were provided where required.

At 12-plus the pupils transferred to secondary schools. Those with high academic attainments were admitted to the Mary Hare Grammar School for the Deaf, whilst boys thought suitable for technical education were admitted to Burwood Park School for the Deaf.

The Partially Hearing

This local authority found that "early ascertainment of very young children, parental guidance and pre-school training has resulted in much better use of the residual hearing that children possess".

Initially it was usual to educate the deaf and partially hearing pupils together—a practice which continued until 1950. But already in 1947 London had set up two special units for partially hearing pupils in normal schools. Pupils with serviceable hearing were separated from those whose hearing loss was so severe as to necessitate special schools. Many partially hearing children who at one time would have been placed in a special school were suitably placed in normal schools, and many children who would once have been classified as "deaf" could now be effectively treated as "partially hearing".

Part of this substantial change in pattern was due to marked advances in electronics and the production of small individual hearing aids with great powers of amplification.

Qualified teachers of the deaf and the partially hearing taught partially deaf pupils in special classes within normal primary mixed schools. The pupils were taught to use their hearing aids and lip-read. They also used group hearing-aid apparatus in specially equipped classrooms.

Some pupils proved able to return to the normal school once they could use their hearing aids and if suitably placed in the classroom. Otherwise, at the age of 11-plus they would be placed in a special unit for partially hearing pupils in a secondary school or there would be some other form of provision (e.g. a non-maintained boarding school). Where a pupil had other handicaps in addition to partial hearing, a boarding school was provided.

The Education of Delicate Children

The early schools for the delicate which were unheated and wide open to the wind once prompted teachers to joke that "delicate children required to have more stamina to survive than did normal ones". The new special schools, whilst aware of the need for fresh air and light, departed significantly from earlier practice and were similar in design to those for normal children.

Medical and nursing services were an integral part of the school life. Beds or folding chairs and blankets were provided so that rests after meals were possible. The main handicaps were defects in respiration (e.g. asthma), whilst about 1 in 4 of the pupils suffered from nutritional deficiencies. The pupils received breakfast and tea in addition to the normal midday meal provided by all schools.

The organization of the school provided a number of problems since some children remained only a short time whilst others remained their entire school lives. Irregular attendance at school or prolonged absences as a result of ill health had accentuated retardation. Whilst the maximum size of classes allowed was 30 pupils, the Authority was able to provide some additional staff for the teaching of reading, and the overall staffing ratio was 1 teacher to 21 pupils. The curriculum was the same as for ordinary schools except that fuller use was made of gardening.

It was found that a school for the delicate was not unsuitable "for carefully selected maladjusted children who find the pressures of a larger school somewhat difficult and for some who cannot face school at all".

Where pupils as a result of their handicap required to live and be taught on the same premises, they were placed in denominational or non-maintained special schools.

Education for the Diabetic

One group of children within the broad category of the delicate was the diabetic. Most of these children could be adequately treated at home under medical guidance. But some homes required help, whilst some children required treatment away from home. Children from all over the country were accommodated in a hostel provided by the Authority. These children were not only helped to understand the principles of their needs but to administer their own injections under the supervision of nurses. Parents, too, visited the hostel and received instruction in the daily care of the children to make possible an early return to the family.

Pupils from the hostel attended the normal day schools in the neighbourhood.

The Physically Handicapped

A great many children with physical handicaps were to be found in ordinary schools. Comparatively few were thought to require special schools, and London's School Plan for 1947 was reduced by two-thirds as far as special school provision for the physically handicapped was concerned.

But the type of provision was now required to be suitable for much more severely handicapped children than the 1947 plan had considered.

> A large proportion of the children are victims of cerebral palsy in one or other of its commonest forms, spasticity or atheotis, with accompanying brain damage. Consequently they often have other defects of impaired sight, hearing, or intelligence. Besides cerebral palsy, other disabilities found in the schools are post-poliomyelitis, muscular dystrophy, spina bifida, congenital deformities of limbs, haemophilia, heart conditions, and brittle bones.

The new schools were suitably planned for wheel-chairs (entering corridors and lavatories, etc.) and for physiotherapy. One school had its own hydrotherapy pool whilst the others were able to use local swimming baths.

371.9 Se37

C. 1

Some pupils were in boarding schools. These had a school vehicle so that the children could be taken on outings of various kinds. One of these schools was for pupils aged 7 to 16 who had dual or multiple handicaps (other than severe hearing loss). "Most of these dual and multiple handicapped children are severely subnormal and need to have a curriculum adapted from that used in schools for educationally subnormal children."

Lack of mobility and serious handicap made these children amongst the most difficult to teach. "Their chances of earning a living are not good in many cases and so learning to read and to enjoy simple crafts is of great importance."

Use was made of facilities offered by the Spastics Society's schools for children who seemed suitable.

Careful attention was given to the possible employment of physically handicapped school-leavers. Some pupils, however, were found to require the further training offered by the Spastics Society, or training to make articles at home, or sheltered employment of some kind.

Epileptics

Severe epileptics were placed in (non-maintained) boarding special schools for epileptics. But where dual defects included a mild degree of epilepsy, pupils would be admitted to special schools which catered for the major handicap.

Treatment for Speech Defects

Speech defects were found to range widely and to pose a growing problem. Many children with speech defects tended not only to keep away from adults but from other children too, resulting in a restriction of development. The problem was increased by delay and the Authority urged that children with poor speech should speedily "be made known to those who can assess and deal with the needs of such a child and so help integration into the general life of the community, home and school or nursery".

Clinics were held in school treatment centres, schools, maternity and child welfare centres, and occasionally in rooms in social centres. Parents, health visitors, doctors, teachers, social workers, or school nursing sisters referred the child to the service. A check would first be made to see if other disabilities, e.g. hearing loss or poor sight, had a bearing on the problem. A speech therapist was in charge of each clinic. Treatment varied as did the causes of the disability. With a child who stammered, contacts were made with the home and the school in an effort to reduce tension in the child's environment. Some children required orthodontic treatment or had cleft palates. Some children talked a great deal but were incomprehensible. Children who did not speak at all required careful diagnosis, sometimes in a hospital.

Some pupils attended a special class for part of the day and their own school for the rest of the time. Where the speech defects were severe, the children were placed in a non-maintained special school which accepted children with acute disabilities.

Education at Hospital or at Home

Where extraordinary circumstances prevented children attending a day or boarding school, local authorities have the power to provide education "otherwise than at school". In 1960 more than seventy London children were receiving individual tuition at home. Each child was examined and recommended for such treatment by the Principal School Medical Officer. Sometimes an accident or a temporary illness made only a short period of home tuition necessary. "Occasionally home tuition may be given in order to determine educability where attendance at school is inadvisable." Between these extremes a child might have dual or multiple disabilities.

The Authority also provided 6 hospital schools, 14 permanent tuition groups, and 37 teachers who worked with individual children in 35 hospitals where there was no permanent group. A teacher was provided if a child was expected to remain in the hospital for at least 3 weeks.

Nursery education from the age of 2 was provided in two of London's centres for cerebral palsied children.

Hospital tuition had not only a therapeutic role but aimed to prevent children falling too far behind their class. Pioneer work in the in-patient treatment of maladjusted children was instituted and developed at the Maudsley and Bethlem Hospital, where teachers, psychiatrists, psychologists, and psychiatric social workers co-operated in the treatment of the child.

Care Committee Services

Reference was made earlier to the Care Committee. All London schools had such committees. A divisional organizer, helped by a committee of voluntary workers, assessed whether parents required assistance towards payment for school dinners, recommended provision of clothing if necessary, attended school medical inspections, arranged appointments at hospitals and clinics, followed up missed appointments, and provided reports on the home background for the doctors. They also co-operated with youth employment officers, made home visits, and kept in touch with young people who needed help and advice about health, general welfare, or leisure activities.

> Care committees are fully aware of any handicapped children and of the problems that they may cause within a family. The workers may help the parents to appreciate the need for special education. They also give much practical help and advice to enable the parents to deal with a severely handicapped child at home, or encourage them to accept boarding education when that is best for the child.

After-care Services

Whilst the majority of children leaving schools for the educationally subnormal or the maladjusted seemed able to hold their own in the community, the Health Authority provided an after-care service to which they or their parents could turn if the need arose.

A good after care service aims to build up confidence unobtrusively by helping the boy or girl to adjust in a setting as normal as possible but in which he or she can become absorbed without a sense of marked inferiority. This applies to recreational activities, to employment conditions and to the home setting. It is a service which helps to offset the effect of an over anxious parent or to develop the understanding of the indifferent one.

Visits were paid to the home by the social worker in the Public Health Department unless this was thought unnecessary. The social worker was in close co-operation with the youth employment officer and was also able to advise ex-pupils and give concrete assistance in certain cases (e.g. by arranging holidays or giving financial help).

The after-care service was a permissive one which the child could refuse. There were exceptions to this (e.g. where the Children's Committee had the rights and powers of the parents or there was a "fit person order" through the juvenile courts).

The Welfare Committee provided general welfare services for handicapped people of all ages (other than those who were mentally handicapped). These services were administered by a Welfare Department which kept a register of those requiring assistance. Even with a school-age child whose needs were largely seen to by the Education Committee, the Welfare Department could make special provision in the child's home to ensure the comfort of the child. Adaptions could be made to the homes of former pupils, and special tuition could be provided in leisure activities, "outings, holidays, special transport, social centres and sheltered workshops".

The Handicapped Ex-pupil

The ultimate outlook of the handicapped pupil and his successful placement in the community are two obvious tests of the value of his educational experiences before leaving school.

The provision so far described was made by a large authority, internationally recognized as amongst the most progressive and generous. If this provision was insufficient to meet all the needs, it was, nevertheless, more extensive, more far-ranging, and in advance of what the majority of educational authorities had to offer. Whilst some energetic authorities could point to this or that branch of special education in which they could claim to have something in advance of London's best, few could claim to have progressed along as broad or as many a front. Nationally, even where a multiplicity of facilities seemed to exist, there was insufficient of each as well as significant gaps in all. So much sheer physical provision was required in many cases that concern for the potential in the more seriously handicapped children had initially to take second place to their care and placement.

Whilst all local education authorities had the power to retain handicapped pupils (if these so wished) beyond the statutory leaving age, there often seemed little point in considering this unless the GCE or some other examination was a goal. Few LEAs could offer suitable additional education except for more able scholars. Nationally, the weaknesses in special provision were most pronounced in three important areas: in the entire pre-school area (outside the education system as well as within it); in the transition from school to work; and in the facilities available after leaving school.

Though one Ministry of Labour survey provided the encouraging information that the majority of registered handicapped pupils had made a successful start in employment, no comprehensive follow-through of pupils in each category could be pointed to. Whether or not special provision in school was adequate for the child's current needs, the transition to work could prove an abrupt change from a protected environment into an unfamiliar and unsuitable one. Fits in the epileptic youth, for example, and a recurrence of asthma or of stammering, could easily be occasioned by the new demands made upon the former pupil in the adjustment to the work situation. The maladjusted pupil who had almost become stabilized might be thrust back several years. Handicapped young people, at the time of transition, were often suffering the additional strains of adolescence. If some felt well-rid of their school and were glad to plunge into semi-skilled or unskilled work in culturally deprived areas, others had an urgent need of support up to at least the age of 18.

The protective laws which had been made were often permissive or inadequately known. The physically handicapped ex-pupil was dependent, in the main, upon his general practitioner or the hospital, neither of which were educationally oriented. Less than a third of employed persons entered establishments which had an adequate industrial health service.

The ESN school-leaver could seek the help of the mental health service. But this service was limited in several ways and as we have seen was entirely voluntary. Whilst some special schools and mental health workers got together before the pupil left school, many pupils on leaving found the mental health officers to be complete strangers.

From the statutory point of view, legislation began with the 1944 Disabled Persons (Employment) Act and the 1946 National Health Service Acts. The former Act, with its amending Act of 1958, gave rise to a voluntary register of all handicapped persons whose condition disabled them from obtaining or keeping employment. The Minister not only had powers to reserve certain kinds of work for the disabled but every employer was expected to employ a proportion of those on the register. Courses of industrial rehabilitation were provided to help enable disabled workers to bridge the gap between leaving hospital and going back to work.

The Minister set up a non-profit-making company (Remploy Ltd.) to provide sheltered work for registered disabled adults "who by reason of the nature and severity of their disablement" were "unlikely at any time, or until after the lapse of a prolonged period, to be otherwise able to obtain employment, or to undertake work on their own account"; and by 1963 there were nearly ninety Remploy factories employing over 6000 disabled persons.

But such centres were not designed as training and rehabilitation centres for handicapped school-leavers. The Acts and the provision which followed were mainly centred upon adults whose work had been interrupted by illness or handicap, etc., and who required rehabilitation or retraining as a result.

The medical requirements were in the main covered by the National Health Service. The National Assistance Act enabled local authorities to make arrangements for the welfare of persons who were blind, deaf, or dumb, or permanently and substantially handicapped in other ways. Local authorities had powers to provide advisory and visiting services, sheltered employment (not for the deaf), and hostels, assistance in obtaining equipment and materials, and supervised work at home. The 1959 Mental Health Act extended the powers of local authorities to make provision for those suffering from mental disorder. But none of these provisions was specifically centred upon the needs of handicapped school-leavers, and there was increasing awareness of the need for a suitable after-care service if handicapped pupils were to be helped through a trying period.

Voluntary organizations were amongst the first to see and attempt to meet the need. The Royal National Institute for the Blind (1956) introduced a centre for "short courses of further education" designed "to improve their maturity together with an assessment and vocational guidance to help them choose between open and sheltered employment and the various types of training for each". This centre at Heathersett, in addition to teaching braille reading and writing and giving social training, provided pre-vocational training in manual dexterity.

The Spastics Society's Employment Department—also directly confronted with the employment problem—provided a series of residential assessment courses. On finding that a few spastics were eligible for the Government training centres (due to the skills and level of educational attainment demanded) the Spastics Society set up its own training centres associated with its own sheltered workshop at Sherrards. Here training was adapted to the needs and abilities of the individual, and placement in employment could be delayed to suit the pace of the individual. The training here was for semi-skilled work from which some might grow sufficiently confident to train for more skilled work. A number in fact were subsequently placed in open employment. The National Society for Mentally Handicapped Children also felt compelled to give a lead here (see p. 165).

The plight of some severely handicapped children, however, remained such that only voluntary bodies, like Dr. Barnardo's Homes, seemed ready to offer them a refuge. In general, with voluntary organizations as with statutory provision, they were only incidentally directed towards the continuing welfare and employment of the handicapped school-leaver. Whilst some special services were available for the blind, the tuberculous, the mentally handicapped, the paraplegic, and the deaf, the shortcomings were considerable.

The Youth Employment Service

The youth employment service was not set up to consider the needs of handicapped school-leavers. Some authorities, recognizing the problem, set up separate sections devoted solely to the handicapped; others did not or could not. Whilst the youth employment officer could obtain help and guidance in placing handicapped leavers from various sources (including good employers and the disablement resettlement officer whose work, however, was mainly focused upon adults whose work had been interrupted), the facilities were inadequate and youth employment officers were in considerable difficulties.

Not all handicapped pupils were sufficiently mature on leaving school to enter government or other training schemes. Some required transport to their places of work, or accommodation near it. Many required help in their social setting if their employment was to be tackled with success. The disablement resettlement officers were usually transitory, and were not trained social workers. And most local authorities did not utilize the full powers bestowed on them by the various acts.

British Council for the Rehabilitation
of the Disabled

Concerned with all who were handicapped, the British Council for the Rehabilitation of the Disabled was founded in 1944 by a group of prominent workers in medicine and social welfare who had come to experience the needs of disabled people. The founders sought to encourage the co-ordination of the many different aspects of rehabilitation into one comprehensive service.

In 1963 a Working Party set up by this Council and under the chairmanship of Dr. Elfed Thomas, the Director of Education for the City of Leicester, provided a detailed report on "The Handicapped School-leaver" and made a total of thirty-seven recommendations of which only two required any change in the law. The first proposed the amendment of the 1944 Education Act to require the school health service to provide continuity of care and supervision for handicapped young people up to the age of at least 18 years, whilst the second sought to enable local education authorities to provide a comprehensive service of personal help for educationally subnormal and maladjusted school-leavers. Having studied all the available evidence it concluded that provision for the blind was on the whole, satisfactory, and that this was true to a lesser degree of the deaf.

> Much progress has been made in recent years, too, by voluntary bodies, in the provision of services for those suffering from cerebral palsy. When we consider other categories of seriously physically handicapped young people, and those suffering from mental disorders, we are bound to say that present provision leaves a great deal to be desired. The statutory and voluntary services which have so far been provided do not begin to compare with those in operation for the blind. . . . We should be lacking in our duty if we did not call attention to the quite serious deficiencies, for example, in the provision of residential care for severely physically handicapped young people, particularly for those suffering also from other defects. The plight in which many of these youngsters find themselves is deplorable and we feel justified in calling for urgent action to relieve this situation.

The National Union of Teachers

Amongst the bodies which gave evidence to this Working Party, was the National Union of Teachers. Surveying the situation in 1959 it suggested:

(1) That there should be provision of a "special designated officer covering not too wide an area" to be "responsible for advising and placing in suitable employment of the handicapped school leaver and for the employment and industrial welfare of handicapped young people who have left school";

(2) That such officers should have "special training which would enable them to give separate treatment to the different categories of handicapped school-leaver";

(3) "That handicapped school-leavers should be placed in suitable employment or training as speedily as possible in order that the steadying and guiding influence of the school" should not be lost.

Other suggestions involved transport, suitable living accommodation, and a satisfactory after-care service. The NUT also urged that "steps should be taken to amend" the National Assistance Act and the Disabled Persons Acts "to transform the permissive powers of local authorities into compulsory duties" so that comprehensive schemes could be operated throughout the country to provide adequately not only for the needs of disabled adults but for the needs of handicapped young persons about to leave or who had left school.

Transition from School to Work

Special schools for the ESN also revealed increasing experiment with the problems of the transition from school to work. This interest brought schools and youth employment officers closer together, and was to extend to the needs of severely subnormal children.

For example, in a conference organized by teachers (the Guild of Teachers of Backward Children, 1965) a principal youth employment officer (H. Z. Hoxtor, Newham) applied to the ESN pupils four questions posed by the former head of the Vocational Guidance Department of the National Institute of Industrial Psychology (Prof. A. Rogers, Youth Employment, Bureau of Current Affairs).

(1) Should we leave young people alone to choose work that interests them?

(2) Can young people afford to make mistakes in choosing work on the grounds that the experience will help to train their characters?

(3) Is it true that we are all so adaptable anyway that, given the opportunity, we could do well at anything we liked?

(4) Is it true that nowadays people generally have to take what jobs they can get?

This youth employment officer had found that the occupational image of average school-leavers was frequently unrealistic or insecure. Still more dependent, and much less well equipped to make a realistic assessment, were the ESN school-leavers. There was, in Hoxtor's view, little justification for the notion that making mistakes was the best way for these young people to learn or was good for the training of their character. As for the third question, he dismissed this with an example of a young adult who wanted to be a cook in the merchant navy but flatly refused to learn to swim. The young man's character and personality defect proved "so severe that he was declared untrainable and incapable of responding to treatment". Finally, jobs depended in some measure upon the nature of local industry, local circumstances, transport, effectiveness of social training, and related factors.

Progressive youth employment officers clearly saw their work as having four main phases. Firstly, vocational orientation (i.e. helping the individual to gain some understanding of the working world); secondly, vocational counselling (guidance in selection of a job and in further education and training); thirdly, actual placement; and, fourthly, follow-up (i.e. providing support and after-care to help the younger worker over any difficulties of adjustment and development).

Hoxtor pointed with interest to the vocational orientation courses, based on direct, first-hand experience of working life, provided in Belgian, Swedish, Swiss, and USA schools. American experiments included full-time release from school to enable ESN pupils to try out a variety of jobs in trades and industries.

Whilst some of these experiments overseas were controversial, a number of other promising developments were apparent by this time in certain schools of different types in different parts of England and Wales. In a discussion on the "transition from school to work", for example, four head teachers described in some detail the programmes at their different schools during the final year. M. A. Jerrold aroused particular interest by describing a Portsmouth project "encouraged as a result of evidence from Clarke, Tizard and O'Connor" that "many young persons of a lower intellectual level than those attending day special schools could take up employment successfully". This evidence had made it "highly probable that the problem ESN school-leaver could also be adjusted to employment conditions, and could become self-supporting, provided the right sort of training and encouragement were made available".

The steering committee for this project not only included youth employment officers but representatives of industry, psychologists, and a member of the Council. The resulting recommendations had included that of constructing a workshop bay, appointing a teacher with industrial experience, as well as a woman supervisor. The aim was to provide for 12 pupils at a time who could stay for about 6 months. There would be pupils who were unsuited for immediate employment or had tried several jobs without success and then wanted training, and others who sought training. The project included simple contract work during working hours (Bleach and others, 1965).

More ambitious still were two developments initiated by the National Society for Mentally Handicapped Children and described by Tudor-Davies. Two "transition" experiments were launched: (Slough 1963) for severely subnormal pupils who were excluded from the school system at the age of 5 and (Pirates Spring) for special school-leavers "at risk" in the work-life setting.

Tudor-Davies (1965) also observed that "the high grade severely subnormal excluded from education" might stand a better chance of getting a job in open employment and keeping it "than the low grade special school leaver. . . . Whilst the severely subnormal may have achieved maturity in vocational skills and social competence, the special school leaver may be a late developer or may be dually handicapped by a non-supporting home life."

At Slough severely subnormal persons aged from 16 to 26 could have periods of intensive and individually directed social and vocational training varying from 6 months to a year. There were purpose-designed hostels and an industrial workshop keyed to individual programmes. (Dr. H. C. Gunzburg, the Honorary Consultant Psychologist, guided the programme and described some of the progress in a paper at the International Congress on the Scientific Study of Mental Retardation, 1964: "The social competence of the imbecile child: landmarks in directed training".)

The Pirates Spring experiment was a 3-month course providing resident, social education for 14 boys and girls aged 17 to 21 who had attended special schools for the ESN.

CHAPTER 3

A Brief History of Special Education

Blessed are Thou O Lord our God, King of the universe, who varies
the form of Thy creatures.
(*Circa* 500–200 B.C. A blessing said by Jews on meeting a handicapped
person.)

Before Binet and Burt

Misfortune is as old as humanity. People throughout the world
at each stage of their different civilizations, have had a proportion
of children who suffered severe and obvious handicaps. The
social-emotional reactions to such handicaps appear to have
taken four major forms, reflecting different degrees of maturity or
different levels and kinds of civilization. The children with such
handicaps were (a) destroyed or (b) neglected or (c) cared for
(institutions being designed as protective asylums) or (d) helped
to improve functionally as human beings.

These four forms of response did not necessarily follow each
other, and some could be found side by side. The Spartans were
not the first, though we may hope the Nazis were the last, to
destroy children who were handicapped, as though they belonged
to an inferior species or endangered the race.

And long before compulsory schooling was introduced, before
religious or voluntary bodies had begun to organize any kinds of
schooling for children of the poor, history sometimes recorded a
remarkable individual who had taught a blind child to read or a
deaf child to write.

But if his own blindness helped to make a teacher of Didymus,
or if compassion for his own deaf sister motivated Dr. Pereira, it
was a philosophy, within an intellectually vigorous France, which

led to the first significant effort to educate a mentally handicapped child.

It was in the social and intellectual climate of France at the end of the eighteenth century, influenced by the philosophies of Locke and Rousseau, inspired with an optimism about human potential which was encouraged by the "sensationist" philosophy of his day, that Dr. J. M. Itard undertook to educate the newly captured "wild boy of Aveyron".

Five years later Itard abandoned the experiment as failure. The child was no "clean slate". If he had not been spoiled by the influences of civilization, he had certainly been affected by their absence. Little was known about his life during the 10 or 12 years which preceded his capture. Living like an animal in the forest, running around on all fours, unable to communicate except by shrieking, "the wild boy" proved much less responsive to Itard's skills than the latter had anticipated. Yet the experiment was not the failure that Itard thought it. Certainly it had not upheld his theory. But others, noting the improvement which had taken place in "the wild boy", saw a positive role for education at a time when medicine could merely add to the description of a condition. From Itard's initiative and one of his pupils—Edouard Seguin— sprang the first professional organization concerned with the mentally handicapped.

Experiments of the kind undertaken by Itard were, before this time, virtually impossible. Such experiments as had taken place were, at best, scattered through time and barely noticed by un-responsive communities. For a handful of children at most, "special educational treatment" can be viewed as having existed for a long time. As for the children of the poor, of those of them who were handicapped in body or in mind, it was the blind and the deaf who first drew the sympathies of humane, voluntary groups. As a nationwide responsibility, compulsory education was not introduced until nearly a century later (in the 1880's). Special educational provision came after this, and came unevenly. Con-cern for the children excluded from schools as ineducable had to wait longer still.

Mental Health

As with the mentally handicapped, so with the insane, care preceded clinical developments. Education was neither a priority nor an unavoidable part of the treatment. The slowly developing interest and knowledge was indicated in the names of sequential acts of Parliament. In 1845 came the Lunatics Act. In 1930 we reached the Mental Treatment Act. And in 1959 the Mental Health Act. But even if one averages out the troughs and peaks in a graph of progress, the result is never a straight line.

The first of these acts reflected a period of reform. Standards in the asylums were improved. Straitjackets, bleeding, and purging of victims were on their way out. But concern for the liberty of the individual and the danger of improper detention gave rise to a new Act (1890). If this Act made it more difficult to deprive a person of his liberty, it simultaneously made it more difficult to accept other than "certified" patients whose condition was obvious. The asylums therefore moved further and further away from being treatment centres towards becoming the despairing last stages. An ever-increasing number of seriously ill people were crowded into larger and larger centres of hopelessness of this kind. The Mental Treatment Act of 1930 sanctioned the principle of voluntary admission once again, along with out-patient clinics and observation wards. But, in contrast to the practice in ordinary hospitals where most of the expenditure went to out-patients, the reverse remained the case with hospitals for the mentally sick, only a tiny fraction of the money going towards out-patients.

Further progress here was not solely dependent upon the changing climate—which, as we saw, sometimes had unforeseen, adverse side-effects—or upon forms of therapy or even upon the remarkable medical advances, notably with tranquillizers and electric treatment, but also upon early ascertainment and new concepts of educational provision.

As Dr. L. T. Hilliard was to remark:

> A century ago only the most severe cases received public attention and segregation in institutions was the only treatment. Gradually a distinction

was made between the mentally ill and the mentally defective, and special training or education was provided for children in the latter group whose ability to learn was limited by an arrested or incomplete mental development. . . . Already following the Report of the Royal Commission there has been a change for the better. The routines of many hospitals for mental defectives are now less rigid and their staff make less pessimistic assessments of patients' abilities and social competence than in the past. . . .

Discovering the Need for Special Education

London appointed its first educational psychologist in 1913. This historic appointment was made only half a century after an extraordinary system known as "payment by results" for teachers had been introduced into our crowded elementary schools. That system soon had to be abandoned. The problems had not been foreseen, and the results were not quite those expected. The school revealed that it was no factory. The pupils demonstrated that whether or not they were originally born with the same academic potential, they were not in equal states of preparation. The same mass processes failed to produce the same end products. And the deceits practised to obtain payment and hide the truth from the inspectors did no one credit.

A scientific basis for a new approach to the physically and mentally handicapped as well as to the "misfits" seemed to be rooted in the work of three men. One, Francis Galton, was a cousin of Charles Darwin. Galton was convinced that intelligence, like physical height or weight, was distributed amongst the population in accordance with the "curve of normal distribution". According to this theory, roughly two-thirds of the population were more or less "average", whilst one-sixth were above average, tailing away to a tiny group of giants, and another sixth were below average tailing away to dwarfs (Fig. 2). Galton's initiatives helped to found the British Child Study movement. A science of individual differences evolved alongside or within the mass instruction system.

The second contributor, Cattell, coined the term "mental tests" in 1895. But it was the third contributor, a French schools inspector, Alfred Binet, who was primarily concerned with developing a practical means for selecting "mentally defective" children in the schools. One of his aims was to provide special help for these children. Binet devised a careful scale of ability against which all school children could be measured. This scale

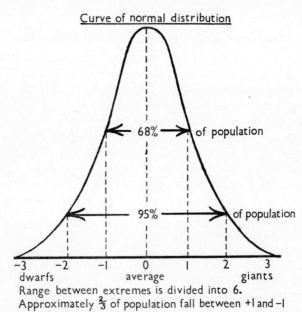

Range between extremes is divided into 6.
Approximately $\frac{2}{3}$ of population fall between +1 and −1

Fig. 2.

subsequently attracted widespread interest and was adapted to the need of many countries outside France, including our own.

There is no doubt that the concept of a "mental age" helped to transform the educational approach. But even Binet's apparently scientific tool for measuring mental ages depended in part for its usefulness on the theories guiding those who did the testing. Binet himself protested against "the brutal pessimism", as he termed it, of those who suggested that intelligence was not educable. This pessimism, however, grew deep roots which were strengthened by work in the USA as well as in Europe.

The Wave of Pessimism

A century after Itard's report on "the wild boy of Aveyron", the nature *versus* nurture controversy had reached a new level, but was far from resolved in the new synthesis.

Around "mental defect" in particular there developed a fog of fear, stigma, and superstitition. Mental defect and mental illness were confused with each other in the public mind, and the fog was in no way dispelled by exaggerated findings from research—research which unfortunately failed to notice important variables or asked the wrong questions.

Accordingly, it was discovered that a substantial proportion of the inmates of prisons and workhouses, and people otherwise dependent upon the community, were below average in ability as measured on Binet scales. Studies of unusual families helped to support the prejudice that social degeneracy was handed down like a trait, running in the family. Distinguished scientists were amongst those influenced both by the social climate of the time and by the evidence from Binet tests which disclosed a greater amount of "feeblemindedness" in the population than had before then been assumed. Professor A. D. B. Clarke quotes the outstanding Dr. Fernald, a respected figure in the history of psychiatry, as saying in 1912 (the year in which H. H. Goddard's study of *The Kallikak Family* was published):

> The feebleminded are a parasitic, predatory class never capable of self-support or of managing their own affairs. The great majority ultimately become public charges in some form. They cause unutterable sorrow at home and are a menace to the community. Feebleminded women are invariably immoral. . . . Every feebleminded person, especially the high-grade imbecile, is a potential criminal needing only the proper environment and opportunity for development and expression of his criminal tendencies.

And this was only one year before the appointment of Sir Cyril Burt. (It was also, interestingly enough, one year before the

Mental Deficiency Act of 1913, which had been pressed for by the voluntary body, the National Association for the Care of the Feebleminded. This Act, whilst centred upon the definition, certification, and detention of the mentally defective, also gave local authorities new powers. They could now set up special committees with responsibility, amongst others, for the care of "mental defectives" who remained in the community.)

Professor Clarke quotes one writer of this period as summing up the situation in the following pseudo-scientific terms: "Our data reveal that illegitimacy, attempted murder, theft, forgery,

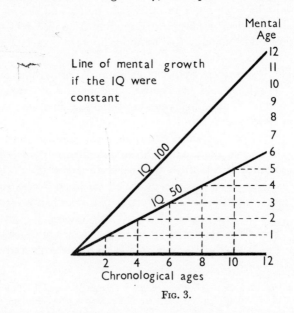

FIG. 3.

arson, prostitution, drunkenness, destitution and disease are salient features of the careers of these incompetents."

This unsympathetic attitude, in marked contrast with the attitudes towards the blind and the deaf at this time, was clearly powerful, dominant, yet confused. On the one hand, intelligence-testing theory implied that the mentally defective were subnormal members of the same species. On the other hand, the prevailing conviction was that the mentally defective were somehow a different species or were both abnormal as well as subnormal, and a matter for doctors rather than teachers.

Professional pessimism was rooted in two findings which had disturbing consequences. Firstly, defect in "intelligence" as measured, seemed incurable (Fig. 3). Secondly, the "high grade mentally subnormal" appeared to be more fertile than average people. The logic was inescapable. Unless something was done about the trend, a decline in the national intelligence seemed inevitable. With eugenists calling for sterilization of the "feeble-minded" there were pressures to have these children withdrawn from the educational system along with the "ineducable".

The educational paralleled the medical approach. If schooling after all, was identified with "the three Rs", those who were unlikely to learn the three Rs or could do so only with great difficulty, were "ineducable". In the setting of the period this was not an unreasonable conclusion. But it was against this that Dr. Cyril Burt began to make his own distinctive contribution.

And it was perhaps not surprising that he published his substantial volume, *The Delinquent Child*, 12 years before he was able to publish his classic volume on *The Backward Child*.

CHAPTER 4

A Brief History of Special Education

*We are not concerned only with minimising the child's disabilities but
with making the most of his abilities, not only with a brain, a sense or
a limb but with a whole person, not only with a child in isolation but
with the child in his environment, including his family circumstances.*
(DR. J. D. KERSHAW, 1962, *Forward Trends*: International Conference
on the Backward Child.)

From Burt to Butler

Sir Cyril Burt's responsibilities did not extend to those children
excluded from the school system or outside it. If theory justified
the continuing exclusion from school of the severely subnormal,
additional special schools were urged for children who were less
severely handicapped. Nevertheless, there remained within the
ordinary schools a substantial minority of children with a wide
range of lesser handicaps. As such handicaps often had an adverse
effect upon school attainments, "the backward" provided a complex problem.

It was Sir Cyril Burt who first studied the nature and extent of
this backwardness in a systematic fashion. His approach was
objective, extensive, and clear. "In education and in science, in
training the mind as in healing the body, efficient practice is to
be achieved only by a scientific approach."

In his role as London's first educational psychologist, Burt
sought to help on a large scale and in a practical way. He began
with such evidence as was then scientifically acceptable. Research
findings were emphasizing "the constancy of the IQ". Impressed
with the evidence that a child's mental retardation, as revealed in
psychological tests, "increases with increasing age, and usually in

direct proportion", Burt saw such tests as of key importance. Test results were his guide to the relevance of other minor handicaps as causes of the child's backwardness. In more than half the cases studied he concluded that "the application of psychological tests proves beyond all question" that the child's whole intellectual capacity was definitely below normal. And, *"since this general disability is inborn, if not actually inherited, the backwardness is irremediable"*.

Burt pursued this line of approach logically, and went on to prescribe provision based upon it. Today, whatever shifts there may be from his theory, there can be no doubt that this provision, made on a more generous scale, could have rescued a great many children (and their teachers) from intolerable school conditions.

Burt did not join those who urged that the "feebleminded" be cut off from the mainstream of education (i.e. along with the "ineducable"). Instead, with the Wood Committee, he saw the feebleminded as part of one broad group, "the backward". Here was the beginnings of the 1944 concept of "educational subnormality".

Burt found that there were specific defects rather than a general intellectual inefficiency in about a sixth of the cases he studied. He pointed out that given "a suitable change of teaching methods" such defects were no real barrier to educational progress.

Having uncovered a multiplicity of causes of backwardness, Burt reviewed the different forms of treatment then possible, describing the classification, the curriculum, the time-table, and the general teaching methods. But he underlined "the supreme essential", *the selection and training of teachers*. If he put strongly the view that the formation of backward classes or, in the senior schools, "of a stream of backward or C classes, was without question an urgent need", he emphasized that this was only a preliminary. "The crucial problem still remains what to do with the backward pupils themselves when we have relieved other classes of their presence."

Unsympathetic as this last clause may sound today, for the times it was both realistic and humane. In addition to pointing out the needs of schools or those who could be ascertained as "feebleminded" and placed in such schools, Burt was pressing the case for special educational treatment for nearly half a million children who were "dull and backward".

Parallel to these activities, it is worth noting that in 1914 the Central Association for Mental Welfare had already suggested to the Board of Education an additional year's training at a training college and—to meet the immediate need—the establishment of short courses for selected teachers. (For a living record of the activities of this association, see Hargrove, 1965.) In the event, 3-week courses followed, but many applicants had to be rejected for lack of vacancies.

In 1935 the Central Association for Mental Welfare was able to initiate a Loan Service of educational psychologists, "heralded by the appointment of Miss Grace Rawlings".

By 1937 a Committee of Inspectors was reporting that where small classes, appropriately staffed, "had been tried, it could be stated with conviction that the chief gain to the children had been an improvement in outlook, a moral and social gain".

Pre-war Theory

Accompanying the IQ was the concept of a mental age. A child of 10 with an IQ of 50 had a mental age of 5, that is 50 per cent of his actual age. At 14, therefore, the IQ being assumed to be constant, he would be no more than 7 years old mentally, i.e. still an infant. His "educability" was accordingly in doubt. Moreover, intelligence, instead of proceeding in the linear way suggested in the graph (Fig. 4), was found to slow down in rate of growth, slowing off earlier in backward children than in brighter ones. The growth seemed to cease around school-leaving age. Whatever physical or other handicaps the child suffered, the results of the intelligence test seemed to be crucial to the educational prognosis.

The accepted goal and ultimate achievement of any teacher became to match the child's mental age with the child's attainments. The "mental age" provided the ceiling or goal.

Fortunately—if in a curious way—since backward children were seldom "working to capacity" (i.e. they had attainments lower than their mental age "ceiling") a positive goal was presented to the schools. This concept of "under-functioning" was even more significant for the backward than for the bright.

On the eve of the Second World War there were, here and there, scattered if limited provisions for some children in each

Pupil aged 10 years	IQ 100	Mental Age 10	Pre-war categories
	85	8·5	
	70	7	Dull and backward
	50	5	Feeble-minded or 'educable'-mentally retarded
			Ineducable

Fig. 4.

category of backwardness described. But in the C-stream classes as a whole, children with a complex mixture of social, physical, educational, emotional, and intellectual handicaps were to be found. And prominent in these classes were the "throw-outs" from other classes, the problem children who after threats were punished by placement in the backward class, the behaviour problems with which the ordinary classes could not cope.

In these circumstances, the dominant theory guiding Sir Cyril Burt and others could not be utilized in practice to the limits of its usefulness. Few teachers of the new C streams—which had replaced the old infant standards—were infant-trained. Fewer teachers still were trained in remedial education, in psychological and educational diagnosis, or could adapt what they did know to the social ages and experiences, the physical, emotional, and intellectual needs and levels of the different pupils within the complex classes. The nation was not yet ready to consider "the supreme essential".

Provision

Under the influence of the 1926 Hadow report, the old elementary schools had been steadily reorganized. The old system of "standards" went, terminating the practice of having wave after wave of bright infants pass through the lowest standards, ridiculing or submerging the older backward pupils who often vegetated there. Promotion according to age, irrespective of attainments, supplanted the system which had disregarded age and emphasized attainments. But what was to be done in the upper years with "the backward"? In place of "standards" came "streams", highlighting backwardness in a new way. Those who pinned their hopes on C streams now discovered other factors or complications. A survey conducted by one progressive local education authority brought the disturbing conclusion that "10% or 15% of the children in the reorganized schools would be so retarded as to prevent them benefiting appreciably when educated in a C stream class" (Hill, 1939, p. 12).

The first real efforts to face up to the problem, made those responsible for provision feel as did this director of education: "like craftsmen attempting to work in a medium the composition of which they did not fully comprehend." Reflecting the whole social climate of the time was the fact that "inside the school there was a distaste among the teaching staff for work with C stream classes". Motivating wider concern and interest in the problem, was the negative consideration that "more than 50% of juvenile delinquents were school misfits".

Behaviour Problems

Nevertheless, many roads led to progress. An interest in juvenile delinquents led to the setting up of the first Child Guidance Clinics.*

In 1909 the Chicago Psychopathic Clinic was founded and was followed 6 years later by the Judge Baker Foundation in Boston. It became increasingly apparent that it was not enough to study the child. Efforts were made to bring in the parents and the home. It became equally clear that "delinquents" were not the only difficult children. The setting up of demonstration clinics was therefore recommended to develop the psychiatric study and treatment of difficult children. The importance of educational methods and of training specialists was now apparent.

The pioneering East London Child Guidance Clinic was set up in 1927 by the Jewish Health Organization. (The Tavistock Clinic, which had been set up in 1920, was largely focused upon functional nervous disorders in adults.) But it was in 1928 that the London Child Guidance Clinic began its work, influenced by the developments in the USA and representing the most significant and substantial development in this country up to that time. Four years later a local education authority followed in its wake—Birmingham. A handful of additional clinics subsequently appeared. All these clinics, however, were concerned primarily not with physical or mental handicaps and difficulties, but with the emotional problem—"unsatisfied inner needs". Until the Second World War created a wider appreciation of these needs, too, the limited provision had to suffice.

* Burt reminds us that Galton and Sully inspired this development and that Cattell (a co-worker of Galton) introduced the idea to the U.S.A. *The Causes and Treatment of Backwardness*, p. 26.

CHAPTER 5

How Many Children need Special Education?

Most countries in Europe recognize that there are children for whom classes in the ordinary primary and secondary schools cannot provide efficient education.

(*Education and Mental Health*, UNESCO, 1955.)

A Ministry Estimate

For children other than those excluded from schools, the 1944 Education Act (The Butler Act) mapped out a new era. A year later the Handicapped Pupils and School Health Service Regulations stated that blind, deaf, epileptic, physically handicapped and aphasic children were seriously disabled by their condition and had to be educated in special schools; but "whether any individual child of the other types is so seriously handicapped that he needs to go to a special school will depend not only on the degree of his disability but also on the adequacy of the provision that can be made for him in an ordinary school".

But how much special school provision was required? And what decided the "adequacy of the provision that can be made" in ordinary schools? By 1946 the Ministry of Education was able to provide "a rough guide . . . useful to authorities in making preliminary estimates" of the extent of special provision required. The first pamphlet on *Special Educational Treatment* (1946), provided the figures as shown on the following page for each 1000 registered pupils.

These figures went far beyond the narrow confines of special school requirements, but could not be more than a rough guide. A considerable health service, forms of differential

52

Educationally subnormal	100
Speech defect	15–30
Delicate	10–20
Maladjusted	10
Physically handicapped	5–8
Partially deaf	1 upwards
Partially sighted	1
Deaf	0.7–1
Blind	0.2–0.3
Epileptic	0.2
Diabetic	no estimate

diagnosis, and an integrated schools psychological service were a necessary prelude to more refined estimates of the size of the problems.

By 1948 it was possible to carry out the first large-scale survey of the standards of reading attainment in the schools and compare them with 1938 standards. As was anticipated, the dislocation of war had led to a marked fall in average standards of reading attainment. After all, the 11-year-old pupil in 1948 had been born in 1937 and spent the whole of his infancy and infant education in war conditions. Far more reassuring were the subsequent reading surveys (1952, 1956, and the special if more limited one in 1961 for the Newsom report) which revealed a general improvement in reading standards and rising average standards. Nevertheless, in 1961, apart from those pupils who were in special or in private schools, 15 in every 100 pupils aged 11 had reading ages below the average 9-year-old; 8 of these 15 remaining below the levels reached by average 9-year-old pupils in 1948. Whatever the causes of their backwardness in reading, a minimum of 15 per cent of the pupils in our secondary modern schools seemed to be in need of special provision of some kind, whilst about half this number seemed to provide a "hard core" requiring specialist and prolonged treatment.

Underfunctioning

With educational sights rising, there was pressure to have attainments match "potential". Dr. Kellmer Pringle was able to

c

provide evidence (supported by other, comparable investigations) that "in a junior school 15% or 20% of children in any age group" were likely to require special educational treatment for "longer or shorter periods". But in her investigations she was reassured by the evidence that the great majority of children whose reading attainments were more than 20 per cent below average at the age of $8\frac{1}{2}$ years were of average or above-average intelligence on individually administered intelligence tests. She concluded that within the ordinary schools, special classes were required for 8 per cent of the total age group in addition to the special school provision then available.

Estimates in the USA

England and Wales were not alone in their developing concern for handicapped children. In the USA, for example, such children were designated "exceptional children". This umbrella extended over categories which were not included under the Ministry of Education's responsibilities here, although not necessarily omitted from provision altogether. Apart from the gifted, the exceptional child included the trainable mentally retarded (equivalent to the children excluded from our schools and placed in training centres under the Ministry of Health), and the socially malad-justed (including children who would be placed in approved schools or similar centres here, under the control of the Home Office).

Whilst there was no equivalent in the USA to our category the educationally subnormal, just under 8 per cent of the school-age population in the USA were defined as slow learners. If we add together these slow learners and the educable mentally retarded (i.e. the USA term for our ascertained ESN pupils), we get a figure near the 10 per cent who are estimated by the Ministry to be educationally subnormal. These apart, experts in the USA estimate that a further 8 per cent of the school population were so exceptional in one or more areas as to require one or more of the special educational services.

Illinois study	Per 1000 registered pupils
Intellectually limited Including 2.7 trainable: 16.1 educable	18.8
Gifted	34.8
Slow learners	79.2
Speech defective	36.6
Socially maladjusted or emotionally disturbed	24.2
Visually handicapped	10
Hearing handicapped	4.6
Physically handicapped	6.7

A Rough Guide

There was increasing pressure in England and Wales to include under the educational system not only the trainable children (who remain excluded) but schools and educational centres now under the Home Office. Certainly no scientific estimate of the need for special training of teachers could be made without considering both these groups. As for the rough guide as to the need for special educational provision, it certainly erred on the side of conservatism compared with pre-war estimates. Sir Cyril Burt, for example, in his pre-war survey of backwardness in our schools, had found "rather over ten per cent" to be in the "dull and backward" category alone, apart from a further proportion who required special schools ($1\frac{1}{2}$–3 per cent) and those of average intelligence we describe today as underfunctioning. Dr. Kellmer Pringle's findings suggested a more objective or realistic rough guide to the need in ordinary schools: 15–20 per cent of the children in primary schools requiring special provision for shorter or longer periods.

Maximum Size of Classes

The Special Schools Regulations (1959) laid down the maximum size of classes—which provided a further rough guide to the number of staff and special training courses required. But perhaps the very size of the problem in ordinary schools prevented early consideration of class sizes and teacher training for the handicapped children who required special classes rather than special schools. If 15 or 20 per cent of the children in primary schools required special provision for shorter or longer periods, what proportion of the teaching profession required special training to meet the needs of these children? This question has still to be squarely faced.

Maximum size of classes			
Deaf pupils	10	Partially hearing pupils	10
Blind pupils	15	Partially sighted pupils	15
Speech defective	10	Maladjusted pupils	15
Physically handicapped	20	Epileptic	20
Educationally subnormal	20	Delicate	30

CHAPTER 6

The New Spirit

For the physically handicapped the first schools had opened in London by 1865, but as soon as "the lower standards of elementary education" had been mastered the children concentrated upon learning a trade. The need for special education for slow learning children was not fully revealed until compulsory universal education was introduced. The Elementary Education (Blind and Deaf Children) Act, 1893, laid upon every school authority the duty of providing education for blind and deaf children. . . . Similarly the Elementary Education (Defective and Epileptic Children) Act, 1899, empowered authorities to provide for the training of physically and mentally defective and epileptic children; these powers were made a duty in respect of mentally defective children in 1914 and in respect of physically defective and epileptic children in 1918.

(Reports of Education, No. 23, Department of Education and Science.)

Individual Differences

The 1944 Education Act reflected a more humane society: a nation more aware of fundamental human values, more ready to open doors rather than bolt them. And if there were new opportunities for children who suffered no physical, emotional, or intellectual handicap, there were also new approaches towards the integration of those who were handicapped.

Backwardness in the Basic Subjects, by F. J. Schonell—a work which was recognized as a classic—appeared in 1942 (the same year that John Watson's informative, practical, and humane book, *The Child and the Magistrate*, was published). Schonell, a pupil of Sir Cyril Burt, differentiated between the four major elements or forces which contributed towards making each child different. These elements, apart from intellectual characteristics, were emotional tendencies, physical conditions, and environmental influences. All these had to be considered in any useful study of the causes of a given child's backwardness.

One might discern in succeeding provision and research, limited though it was, a separation outwards in emphasis in the four directions.

In 1945, a year after the Act, a Diploma of Child Psychology (first introduced by Valentine before the war) was revived in Birmingham University. Here was a general course of training in applied educational psychology, but with its emphasis on the causes and treatment of educational failure in children who were otherwise normal. In 1948, Birmingham's Institute of Education incorporated as a part of its Research Department, a new Remedial Education Centre headed by Professor Schonell. Schonell's deputy was Dr. W. D. Wall who was later to become an outstanding Director of the National Foundation for Educational Research—itself a post-war organization. A psychologist and a psychiatric social worker completed this pioneering team. (It is interesting to note that Dr. Kellmer Pringle succeeded Dr. Wall at this remedial centre when Dr. Wall took up an appointment with UNESCO. Similarly, Professor Peel succeeded Professor F. J. Schonell.)

Two years after the setting up of this remedial centre, diploma courses for teachers of handicapped children were introduced at the University of London Institute of Education. One of these courses was set up with special reference to the educationally subnormal; the other had special reference to the maladjusted. Whilst only a handful of teachers could be accepted on either of these 1-year diploma courses, they initiated a significant new development.

Research: Shifting Theory

The concept of a mental age had drawn attention to major differences to be found in children of the same chronological age. It suggested an organizational framework within the school system, the school, or the class. It provided a starting point for special educational treatment. Lastly, it suggested an expected rate of maturation and school progress. This latter consideration was a particular caution to those tempted to press too hard in directions likely to reinforce failure and dislike of schooling. On the other hand, the theory also discouraged helplessness or mere "baby-minding".

With literacy defined as a reading age of 9 years, it became generally accepted that any child who could reach a mental age of 9-plus should be capable of being literate. An IQ of 60 made literacy possible by the age of 15, and IQ of 70 made literacy possible by the age of 13. All this assumed what the limited research on intellectual development had tended to confirm, that the IQ was constant and that mental growth terminated at 16 years (with a tendency to decline earlier in dull children). In the new climate, provision based on existing theories could be more generous. Intelligence tests and testing subsequently grew into something of an industry. With the growth of intelligence testing, provision, and research, came a deeper insight and a shift in theory, a shift in emphasis at least if not yet in substance. An increasingly flexible and subtle approach became possible, with teachers changing their practice if not the actual statement of their theories. By 1951 the shifting viewpoint was apparent in a revised version of M. E. Hill's pioneering, pre-war book *The Education of Backward Children* (1939). She now drew attention to the fact that "In the early days of intelligence testing, there was a tendency to accept the results uncritically as predictive of the child's capacity to learn. However, it became apparent, as discrepancies multiplied, that the IQ could prophesy falsely."

There was no longer the statement, formerly in italics, which had guided a generation of progressive teachers: "a measure of the child's intelligence or innate capacity to learn should set the ideal standard of attainment for that child." But there was still reference to "considerable statistical evidence" which showed that "for the vast majority of children the IQ fluctuated very little and that it is a reliable predictive measure, at least over a period of two or three years". Whilst this latter conclusion would still be accepted by many colleagues, its relevance could be seriously questioned.

As the IQs had been estimated from age groups whose environments could not be expected to alter much in "two or three years", there could be little reason to expect significant rises in IQ for the majority of the population over a short period. Moreover, such a fact—if so proved—was of little practical use except perhaps to administrators. For special educators it was far more important to study the changes and consider their relevance to special education.

In 1954 an expert international group called together by WHO and UNESCO stressed the possible modifiability of the level of intelligence as well as their conclusion that most mentally handicapped or educationally subnormal children were in no way defective.

Searching summaries of the influence of heredity and environment inevitably followed (see Vernon, 1960). Studies of intelligence testing led Professor Vernon to conclude that 25 per cent of children *at some time* in their primary schools career could merit inclusion in the most backward 5 per cent, whereas only $1\frac{1}{4}$ per cent of the school population were likely to remain within this subnormal group throughout their primary school careers. Flexibility of school organization was accordingly urged by him. "Intelligence", he pointed out, operated in a context of personality, and especially in a framework of motivation and learned behaviour. He argued that some of the pessimism about the modifiability of the IQ might be due to the nature of the measures used: "our current intelligence tests make no attempt to measure modifiability or learning capacity as such."

In the same year (1960) the most widely accepted of all individual intelligence tests (the Stanford–Binet Intelligence Scales) had been extended to the 18-year range "on the assumption that mental growth extends beyond the age of sixteen" (p. 45).

The Inconstancy of the IQ

Whatever had been the evidence for the constancy of the IQ, doubts now grew. Even allowing for a margin of error in testing and fluctuation in the functions measured, this constancy was seen to break down astonishingly when individual intelligence tests were given to children in the special (ESN) schools. In 1954 London's Senior Educational Psychologist (by then the LCC had a small team), H. A. T. Child, gave the figures for one primary special school. These figures had been shown to him by Frances Lloyd, the author of a book which appeared in 1953, *Educating the Subnormal Child*. Frances Lloyd had not only recorded some dramatic changes in IQ (which she attributed to wrong diagnosis or to failure to detect emotional difficulties, as with one child who leapt from being in the ineducable range, IQ 45 to beyond the range for the special school, IQ 89) but revealed that 24 per cent of her pupils had made a steady but significant increase in IQ, 19 per cent a steady fall, whilst 50 per cent showed an irregular pattern of IQ development. This inconstancy was confirmed in a secondary (ESN) school, too, in an unpublished thesis by George Sadler. His pupils altered within a range of minus 13 points to plus 26 points. Another headmaster, who listed the IQs of his pupils over a period ranging from 2 to 9 years of special schooling, found that 75 per cent fluctuated by more than 5 points, 41 per cent by more than 10 points, 20 per cent by more than 15 points, and $5\frac{1}{2}$ per cent by more than 20 points.

Dr. D. H. Stott, studying the results of such retesting in another part of the country, found the discrepancies "considerably greater than those obtained from the standardization of the Binet" test by Terman and Merrill. In fact the shifts in IQ reported as a result of tests used in the ascertainment procedure were found to be sufficient to reclassify a substantial group of children according to (a) the significance attached to a single test, and (b) the year in which the test was given. Whether or not intelligence was thought to be improvable, these fluctuations were at least a considerable challenge to inflexible administrative procedures.

Stott, for example (1964), found that the only consistent criterion used in the exclusion of children from schools in one large authority was a ceiling IQ of 50. Whilst it might not harm a child to be wrongly classified for a special school (and might do him a considerable amount of good by ensuring a child-centered educational programme), moral as well as educational issues became involved if a child was excluded from school on the basis of his IQ.

Considerations such as this led the Ministry to urge that a satisfactory trial in special schools or special units should first be given to any child bordering on the "ineducable range". It became increasingly clear that however necessary the classifications were for administrative purposes, they did not necessarily square with educational potential or with the developing theory.

Some Practical Considerations

Whether one criticized the tester, the test, or the person tested, implicit was a recognized weakness in the entire ascertainment procedure. Moreover, as provision was made, it became increasingly apparent that the same IQ in two pupils of the same chronological age masked a wide range of individual differences and of educational possibilities. There followed a natural reaction against doctors being responsible for the diagnosis. If IQs could no longer be used prognostically, the doctor's role in the ascertainment procedure was replaced or undermined. More than a brief training in the use of psychological tests was imperative if the tests were to be used diagnostically. Educational psychologists were seen as being essential if the tests were to be administered wisely, the results evaluated, placement for the child suggested, and lines of action for the teacher suggested.

There were practical considerations pressing against inflexible provision. Whilst fluctuations in IQ led to general acceptance that there should be a regular review of each case of educational subnormality in special schools, it became apparent that such reviews were of limited value unless they could be followed where necessary by more suitable placement.

In 1962 the Chief Medical Officer, Ministry of Education, revealed that only 63 per cent of pupils in special schools (ESN) had IQs of 50–69, more than a third (34 per cent) having IQs of 70-plus. In rural (ESN) schools the IQ of 70 was virtually the mean.

But transfer back to an ordinary school, for example, posed for educationalists such a problem as "Which ordinary school?" Climates in the different schools varied. Provision in the different schools varied. Moreover, could the school desired provide a place? Transfer within a streamed school might be obstructed by the need to demote another to promote this one—the size of classes affecting educational opportunity. If streaming itself was under fire within the teaching profession as well as outside, the form that provision took could too easily be confused with its content.

The stated advantages of the unstreamed class for the majority of pupils in no way solved the problems relating to class size and teacher training which had made special educational provision within them almost impossible.

There was a further challenge arising from the obvious inconstancy of the IQ. How far could one accept the IQ as revealing the relevance or otherwise of physical or other handicaps in a child who was backward?

Changes in Practice, 1945–65

It was during the two decades following the end of the Second World War that a number of new organizations gave expression to new trends. Some of these trends came up forcibly against administrative practices. Some saw the evolution of our educational system into grammar, secondary modern, and special schools as an obstacle to easy transfer. These critics were not necessarily critics of the theory of intelligence and its distribution which reinforced the theory of "streaming". They saw, however, that there were less transfers between grammar and secondary modern schools, for example, than might have been anticipated on the basis of errors, IQ shifts, or theory.

The tendency towards one-way traffic between secondary modern and special schools was paralleled by a similar one-way route between special schools and occupation centres (or, now, training centres). In fact the dichotomy between the latter two was even more pronounced. Nevertheless, some impressive pioneering against the trend became ever more apparent. The remarkable mental deficiency institute, Fountain Hospital, proved able to feed into the school system a substantial group of the children who had formerly been diagnosed mentally defective. Experiments—inadequately publicized—began to take place in training centres as well as in schools. A survey conducted in 1960 by the Guild of Teachers of Backward Children revealed a totally unsuspected if small interchange between training centres and special schools as well as between ordinary and special schools. Notably in Wales, a number of training centres were evolving programmes with an educational bias. A remarkable example of the way legal problems could be overcome where the spirit was willing, was provided by Birmingham, where the Health Authority delegated responsibility for the training centres to the Education Authority. And by 1963 Gloucester was able to pioneer an experiment in which a purpose-built training centre and special school were sited together, the headmaster of the special school having responsibility for the training centre.

Throughout this period there had been growing pressure from professional workers as well as from parents for the responsibility for training centres to be handed from the Health to the Education Ministry. Both the National Union of Teachers and the British Medical Association in their evidence to the Royal Commission had proposed such a transfer. By 1956 an interdisciplinary professional organization, the Guild of Teachers of Backward Children, was spanning the entire field of "backwardness" from the school failures within the ordinary school to the mentally handicapped outside the school system. Two remarkable parents' initiatives resulted in the powerful Spastics Association, on the one hand, and the National Society for Mentally Handicapped Children, on the other—both almost inconceivable during the miserable inter-war years.

In challenging public attitudes towards their handicapped children, they questioned both the existing provision for them and the evidence or theories which had justified this provision. Within the educational orbit, several voluntary and professional developments became apparent. In 1951, for example, almost at the time the Guild of Teachers of Backward Children had its origins, an Association of Workers for Maladjusted Children was formed. An Association of Educational Psychologists became possible in 1961.

Whilst the College of Teachers of the Blind, and those concerned with the deaf, developed further along their own lines, the old Special Schools Association, which had formerly linked together those working in the remaining special schools, now became reorganized and revitalized as an Association for Special Education.

Moves towards bringing together all organizations concerned with handicapped children were initiated by the Guild of Teachers of Backward Children in 1960. Agreement that a National Council for Handicapped Children should be established was gained at a meeting chaired by the Director of the Institute of Education in London. A parallel development with an apparent "care" bias resulted in the establishment of a National Bureau of Child Care under the directorship of Dr. Kellmer Pringle, and this led to a re-examination of the need for a National Council. At the time of writing new discussions were proceeding with a view to setting up some linking educational committee for handicapped children inside the National Bureau.

CHAPTER 7

Juvenile Delinquents

I myself have been present in a Juvenile Court when two boys already classified as E.S.N., were committed to an Approved School simply because there were no vacancies in Residential Special Schools for E.S.N. Children.

(R. HARRISON (Editor) *An ABC of Social Problems and Therapy*, vol. 2, 1963.)

The Principle of Guardianship

Whilst special educational provision for most handicapped children was recognized as a responsibility of the education authorities, special provision for "juvenile delinquents" came under the Home Office. The barriers between the flow of educational ideas here were substantial if not as acute as between the education system and the former occupation centres.

Although the basic function of the juvenile court in the USA had been seen as that of guardianship, as opposed to punishment, our juvenile courts (1908) were viewed primarily as criminal courts. Provision, instead of being a part of special educational treatment, guided by specially trained teachers and offering a range of provision within which pupils might be transferred according to their needs and development, evolved along its own path. The disturbed, the maladjusted, the educationally subnormal, and the badly trained could easily find themselves treated in identical fashion.

One juvenile magistrate, John F. Watson, described a visit in the middle 1930's to one of these education centres—an approved school. He went in the company of Miss Margery Fry who was then a chairman of the metropolitan juvenile courts. And he commented (Watson, 1965):

> We disliked everything about the school, not least the headmaster. Eventually we reached the dining-hall, an ugly bare room furnished with rough wooden tables. It was empty when we entered, but on the tables were enamelled plates each bearing two sausages reposing in a pool of congealed fat. There was a pause for a few moments. Then the boys were marched in, made to stand to attention at their places, and ordered to say grace. They were then allowed to sit down and eat. Margery Fry turned to me trembling with indignation: "If I were God", she said, "I would be furious."

In 1927, however, some years before this visit, a departmental committee on the Treatment of Young Offenders had seen "the principle of guardianship" at the root of all juvenile court procedure. The resulting 1933 Children and Young Persons Act (section 44 (i)) had laid down as a guiding principle for magistrates in juvenile courts that:

> Every Court in dealing with a child or young person who is brought before it, either as being in need of care or protection or as an offender or otherwise, shall have regard to the welfare of the child or young person and shall in a proper case take steps for removing him from undesirable surroundings, and for securing that proper provision is made for his education and training.

Certainly, the juvenile court was increasingly seen as a part of special provision within a welfare state in the sense that its role was not limited to criminal matters. A considerable amount of its time was devoted to children found to be in need of care or protection, to persistent truants, and children in the care of local authorities who proved refractory.

A significant increase in juvenile crime from 1956 aroused considerable public concern and prompted conflicting views about prevention, deterrents, and treatment.

John Watson, for example, found it necessary to underline the corresponding increase in crime by people of all ages (Watson, 1965): "confirmation—is it not?—that the behaviour of children, like the attitudes of children, is a reflection of the behaviour as of the attitudes of their parents." But, simultaneously, he pointed to another depressing trend, an apparent fall in the proportion of young offenders dealt with in the courts "where the treatment ordered may be said to have succeeded".

Research

Research appeared to offer little more in the way of help or guidance. L. T. Wilkins (1963), in a critical review of research and theory, ironically pointed to the conflicting conclusions regarding the causes of delinquency and its increase: "poverty and high standards of living; both broken homes and the spoiling of children; both bad companions and loneliness; biological factors and social circumstances; in fact almost all the features of life itself have been mentioned by some writers, whether singly or conjointly, as suggested explanations." Wilkins did bring out strongly, however, the importance of definition of delinquency. He stressed that what was viewed as delinquent in one country, one culture, one period, one age group, etc., might not be viewed as delinquent in another. And since "causation is a concept which has little meaning except in terms of something which if changed changes the outcome", Wilkins concluded that none of the studies to date had demonstrated the causes of delinquency.

The "age of criminal responsibility" was another revealing topic and subject of controversy. Before 1933 it had been 7 years of age. The 1933 Act raised it to 8 years. The Ingleby Committee recommended that it be raised to 12 years (with the possibility of becoming 13 or 14 at a later date), but this recommendation proved too controversial even in 1963 when the age was fixed at 10.

A relationship between truancy, "the streets", and delinquency had long been warned about by experienced educationalists and enlightened magistrates. A relationship between mental handicap and delinquency was debated, although it was recognized that some handicapped children might be easily led. A relationship between school failure and commitment to approved schools seemed to be well established. But research was limited.

By 1958 one of the first surveys in a rural area (Somerset) sought to examine the relationship between "certain factors in the education of children and delinquency". The Director of Education, W. J. Deacon, noted that it had been said that one could distinguish seventeen different factors which could contribute towards a child's delinquency.

Whilst the survey did not provide the required answers it produced "a considerable amount of information" which would assist "in pointing to factors and contributory causes of delinquency".

A substantial research project was begun in 1964 when the Home Office, jointly with the Minister of Education, commissioned the National Foundation for Educational Research to study the factors in the organization and life of a school which might affect the attitudes, behaviour, and attainments of children with the aim of discovering how "variations in these factors may exert a positive influence on educational attainment and on personal development and social adjustment. Juvenile delinquency will be one of a number of variables included in the study". (This 8-year "constructive educational project" was briefly described by McNally, 1965.)

Teachers, however, have frequently protested on the basis of their experience that what the school could do in prevention depended in some measure upon the size of classes, the range and extent of special provision, the availability of specialist advice from a range of disciplines, the training of special teachers, and the links between the school, the home, and the various agencies working in the community (including, no doubt, the probation service).

Whatever the causes of delinquency, some distinction has suggested itself in practice between those children for whom one caution or one court appearance proved a sufficient check and the tiny fraction of offenders whose social circumstances or personal condition prompted more than one appearance and revealed an urgent need for help.

Provision, Treatment, and Punishment

In practice, it was the acute shortage of special educational provision, allied to the dichotomy between the school system and the Home Office administration, which resulted in such unfortunate decisions regarding handicapped children as that quoted at the head of this chapter. But whilst a number of children were unquestionably getting the wrong kind of treatment through the courts, a number were also getting their first reference to special educational treatment as a result of a court recommendation. Significantly, it was a juvenile magistrate—John Watson—who in 1965 suggested that he saw a prima facie case for obtaining the advice of a psychiatrist where—amongst other things—the child was (a) in need of care or protection or control, (b) had suffered a severe illness or accident or there was a history of serious illness (mental or otherwise) in the family, (c) had any physical defect or deformity, (d) was unduly backward at school, (e) was said to be a truant, wander from home, pilfer, or unable to make friends, and (f) was solitary, irritable, or depressed.

A similar application to the psychiatrist was recommended where the court was considering a drastic step such as removal from home.

The Guild of Teachers of Backward Children, in its evidence to the Royal Commission on Penal Reform (1965) recommended amongst other things that all educational provision, including approved schools, should be under the education authority.

Meanwhile M. Chazan (1963), reviewing "trends in post-war theory and practice" with relation to maladjusted children, not only recognized that there were "many gaps in the facilities required to help maladjusted children" but "perhaps the major need" which was "for knowledge which will enable clinical and social services as well as special educational provision to be realistically planned".

The Child, the Family, and the Young Offender

By the second half of 1965 the Home Office had published a new White Paper on *The Child, the Family, and the Young Offender*. It represented a new look at the problem, setting out the Government's provisional proposals for practical reforms to help the family, prevent and reduce delinquency, and revise the law and treatment of offenders up to the age of 21. It was recognized that a high proportion of adult criminals began as juvenile offenders, and that every advance in treating early offenders therefore helped in the prevention of adult crime.

The Family

It was interesting to note that at about the same time as this paper was being published, a report from the Moscow region on juvenile crime pointed out that in more than 70 per cent of the crime committed by juveniles there was "an abnormal situation" in the homes of these young people.

In Britain, according to the white paper, much delinquency could be traced to inadequacy or breakdown in the family.

Local authorities had already been required by several Acts (1946, National Health Service, 1948 Children Act and National Assistance Act) to provide services in support of children and the family. By the 1963 Children and Young Persons Act, they were required to "make available such advice, guidance and assistance as may promote the welfare of children by diminishing the need to receive them into or keep them in care, or for them to be brought before a juvenile court".

This preventive work was seen as of cardinal importance not only for its positive social value but as a means of exposing situations which might give rise to delinquency. It was proposed to improve the structure of the various services connected with support of the family, etc., and that these should be organized as "a family service".

Special Arrangements

Those young people who in spite of the above still needed special facilities were to be divided into two groups, those under 16 and those between 16 and 21. It was proposed that the sanctions of the ordinary criminal law apply to those over the age of 16.

Under 16 Age Group

Radical changes in the juvenile court system were proposed to: (a) spare children the stigma of criminality, (b) provide a better means for directing social inquiries and discussing treatment with parents and social workers, (c) persuade parents to assume more personal responsibility, and (d) allow more flexibility in developing treatment according to the child's response.

The under-sixteens were to be removed as far as possible from the jurisdiction of the court and to be dealt with by family councils. Such councils would be appointed by the local authority and try to reach agreement with parents concerning the facts of the case and the most appropriate treatment for the child. Observation centres would be provided to which local authorities could send children for examination and assessment. These would replace the present remand homes and classifying approved schools in this respect.

Family Courts

Where the evidence was disputed it would be dealt with in a family court. These courts would also deal with grave or difficult cases. Specially selected juvenile magistrates were to be appointed for these.

Methods of Treatment

It was proposed that responsibility for the child might be left to the parents or (a) the child might be ordered to attend an attendance centre for a given number of hours, or (b) be put under supervision of a social worker for 1, 2, or 3 years, or (c) sent on short-term training to a detention centre provided and administered by the Home Office, or (d) if in need of longer training, would be placed in the care of the local authority whose children's committee would decide with the parents the most suitable residential home or school for each individual. Approved schools would become part of a comprehensive range of residential establishments and, for the most part, would be taken over by local authorities.

Older Offenders (16–21)

The same panel of magistrates as at the family courts would exercise jurisdiction over the 16–21 age group. A legally qualified chairman would sit for all indictable cases. Serious cases, e.g. murder, rape, or robbery, would be committed for trial to a superior court. The courts would sit separately from the family courts or on another day if in the same building. Treatment included probation, detention, training in a youth training centre (Borstals and senior approved schools becoming part of a comprehensive system of residential provision), and long-term training (now dealt with by prison sentences).

It was hoped that the proposed changes would take young persons outside the ambit of the criminal law and of the courts, and make it easier to organize such arrangements for their welfare as were most appropriate. Also, they would divorce the arrangements for the trial and treatment of those aged 16–21 from the ordinary criminal courts and from the penal system as it applies to adults.

The spirit behind the white paper was widely approved although the proposed new structure was subject to searching criticism.

CHAPTER 8

Provisios for the Mentally and Educationally Subnormal in 1964

Improved medical skills, more dextrous therapy, more humane nursing, more efficient optical, auditory and mobility aids will tend still more to reduce the number of those children who are now termed physically handicapped, either in sensory or motor-modalities, or to reduce the effective handicap to such small proportions, so that more children so affected might manage within the normal sphere of education. This will leave the mentally handicapped as the numerically predominant category and the emotionally handicapped as a close second.

(National Union of Teachers, 1960.)

A NUT Survey

With the increase in special (ESN) schools came several developments. Summarizing the replies to a questionnaire (1958) from 144 special day schools for ESN pupils, the NUT pointed to the changes as well as to the variations in provision. For example:

1. The use of the terms "ESN" or "Special" in the name of the school was being displaced by names like "House in the Garden", "The Wishing Tree School", etc.
2. The majority of the schools were all-age and for both sexes.
3. The age at which pupils were accepted differed substantially. For example:

    32 schools began with 5-year-old pupils.
    17 schools began with 6-year-old pupils.
    51 schools began with 7-year-old pupils.
    15 schools began with 8-year-old pupils.

> 3 schools began with 9-year olds. ⎫ these were prob-
> 4 schools began with 10-year olds. ⎬ ably "secondary
> 22 schools began with 11-year olds. ⎭ age" schools.

4. The size of school ranged from 20 to 220 pupils, with an average of 100.

5. The IQ range was from 30 to 115, more than half the schools having some pupils with IQs below 50 whilst three-quarters had some pupils with IQs above 75.

6. The majority had the services of a speech therapist for "rather more than half a day a week", psychiatric advice and treatment, and facilities for home visiting.

7. Additional equipment (e.g. for physical education) varied from "nil" to "anything required". A quarter of the schools stated that they received no fund for visits or school journeys, whilst more than three-quarters listed deficiencies which ranged from "no playground" to "class in hall".

Amongst the quotes from replies were: "We are fortunate to work for a first-class authority who give us every backing and support. This type of school is new to them, but I can think of no point of substance where they have not gone out of their way to meet our point of view. Would this were so everywhere."

Special schools, however, were only a part of special provision, and practice more than theory seemed to follow the lines of Stott's James Wycombe experiment in that "there was no quick and easy way of sorting out those children who require long term, all round treatment, from those likely to respond quickly" to suitable remedial measures. In Stott's experience only the child's actual progress within the remedial setting and under skilled guidance could decide this. Such a setting and guidance was not everywhere available.

146 Varieties

The range of provision for handicapped children made by one authority has been indicated. But nationally what provision emerged for the largest category, the educationally subnormal, and for the overlapping category, the mentally handicapped?

The multiplicity of local educational authorities, of course, had each developed at its own pace, motivated in different ways, and subject to different local complications. In an effort to gain some picture of current provision for evidence to the Plowden Committee, a circular was sent by the author to all local authorities early in 1964 requesting published reports of other helpful information on:

1. Special educational provision available within ordinary infant and primary schools.
2. Other forms of special educational provision available for pupils under 11.
3. Experimental provision for infants who "did not fit into the normal school pattern".
4. Experimental educational provision for children excluded from schools in training centres.

From the replies received from more than half the authorities the following pattern emerged.

Within Ordinary Schools

(a) Some LEAs made no planned provision within ordinary schools or "such provision as they are able". This group might extend to those who felt that the situation was adequately served by streaming or who were influenced by this theory. "In the three form entry schools, the third stream in each group is usually small enough to undertake useful remedial work, but in general the surge of infant children and the forecast of scarcity of primary teacher supply may endanger this practice."

(b) A second group used part-time teachers for small groups or had small classes for remedial work.

(c) A third group had remedial centres to which children went part-time.

(d) A fourth group used peripatetic teachers to visit the junior schools. Here, too, provision ranged from one or two peripatetic teachers to a substantial, centrally planned operation.

(e) More arresting were such situations as that reported in Carmarthenshire, where there was "a well integrated School Psychological Service" which worked in close consultation with the school health service. All special educational treatment was carried out under the aegis of the School Psychological Service "so that proper arrangement can be made for both diagnosis and treatment". Routine surveys were carried out of all age groups and the children eventually referred were assessed

> in a Central Diagnostic Clinic which serves as a base for the various agencies working under the aegis of the School Psychological Service. After diagnosis by the psychologist arrangements are made for the children to receive special educational treatment in various types of units in primary, secondary and residential schools. At primary level there are Remedial Units for (a) Dull children. (b) Backward children. (c) Retarded children. (d) Maladjusted children.

Similarly, in Glamorgan, ESN pupils were informally ascertained following upon surveys conducted by educational psychologists with the co-operation of teachers. The entire 8-year age group was covered. Special classes were established in 119 schools.

Whilst not all the replies suggested so integrated, so widespread, or so organizationally consistent a system, the following ungraded selection indicates the concern, the difficulties, and the trends. Derbyshire had set up a number of special classes in primary schools. Some of these classes catered for children who might otherwise be in a day ESN school if there were one in the area.

East Sussex had special classes for ESN pupils in "practically all the larger primary schools".

Essex had "a large number of special classes in junior schools throughout the county. These were arranged by Divisional and Borough Education Officers in consultation with the psychologists concerned. . . . This provision varies from time to time according to the teachers and the space available in the various schools." Remedial teachers were employed in every division and borough, and usually worked in conjunction with the child guidance clinic.

Grimsby had set up sixteen remedial teaching classes under the aegis of the educational psychologist.

At selected schools in Hampshire there were 2, 3, or 4 classes accommodating children aged 8–11 from surrounding rural schools.

In Kingston upon Hull "all the opportunity classes have been specially furnished and decorated and they are all appropriately and adequately equipped, and for this purpose an extra allowance is granted for each class". The psychological service provides an active remedial unit which children aged 9–14 attend each afternoon.

Leeds had special classes, a child guidance centre which provided individual help in reading and number, small remedial groups within ordinary schools, and an advisory service for class teachers having backward pupils.

Leicestershire had twenty-seven special classes in primary schools for 619 pupils. "Opinion has radically changed over the last 15 years on the question of moving educationally subnormal children out of their natural environment. But equally important, methods of teaching have changed too and particularly in the County where there is reason to suppose there is a larger aggregate of forward looking teachers in the primary schools than is normally to be found."

Lincolnshire had a team of seven remedial teachers who, together with the education psychologist and psychiatric social worker formed part of the school psychological service. The remedial teachers were paid as group 1 head teachers with mileage allowances and "the Authority has been able to make good appointments of experienced teachers who in addition to the usual teacher-training have taken an additional course at a University Department of Education in the teaching of backward children". Teaching was given in groups of not more than 8. One or two pupils might be taken in the teacher's car to join a group in the next village. The majority had two sessions a week.

"Because we have not yet been allowed to build our quota of special schools the IQ range of the children given help varies from as low as 55 to as high as 120." Also, "we have noted with pleasure in the Ministry's circular 11/61 that the need for more separate rooms for teaching small groups of backward children is recognized but find it well nigh impossible to provide these in new schools, particularly small primary schools, within the current cost limits, if we are to have proper regard to the need for spacious teaching conditions for primary children".

Other authorities also made reference to more such provision being made "if suitable teaching staff and accommodation were available". Lincolnshire (Lindsey) encouraged the formation of special classes and paid an allowance for the teachers. The school psychological service (with four educational psychologists of whom two were shared with neighbouring authorities) advised in methods and equipment as well as testing children and providing remedial teaching. Remedial teachers visited schools at the request of head teachers and taught groups of not more than 6 pupils. Middlesbrough employed a number of peripatetic teachers who visited primary schools at least twice a week to do remedial reading work with small groups. The children attended until they had made up lost ground. Part-time teachers were also used to this purpose. There were remedial classes in some of the larger schools. Newcastle had remedial classes in five junior schools.

Large primary schools in Northamptonshire (with 240 or more on roll) were able to get one teacher for the first 20 pupils and then further teachers "at the rate of one for each 40 or part thereof". It was hoped that this formula would allow for the provision of a class for backward children in the larger schools. In two of the more rural areas with many small village schools, there was a peripatetic teacher who gave special tuition to small groups of backward pupils for two or three periods a week. At one junior school in Kettering there was a class for children aged 7 or 8 who were of normal intelligence but were backward due to absences, maladjustment, or specific disabilities. Children were drawn from the whole of Kettering. The aim was to transfer these children back to their own normal classes after a year or two of special provision.

Oxford provided remedial reading classes for children of near average general intellectual ability, the children attending for part of each day until their reading difficulties were overcome. The teachers in charge of these centres were members of the school psychological service and had specialist qualifications in addition to normal teacher training.

Oxfordshire had one class for 12 ESN pupils attached to a primary school. In many other large primary schools teachers were appointed to take charge of retarded children in smaller groups than the normal class size. Seven peripatetic teachers gave help to children aged 8- to 9-plus who revealed backwardness in reading. Pembroke had two classes designated as ESN, and a remedial centre. Portsmouth had

> always had a few special classes in junior schools and in some schools we have had positions of special responsibility. A lot of this work, however, has been cut down because of staff shortage. We have just begun a new scheme whereby we find out how much special educational treatment is required in school and are allocating teachers for special classes in such schools. These teachers are to be paid special schools allowances. So far we have three of these teachers. We had planned for more but were *unable to get sufficient applicants*.

Three tutorial groups and four remedial classes functioned within the framework of the school psychological service.

The above is sufficiently indicative of both the range and the difficulties. Again and again local education authorities found themselves up against substantial problems related to geography, space, finance, and appropriate teachers or other specialists. The following replies are examples of this.

1. "Other than this, with staff changes and shortage in primary schools no permanent pattern of special class or other provision in ordinary schools has so far been possible."
2. "Much of what we do is of an *ad hoc* nature owing to the rural nature of the area and the fact that the population is scattered."

3. "More such provision would be made if suitable teaching staff and accommodation were available."
4. "So far we have three of these teachers. We had planned for more but were unable to get sufficient applicants."
5. One PSMO saw in juvenile delinquency "another aspect of the inadequacy of the school psychological service . . . too few educational psychologists. Almost always I feel that an adequate psychological service could have rescued them, by discovering their problems at an early age."

Experimental Provision for Infants

A number of the authorities were clearly guided by theories which are now suspect. Many of them did not permit children to enter special schools until they reached the age of 7 or 8. The reasons for this varied. Worthing, for example, argued that admission should not take place until the age of 8 "on the principle that each child should have the opportunity first of attending an ordinary school". Emphasis there was placed on the return of the child to the ordinary school at the secondary stage, if this was possible, and great weight was placed on the head teacher's opinion.

Another authority, however, replied that there was no provision within ordinary infant schools. Some ESN pupils were "mothered along" by interested teachers. "Some children who appear clearly ESN and are also emotionally and socially backward at this stage, 'were excluded from the infant school', some attending nursery schools, some the training centre, and some *awaiting maturation at home*."

Side by side with this approach were other developments of which the following are indicative.

In Bradford all the special schools admitted infants. One of these schools also had a nursery class. Some authorities, like Berkshire, had set up a small assessment class for "a maximum of ten children" who would otherwise have been ascertained as unsuitable for education. Cambridgeshire set up a special unit for children with Down's syndrome (mongols). This unit accepted children from the age of 5 and diagnosed—over a period of not less than 2 years—whether such children could be given education in special schools or should go to training centres. Essex built an assessment unit in every new special school. Glamorgan set up observation units for children aged 4–7.

> The Units allow the children to be taught and kept under observation by the Educational Psychologist, Medical Officers and others with a view to determining the best course for their future education. Each educational psychologist himself has one specialist third-year trained teacher to whom will be referred children with learning or behaviour problems who cannot be admitted to convenient special groups or classes.

The Hampshire Diagnostic Unit at Compton accommodated 40 "borderline ineducable children" from the age of 5 to 7 or 8. Portsmouth included half-time provision "partly because we feel the children concerned can benefit more by attending half a day than a full day, and also because we are not able to get a teacher for a full day. The five-year-old unit is housed in a Remedial Centre which also has a Tutorial class and a Remedial Teaching Unit." They placed children, in the ordinary infant school, "in this class and from there they go either to a special school, tutorial class, day training centre, or return to the ordinary school. Their period of stay tends to be anything from one to two years."

The provision appeared to range from virtually none to:

(1) younger admissions to special schools;
(2) the setting up of special, purpose built units within (a) an ordinary school, (b) a special school, or (c) some separate remedial or similar centres.

Provision for the Severely Subnormal

Efforts within training centres have included the most depressing and haphazard as well as the most inspiring. The setting up of a Central Training Council to approve courses for staff of training centres marked a new direction, but only a fraction of the staff had opportunity to attend even a 1-year diploma course provided voluntarily by the National Association for Mental Health, and the 2-year courses did not commence until 1963.

Curzon (1960) found:

> The very young pre-school children (the under fives) are accepted in some cases in ordinary Nursery Schools and Day Nurseries, where they fit in easily and unobtrusively with their own age group. Unfortunately only very few places are available, although it is understood that 10–15% of the total can be accepted without disruption. There is not only a great need for some pre-school provision, for the training, observation and assessment of the child, and to give help to parents, but also for more education of teachers and doctors, local committees and the general public in the realisation of the needs of this age group.
>
> The first Occupation Centre as it was then called, was opened in 1909 . . . it is not such a new idea as many folk seem to think. One might even say that a few of the Centres in 1960 seem to look and behave as that earlier one.

She saw a need for rethinking here on "the kind of educational niche the child needs" and a need for "considerable re-assessment and experiment in training methods and organization".

However, apart from the staff-training question, there were outstanding local authorities like Monmouthshire where programmes began with a "backward babies clinic". By 1957 Monmouthshire was able to claim that not more than 20 per cent of these children would ultimately prove to be custodial cases; 50 per cent would be able to contribute to their upkeep in sheltered conditions, whilst 30 per cent would be able to work within the normal population.

The John F. Kennedy Training Centre in West Ham with its special care unit represented a purpose-built centre of a new type (Didsbury, 1962). And in general, whether the health authorities remained separate from the education authority or found ways of co-operating, provision might be subdivided into the following:

(a) Traditional "occupation" or babyminding without particular evidence of alertness regarding teacher training, the content of the day's activities, the hampering and depressing effect of an inadequate building, and the effect of impossible loads upon the staff.

(b) Some educational orientation in the programme, if only of a limited, half-hearted type.

(c) A structured organization and programme by a health authority (e.g. Monmouthshire) with a graduated system of four progressive classes from the age of 5–16, and the addition of a special class for academic work.

(d) Closer relationships between health and education authorities, ranging from a reduction of administrative barriers (e.g. allowing easier transfer of children) and the use of educational psychologists by health authorities and extending to:

 (i) the delegation of responsibility for the training centres by the health authority to the education authority; and

(ii) the building on the same site of a joint special school and training centre, the qualified head teacher of the former having oversight, too, of the latter.

Some Parents' Views on Current Provision

Replies by parents in one branch of the National Society for Mentally Handicapped Children, to a questionnaire sent out by one of its officers, brought the following responses. It is interesting to compare the pre-war hostility to ascertainment of children for special schools with the attitudes expressed here by parents of children who would otherwise be deprived even such provision.

PROVISION FOR CHILDREN UNDER 5 YEARS OF AGE

A third of those replying reported difficulty in getting guidance, but the majority reported no such problem. Some of the latter, however, qualified their replies with such comments as: "provided one went out of one's way to find the right place." The majority found difficulty in getting provision.

PROVISION FOR CHILDREN OVER 5

There was little difficulty in getting guidance but replies included: "It was conflicting." "The guidance was given by the head of the school." "Did not ask for any." Half reported difficulty in getting provision.

In reply to the question: "If it is felt that good provision was made, can you state personally what form it took?", the following replies were representative.

(a) Our daughter is now at an excellent special school.

(b) Entrance to an ESN school was obtained by continuous pressure by parents on local education authority.

(c) Excellent teachers but their good work impeded by antiquated school and overcrowded classes.

(d) The headmaster and teachers there are kind and gentle, doing all they can to help Jean to learn all she can to be a useful person. My husband and I are very grateful that such a school has been provided.

(e) The Supervisor of the training centre felt that Karen was too high-grade and gave every assistance in obtaining a place for her at a special school.

(f) My child went to a junior training centre when aged 4. When he was 5-plus the county education department sent a psychologist to test him and found him an ESN place after a wait of 5 months.

(g) At first yes, but now it is difficult. She is at home at present waiting for a place.

(h) Difficulties began after she reached the age of 7. There is no maladjusted school in this area.

(i) Some advice obtained by sheer chance from a child therapy clinic. Otherwise county psychologist only stated that the child was backward. No other facilities or guidance at the age of 5, thus creating quite a problem.

(j) It was mostly a case of waiting for a vacancy in a suitable school and the authorities, though slow were always extremely helpful.

D

At a public conference Janet E. L. Barclay described the child
"permanently at home," graphically revealing a mother's plight.
She considered herself fortunate that her child's handicap was
recognizable at birth (the child had Down's syndrome). "I knew
at once that she was not normal and pestered all the nursing home
staff but they were not allowed to tell me the truth and so lied or
avoided me. In all fairness, I had not the courage to ask the
Specialist, Doctor, or Matron when they stood at the bottom of
my bed."

She had found that "agencies, advertisements and Nursery
Training Colleges produced no help when it was known that the
child was a Mongol. . . . Daily help was easier to come by. Most
daily women seem to be fundamentally kind and sympathetic and
readily accept our problem." She found that

> her first real friend was herself the mother of a mentally handicapped
> child who happened to live in our road. She took me to the local branch
> meeting of the National Society for Mentally Handicapped Children and
> I am convinced that that introduction was my turning point as I realized
> I was not alone with this problem, and I know of other mothers who have
> felt the same. Would it not be possible for all doctors and nurses to tell
> new parents of mentally handicapped children about this society, and put
> them in touch with other parents with like children in the neighbourhood?
> It is in the first few months that we need help from someone who has been
> in the same situation. . . .

Her plea was (and she thought she spoke for all mothers of
"mongol" children)

> treat our children as children first and mongols last. Check the heart and
> eyes and other possible defects at once, not wait for the mother to query.
> Tell the parents the positive things about them. Aim at training them
> normally. They are worth it and the reward is the love and affection and
> friendship they give and bring in return. Our child has brought untold
> blessings that we should never have dreamt of eight years ago.

Educational Guide Lines

Just as the schools and local authorities varied so did the skills
and training of teachers. Whilst staff in many training centres
and teachers in many special schools and classes for backward

pupils were left to devise their own curricula or programmes, two broad approaches could be discerned in the education of their pupils. The one was a "child development" approach, and stemmed from the needs of "the whole child". The other approach was more narrowly remedial. Efforts to integrate the two approaches have been attempted in varying ways, but we are still far from offering a rounded programme for more than some pupils for more than part of their school life.

Dr. Tizard's "Brooklands experiment" with severely subnormal children demonstrated the positive role to be played by a nursery-school type programme (1957–60). Thirty-two children from Fountain Hospital were divided into sixteen pairs matched for sex, age, IQ, and, as far as possible, type of defect. "Children with severe physical problems and those suffering from psychosis were excluded, since in a pilot study with largely untrained staff it was not practical to include children who present special problems."

Whilst one of each pair remained at the Fountain Hospital, the other went into the experimental centre at Reigate. Eight boys and girls aged from 6 to 12 years were in a "family" with two staff members to look after them. An "activity" approach, or "learning through doing", was encouraged.

Despite many physical difficulties and staffing problems, and initial retrogression of the children, striking improvements became evident, and the positive value of "individual attention" in small units was brought out. The experiment challenged "the type of educational programme used generally in training centres for mentally handicapped children . . . the form of teaching, not the realist and agreed aim of independence and the fullest economic productivity".

Goldstein and Seigle (1958), describing the primary and secondary characteristics of mentally handicapped children, drew attention (as part of their "curriculum guide") to the needs of all children for love, security, recognition, and a sense of belonging.

It is important that the administrator and teacher recognize the relationships between the educable mentally retarded child's basic psychological needs, certain aspects of our culture, and the child's intellectual subnormality. Our culture generally smiles on the bright. . . . Conversely it frowns upon the incompetent and the laggard and confirms upon him the very antithesis of his basic needs—rejection. It is obvious that the educable mentally handicapped child's intellectual subnormality must, in all too many cases, operate to prevent the fulfilment of his needs for attention, acceptance and security, if not in the home, at least in the competitive and depersonalized activities in the school setting.

Secondary characteristics result from the conflict between the child's primary characteristics and his physical and social environment and "most frequently take the form of behaviour and attitudes". The source of the conflict, however, was not only in the school but in the home and the locality. The school was only one of the environments capable of influencing, positively or negatively, the child's intellectual or other growth.

These secondary characteristics were said by Goldstein and Seigle to include frustration-proneness and self-devaluation. Learning disabilities included (a) oversimplification of concepts, (b) limited ability in generalization, (c) short memory or attention span, (d) limitations in incidental learning, and (e) retarded language development.

Earlier Contributions to Theory and Practice

Earlier contributors to theory and practice came from several countries and spanned more than a century. Dr. J. M. Itard, who set out to educate "the wild boy of Aveyron" via the senses, influenced Dr. E. Seguin, another medically trained pioneer. Seguin based his educational methods upon a neuro-physiological approach. His two books describe this approach: *The Moral Treatment, Hygiene and Education of Idiots and Other Backward Children,* and *Idiocy: Its Treatment by the Physiological Method.*

Dr. Seguin brought out the importance of the physical comfort and condition of the child, the child's needs which required to be considered before any question of proceeding to "teaching" the child could be seriously entertained. The need for a healthy relationship between teacher and child and for the individualization of instruction was also brought out—more than a century before the 1944 Education Act.

Just over a decade after Seguin's second book appeared, Dr. D. M. Montessori (as assistant in the psychiatric clinic in Rome) became interested in mentally handicapped children. If in some respects she appeared to narrow down Seguin's approach, she ascribed considerable importance to sense and muscle training in the early years. Her didactic material encouraged considerable interest and innovation. Her system of "auto-education" utilized twenty-six different items which were intended to train the senses of touch, sight, hearing, and speech. If France and Italy had now made significant contributions to the development of theory and practice in this area, a Belgian, Dr. O. Decroly, encouraged the next step forward. Montessori's techniques appeared too formal. Dr. Decroly emphasized the relevance of a natural setting for teaching, and developed games and a curriculum which were extended by a pupil, Alice Descoeudres. She was guided by principles which included (a) utilizing the natural activities of pupils, (b) enriching verbal expression via social activities, (c) grouping together certain "subjects" so that each could strengthen the others, (d) individualizing instruction, and (e) using knowledge gained or the learned activity in actual life. School walls were being pushed down and the relevance of what was taught was being made more apparent to teacher and taught.

The grouping of subjects, the development of "projects" or "units of experience" had their roots in the work of Alice Descoeudres, and were developed further in the USA by C. P. Ingram (1924) and E. H. Martens (1950).

In Britain a somewhat different approach was developed by John Duncan, a headmaster of a special school (*The Education of the Ordinary Child*). This was rooted in the theory of intelligence developed by Spearman. In practice, a step-by-step, carefully graded scheme was devised in handwork and other areas, seeking to encourage observation of similarities and differences, and a development of the mental processes.

In the post-war years the USA developed interest in this area of work, further producing a number of textbooks for teachers. Not until 1960 was a post-war research-based rounded textbook for teachers of such children in this country, published by Tansley and Gulliford (1960).

Remedial Treatment

The remedial treatment of backwardness in basic subjects had, however, attracted wider interest here, accelerating the work by Schonell (1942). Reading had always been a particular source of anxiety. A study of research in this area by Professor M. D. Vernon (1957), concluded that the methods of experiment and clinical diagnosis so far employed had "failed to isolate any factors which appear universally in all cases of reading backwardness other than inability to read easily" (p. 186). She added: "if the Chinese, according to Elia, could discover how to roast pork without burning their houses down, it may be possible for us to attack and remedy the fundamental cause of reading disability without applying excessively lengthy and possibly irrelevant remedial procedures" (p. 197).

Teachers in the situation had to teach as best they could. Their difficulties and those of their pupils gave rise to a "number of significant reading schemes". Gertrude Keir's "Adventures in Reading" brought in a series of small, graded readers, linked with work-books, activities, and based on the sentence method. These proved extremely popular with teachers and children. A phonic-word method was introduced by Daniels and Diack, "The Royal Road Readers". The advantages of a word whole and phonic system were integrated. Dr. D. H. Stott produced a "Reading Kit", a systematic phonic approach, utilizing games and activities which motivated pupils and held their interest. All these approaches showed an awareness of the nature of the child as well as of the "subject".

ITA

To these might be added Sir James Pitman's *Initial Teaching Alphabet*"* which could be used with any method and which saw as a major cause of reading backwardness the fact that the twenty-six letters of the alphabet had to change their sounds and even their shapes in a manner confusing to the child. This medium aroused considerable interest and widespread publicity.

There was no doubt that the mere act of experimenting in education produced better results for the class undergoing the experiment than for the control class. As Vera Southgate (1965) pointed out, experience indicated that "any pronounced drive in the teaching of reading produces improvement, almost regardless of the method or scheme employed". She found it important to relate this knowledge to the fact that

> there has never been, in this country, a reading drive which in any way approaches the magnitude of the current one regarding i.t.a. Furthermore, one should bear in mind that there are other new approaches to reading which are giving good results but which have not had the opportunities for research and publicity open to i.t.a. Consequently, good results in i.t.a. classes cannot be attributed solely to the new alphabet.

Nevertheless, ITA was recognized as an important and interesting approach to the teaching of reading. Whilst it was not then possible to determine how far its successes had been due to its alphabet or content rather than to the surrounding motivation and drive, it was plain that a number of children had benefited considerably from the innovation. If for this reason alone, many children had reason to be grateful to Sir James Pitman.

But unless treated early or prevented, the problem of backwardness in reading became pronounced and complicated at the secondary stage. This problem afflicted a range of special as well as ordinary schools. Concern with the many implications led to a Nuffield inquiry (National Book League, 1961) into the availability and suitability of reading books for older pupils who were

---

* See also H. Johnson's system of diacritical marks described in *Teaching Backward Pupils* by S. S. Segal (Evans), and *Words in Colour*, by Dr. Gattegno, described in *Forward Trends*, October 1965, by T. Lee.

backward readers. As books specifically designed for such pupils were then found to be very few, they had to be supplemented by books for normal, younger readers, which were not too infant in illustration or content.

Such was the hunger for suitable books, and so inadequate were those in actual use in many schools, that books exhibited for the "inquiry" were treated as a recommended range—many schools aware for the first time apparently, of such material as was in existence.

Dr. D. H. Stott and T. Pascoe made studied, critical analyses of all series specially designed for backward pupils, and their "survey of books for backward readers" led to further interest on the part of publishers and interested teachers.

Frequently schools practised a narrow remedial approach to reading, but this was not always a happy arrangement. It was extremely difficult to integrate the "child development" and remedial approaches without smaller classes and suitable books. A number of teachers set out to produce attractive, well graded, reading series, and publishers were quick to respond to the growing interest. But this was only one aspect of the need.

The effect of school failure created an increasingly difficult social, organizational, and teaching problem in secondary schools. One attempt to provide a balanced curriculum for secondary pupils led to the "Working World Series", a range of dove-tailed textbooks designed for "dull and backward" pupils. This 4-year course was oriented towards the pupil's current and future needs in the working world. It took note of the variable forms of organization to be found in secondary schools, which in the main had subject teachers moving into and out of the forms. The social ages and interests of secondary pupils were also important considerations and, to ensure a successful start, a reading age of 7 was assumed for the 11-year-old pupils' first-year books. The series proceeded along the well-known pedagogical lines of working outwards, beginning with "the home" in the first year and moving on to "the locality", "the nation", and "the working world". Each year's range of books included consideration of applied basic skills, health, and hygiene, safety, leisure training, citizenship, religious instruction, and vocational guidance.

Broad approaches of this kind were dictated by the gross and practical problems arising from backwardness in our secondary schools and faced by thousands of inadequately equipped teachers. For the more complex problems of reading disability there was still a need for specialists, familiar with all approaches and techniques, who could bend or change available material to meet a child's specific needs.

Machines and Programmed Learning

Increasing value was seen in the use of audio-visual aids in schools, notably television, radio, tape recorders, film strips, and films.

> A fresh approach was outlined by the headmaster of a day school for educationally subnormal children: I believe that many of the problems of the socially handicapped child can be overcome if more use is made of Programmed Learning. We have had an extended and comprehensive test of programmed learning here—lasting over two years. Apart from its efficacy as a learning technique, we find that it will by-pass emotional problems and motivate intensely dull and difficult children, for long periods.   [Reports in Education.]

Programmed learning was not automatically tied to a teaching machine. It provided a carefully graded series of experiences, and there were three important elements in this controlled learning process.

Firstly, the learner was presented with a stimulus which gave him information, demanded a response, or did both. Secondly, the learner had to utilize the information in making some decision or response. Thirdly, after responding, he was presented with some information ("feedback") which helped him ascertain how appropriate the response was.

Reviewing research on *Teaching by Machinery*, Leith (1963) described the three rival approaches to automated teaching which derived from Pressey, Skinner, and Crowder, and interpreted the findings of a number of studies bearing on ten categories of research on programmed learning. He concluded that with many kinds of subject matter and different age groups of learners programmed instruction secured as much or better learning than did conventional methods, "sometimes with a saving of from a third to two-thirds of the normal time spent". This efficiency was possible with a programmed textbook although "it would be unwise to assert without further evidence and without careful cost analysis, that the hardware of automated teaching has no significant role to play in teaching and training".

He found that programmed learning, prepared and guided by well-informed teachers, was an effective mode of instruction of which the possibilities had not been fully revealed. "It has already shown itself to be a helpful adjunct to other methods of teaching."

By 1965 several large British engineering firms, for example, were collaborating in publishing a series of training programmes designed to improve current practices in apprentice training and basic engineering education. Birkbeck College in London was linked with a substantial experiment in Surrey schools, and the Institute of Education in Leicester had an active Programmed Learning Research Unit.

Leedham, at this latter unit, saw that the isolation of the person using the teaching machine might involve a loss of some of the benefits of the group situation. In a research note (Leedham, 1965), he revealed that he had created and examined a group situation which allowed flexibility and made some adjustment to meet individual differences in the speed of learning whilst using a programme. This experiment—like the others so far described—was not centred upon ESN pupils.

The first study of programmed instruction by the Institute for Research on Exceptional Children (USA) began in 1959, and a series of experiments in this direction have been summarized in the report *Ten Years of Research*, issued by the Institute in 1963.

As is the case with programmed instruction in general and not solely for handicapped children, provision is still in its infancy even if it promises exciting possibilities (e.g. in the Research Institute of Defectology's machine for the blind, referred to elsewhere, and the USA Edison Responsive Environment System).

An interdisciplinary centre may well encourage the invention of new machines, just as some machines already bypass the loss of one sense. With mentally handicapped children the role of teaching machines will only be evaluated healthily after sufficient programmes have been devised.

CHAPTER 9

The IQ under examination

> If it is true, as we maintain . . . that I.Q. tends to remain constant for the same child from test to test, then we can draw two very important conclusions from this state of affairs. In the first place, one test of a child serves not only to let us know the present level of his intelligence, but also enables us to prophesy with a high degree of reliability his future rate of mental growth.
>
> (PROFESSOR D. KENNEDY-FRASER, *Education of the Backward Child*, p. 25 (1932).)

> Speaking of mentally handicapped children one must be aware that terminology in this field is in a particularly confused state at present. Mentally is the most inclusive term, *mentally retarded* refers to the highest grade, *mentally defective* refers to the educable grade and *severely mentally defective* refers to the trainable grade. Translated into terms of I.Q. it means that we have to deal with persons with an I.Q. ranging from 90–80, from 80–55, and from 55–40.
>
> (N. Y. VLIETSTRA, Chief Inspector of Special Education, Netherlands, 1963 Congress.)

Constancy of the IQ

For a long time great hopes had been placed upon intelligence tests and the IQ. Kennedy-Fraser (1932), for example, reflected the views of his generation when he declared with some enthusiasm, discussing the problem of distinguishing between the temporarily and permanently backward child:

> The backwardness in either case has first been noticed in the child's failure to respond effectively to the ordinary situations of his school tasks, and we want to know whether this is due to some inborn causes or merely to some unfortunate hindrances, such as prolonged or frequent absences from school, frequent changes of school, or even actual bad teaching or a physical disability. If we have two such cases and apply mental tests to each (requiring from twenty to forty minutes per child), and find in the one case that the child has an I.Q. of 100 or over, and in the second case

that the I.Q. is 80 or under, then we can at once say that the first is a temporary and the second a permanent case of backwardness, and proceed accordingly with our remedial educational measure. Without some such method we are merely proceeding in a hit-or-miss fashion. . . .

Not only before the Second World War but since its conclusion many teachers are still guided by such concepts. Here seemed to be a scientific measure—a step towards a science of education. The Ministry's pamphlet on special education (1946) was slightly more guarded.

It is a matter of general agreement that intelligence cannot be substantially improved by any methods known to us at present, and that aptitudes verbal or practical, are not readily alterable except, perhaps, by skilled teaching over a long period. Retardation due to limited ability is not likely to be quickly or easily overcome even by the best forms of special educational treatment, and where the limitation is in general intelligence, the retardation is likely to be permanent.

If few took exception to this cautiously stated view, the most powerful criticism of current practice stemmed from a consequence of this theory—its weakness in relation to the pre-school child and infant.

M. E. Highfield (1951), for example, in her chapter on the infant school special class, was clearly influenced by the then prevailing views on "mental age" and "maturation". She wrote:

it is clear why a dull child should be retarded, simply because his thought processes are at too immature a stage of development to enable him even to assimilate the material of formal training in number and reading. . . . In extreme cases he may be a defective whose mental age when he enters school at 5 years of age will be 3 years. No more can be expected from him than is demanded of a child in the younger section of a nursery school. It is a waste of time and injurious to the child to attempt formal training in such cases.

This view would have been universally applauded before the war. Today it would be criticized as negative or as encouraging "waiting" for suitable maturation. In some countries this concept resulted in children being excluded from nurseries as well as from infant schools to await maturation.

As Professor Kirk pointed out, this practice assumed that kindergartens did not aid mental and social maturation, and that cultural influences of the home were not important factors in mental development.

It was at this stage and in this respect that theory required the closest possible examinations, for many experts in the field emphasize the lasting and possibly determinate importance of educational influences brought to bear upon the child under the age of 7.

Similarly, if not quite of equal importance, is "what happens to the children after they have left school?" The relevance of the IQ is under examination.

Worldwide Developments from this Base

It is interesting to note the variety of different forms of practice which evolved from similar theoretical bases in different countries. The situation in 1960 was clarified in the 23rd International Conference on Public Education Report. This put forward classifications of "educable mental defectives" which in some cases gave ceilings higher than IQ 75. One group of countries, our own along with some Commonwealth countries, China, France, Sweden, Israel, Japan and Thailand, were reported as providing special schools for children within the 45 or 50 to 70 or 75 IQ range. The lower IQ floors in some countries indicated how arbitrary the lines of demarcation were. A second group (Norway and Philippines) distinguished between the 50–70 IQ range (in special schools) and 70–80 range (special classes). A third group widened the band of special school children to the 50–80 range (Australia, Argentine, El Salvador) or even the 45–60 IQ range as "imbeciles" (the Netherlands) or would only allow children with IQs above 65 to enter special schools (German Federal Republic). There was a fifth group which fell outside the above in not using intelligence tests at all (USSR, Hungary, Rumania, Byelo Russia, Ukraine) or in using them only as "an auxiliary criterion" (Czechoslovakia). There was, however, everywhere, the report noted, a marked shift away from the IQ as the sole or even the predominant element in a decision to place the child in a special school or class.

The Significance of the IQ

By 1964 Dr. A. Kushlik had concluded:

> The I.Q. range of 50 to 70 or 75 has been suggested as diagnostic of the grade of mild mental subnormality. This has not proved useful either clinically or administratively. There are many people in this IQ range who are never dealt with as subnormal and who do not appear to have problems arising from their low intelligence, and there are people of IQ well over 70 who are being dealt with by the services for the subnormal. . . .
>
> There is much evidence that unlike severe subnormality, mild subnormality is a temporary incapacity related largely to educational difficulties experienced at school. After leaving school the majority of these people become socially and economically independent and indistinguishable from the rest of the community.

But whilst he seriously questioned the use of the IQ clinically or administratively for diagnosis of "mild subnormality", after a thorough appraisal of available evidence he noted that "an IQ of under 50 appears at present to be a severe incapacity leading to permanent dependence among about 90% of affected individuals. Those subjects who do not die at an early age appear eventually to be admitted to hospitals for the subnormal. Once admitted they tend at present to remain there until they die."

Moreover, despite revaluations of the importance of the IQ in the USA, Dunn and Capobianco in their review of research the year before the 1960 Conference, could state that in practice: "mental retardation is coming to mean an IQ score below 75 or 80 on valid, repeated administrations of an individual intelligence test."

The term "mental deficiency" was reserved for those who as adults, were likely to be "socially incompetent". The functional though tentative divisions of mentally retarded children in the USA had become: "(a) the educable mentally retarded (IQs approximately 50–75), (b) the trainable mentally retarded (IQs 30–50), i.e. children able to communicate orally, to care for themselves physically, and to become economically productive in sheltered environments, yet who cannot be expected to become literate", and, finally, (c) the custodial mentally retarded with IQs below 30 who required permanent help.

It is, of course, impossible to estimate how rigid or fluid the organization of schools were with respect to these categories. Certainly, a new interest in the category which Burt had defined as "dull and backward" was also evident in the USA. The Professor of Special Education at Syracuse University (Johnson, 1963), saw reason to produce a substantial textbook on the education of such children. For him, the lowest quartile of the population intellectually formed at least three broad and rather distinct groups: "the mentally deficient, the mentally handicapped, and the slow learners." The first group comprised about a half of 1 per cent of the population; the second group 3–4 per cent; and the remainder of the quartile were "slow learners". Of this last group a quarter were estimated to come from adequate homes and to make a "reasonable although somewhat difficult adjustment to the traditional school and instruction". The remainder, 14 or 15 per cent of the population, formed the group which gave rise to the textbook.

McLeod, in Australia, drew some interesting conclusions from a symposium. In *Segregation or Integration* there were contributions from a number of countries which made provision for the "educable mentally retarded" as they were termed outside Britain, or the educationally subnormal here. In this symposium the social effects of various kinds of provision were considered not solely from the viewpoint of the needs of the rest of the community, but from that of the needs of the handicapped child himself. McLeod found a general consistency on certain matters although "more research is needed". He found that "educable slow learners" tend to divide into two categories: "one group which is likely to be competent in adulthood, and the other which is not." For the most part, children with an IQ above 60 belonged in his view to the former group, but he considered the IQ alone as inadequate as a diagnostic tool. "Moreover the threshold of intellectual ability necessary for educability may be pushed down as a result of improved techniques of teaching. Variability of measured IQ and educational achievement means that assessment cannot be a once-for-all affair; instead diagnosis must be continuous and cumulative."

As one USA reviewer concluded, the concept of the "constancy of the IQ" was no longer defensible. For Dr. Buckle it was "a nihilist concept". Alongside this developing belief was the discovery from follow up inquiries of mentally retarded adults that in the adult world most of them made out unexpectedly well, even without special education. (A summary of these studies was made by Professor Tizard in the book, edited by A. D. B. Clarke, *Mental Deficiency, the Changing Outlook*.) Full employment had helped to modify the attitudes of the public towards the mentally handicapped.

The IQ then, had lost its central importance in theory, but in practice one found at the extremes one group who believed the IQ to be educable, but who continued as if it were constant, and one group who considered the IQ to be constant, but rejoiced at any variation upwards.

A further complication is provided by Williams (1965):

> The background to the term "educationally subnormal" would not be complete without a brief reference to developments in the adult field. Here the 1957 Report of the Royal Commission on the Law relating to Mental Illness and Mental Deficiency (1957) was followed by the 1959 Mental Health Act. This Act replaced the traditional categories of idiocy, imbecility and feeble-mindedness based on ideas of social competence, with categories of defect based on subnormality of intelligence. A recent report from Castell, Clarke, Mittler and Woodward (1963), recommends defining psychometrically the new categories of subnormality and severe subnormality, so that the upper limit of subnormality of intelligence should be considered to be I.Q. 70, and that of severe subnormality of intelligence I.Q. 55, where the mean I.Q. is 100 and the standard deviation is 15. . . . Thus, while in this country the approach to backwardness in children has been moving away from criteria based on psychometrically determined levels of intelligence to criteria which emphasise educational— and, more recently, social—competence (*v. infra*) the approach to backwardness in adults has been moving in the opposite direction.

An Elastic Measure

If the IQ was not as relevant to a diagnosis of "mild mental subnormality" as had formerly been thought and in practice still widely assumed, it nevertheless measured something. Could this something grow—or were the variations in IQ due to faults that lay with the test, the tester, and the emotional or physical condition of the person tested?

Professor S. A. Kirk, summarizing a study of the effects of early educational procedures on the child, found that children from underprivileged homes tended to stay at the same rate of development or drop in rate as they grew older, *but that this was reversed if pre-school education was given, the majority increasing their rate*. With pre-school education all were found to increase in rate of development. With institutionalized children, *those who had pre-school education* tended to *increase* in rate of development, whilst those *remaining in the ward tended to drop* in the rate of development as they grew older. He concluded that the rate of mental development, particularly with *non-organic mental defectives*, was partially dependent upon *early environment including school experience*. This suggested a strong socio-cultural element in growth in addition to a purely genetic one. Sarason and Gladwin (1959), pointed out that there was a growing recognition that the IQ did not tell the whole story of potentials, "for every small gain the retarded can make is significant. . . ."

Oliver found rises in IQ to be in the nature of a by-product of a programme of physical conditioning. Mundy was able to prepare a number of children for special school entry, whereas without her programme they might still have been considered "ineducable". L. W. Sontag, 1958, found that 62 per cent of children changed more than 15 IQ points sometime during their course of mental development from the age of 3–10. He ascribed these changes to the interaction of training and experience of the children, their changes in personality and interest, and errors in measurement. Stein suggested that the nature of the family background of values was of importance. She differentiated among the ESN according to whether they came from "aspirant" or "demotic" families. In the first group—the "upper" group—some organic lesion could be expected. In the second group there would be some cultural deprivation rather than (or in addition to) organic lesion. She found that the organic showed little change as they grew older (other than a possible deterioration), whilst the other group could be significantly improved. Kushlick found people categorized as mildly subnormal or ESN continued to make IQ increments for some years after IQ growth was thought to be complete. He found this observation important for several reasons:

(a) it questioned the concept of the constancy of the IQ as an assessment of innate "intelligence" among the "mildly subnormal";

(b) it complicated further any attempts to measure the prevalence of "mild subnormality" (i.e. educational subnormality) on the criterion of IQ;

(c) this growth appeared to be characteristic of mild subnormality *in the absence of brain damage* and might partially explain the good prognosis for such children after they leave school, and *"emphasizes the need to provide them with adult education on leaving school"*.

On a broader front, the influence of unusual environments upon the IQ was becomingly widely recognized (e.g. Negroes in the north who had higher IQs than Whites in the south of the USA). In Britain, the Scottish surveys and Cattell's two surveys of Leicester children (1950 and 1957), confirmed what became common experience at the 11-plus examinations—there was a small but significant rise in mean IQ on the same test given to otherwise similar groups of children separated by a generation or so. Whilst test-wiseness was thought to be responsible for some of the improvement, it could not be the whole of the explanation now that the school population had been exposed to these tests for some years. It was reasonable to conclude that the change in general environment of the schools and the homes was having some effect.

Dr. Wall (1960), lucidly summed up the new thinking by concluding: "Human nature could be changed; intelligence could be changed; environment could be changed and organized to create intelligence and personality. Change was the purpose of education."

CHAPTER 10

Physical Conditions

> We know well that the child with defective hearing, because he does not hear other people talking, may not learn to use his organs of speech. Similarly, for example, the physically disabled or blind child runs a risk of being robbed of normal experience of living and may not learn to make full use of his intelligence. Any handicapped child, because of the special difficulties which life holds for him, is exposed to serious emotional risks and may become grossly disturbed.
>
> (Dr. J. D. Kershaw, *Forward Trends*, 1962.)

Some Chemical Disorders

Professor A. Moncrieff, CBE (1960), described four discoveries of chemical disorders which were thought to cause mental handicap. One was concerned with water, two with sugar, and one with amino acids.

He explained that proteins in our bodies were broken down into amino acids and then built up again into muscle and other parts of the body. A Norwegian physician discovered an abnormal chemical (derived from an amino acid) which these patients could not utilize in the urine of some mentally handicapped patients. This was called phenylketonuria, and the amino acid, which was essential for life and growth, was called phenylalanine. Since the phenylalanine was not being utilized properly, it built up and poisoned the brain. This had been known since 1934, but it was not until after the Second World War that both the USA and Britain began to think in terms of a possible synthetic diet. An organic chemist working at Great Ormond Street devised a special diet which removed phenylalanine except for enough to keep the child living and growing.

Children with phenylketonuria can be detected early and treated with the special diet, thereby improving their condition and preventing them becoming more handicapped. Professor Moncrieff gave an example of a child who was picked up at 10 months because of a nasty eczema, and proved to have phenylketonuria. "His IQ then was 30, he is now four and a half and his IQ has risen to 74 and he can of course go to an ESN school if not to an ordinary school in time."

Of the sugar disturbances, one concerned lactose, the special sugar in milk, which in some children is not properly digested and piles up to become rather poisonous. It has proved easy to remove this lactose from milk and save children from mental and physical handicaps which might otherwise arise.

The other sugar problem arose from the sugar content of the blood being too low. The discovery of cortisone made it possible to keep the blood sugar up and save children from mental handicap. This treatment becomes unnecessary after a few years, and by the time the child has left the infant school the condition has righted itself.

In some infants the kidneys fail to regulate the flow of water which comes from the blood. They have a tremendous thirst which older children can make apparent but babies cannot. 'Discovery of this need early enough prevented early deterioration arising from the lack of sufficient water."

Children at Risk

It was recognized that certain physical causes gave rise to varying degrees of mental deficiency or psychological disorder. Detection of these causes was accordingly of the utmost importance—although no assumptions could be made that mental handicap necessarily followed the untreated or (then) untreatable conditions. Dr. M. Sheridan stressed the need for early identification of handicapped children. It was estimated that 1 per cent of the children in England who survived the hazards of the neonatal period, would later "need special care, treatment and parent guidance for severely handicapping conditions". Whilst some of these conditions were apparent at birth (e.g. deformities of the limbs, Down's syndrome (mongolism), cleft palate, spina bifida, and meningicolae, others had to be looked for (e.g. blindness, deafness, cerebral palsy, and metabolic disorder). The majority of children who were handicapped were found to come from certain vulnerable groups.

Professor Tizard (1963) summarized the situation in this way:

> Experience suggests that children in these five categories, those with an unfavourable family history, those who have been exposed to adverse circumstances in pre-natal, peri-natal and post-natal life, and a symptomatic group whose developmental progress is in any way retarded or abnormal, make up about ten per cent of all children who survive the neo-natal period. It is these children who constitute the infants most at risk of handicapping conditions.

A special watch, therefore, needed to be kept on these children, and there was increasing evidence of "at risk" registers being kept by health authorities. Professor Tizard foresaw that a public health programme (which needed to be related "to the possibility of treatment and the age at which such treatment should be instituted") would make possible "the early discovery not only of children who are mentally subnormal but also of the deaf, blind, spastic, delicate, dysphasic, autistic and other types of children who require special care and attention".

By 1963 Tizard was able to point out and urge that we had an appropriate treatment for hearing loss "which is most successful if begun within the first four months of life". Early diagnosis was also possible and essential in cretinism and phenylketonuria, both of which could be treated. Early treatment of cerebral palsy was essential, as was early surgical treatment of hydrocephalus ("water-on-the brain", as it is often known colloquially).

Unknown Causes

But causes were not always known or detectable. Dr. J. M Berg and Dr. B. Kirman (1959) examined the records of 20(

consecutive admissions to Fountain Hospital. They found that in 31 per cent of the total no causal factor of the condition was identifiable.

With "mildly subnormal" subjects, Z. Stein and M. W. Susser found that those without neurological signs, epilepsy, EEG, bio-chemical, or chromosomal abnormality, or sensory defects, were almost confined to the lower social classes.

Mental Handicaps

Dr. Stott (1964) found it "reasonable to assume" that the great majority of backward children were in some way functionally impaired. "In the last resort this amounts to saying that they have suffered organic lesion, if presumed neurological impairment not at present anatomically verifiable is included in this term." Accordingly, such damage had to be bypassed or, as far as possible, compensated for.

Dr. Lise Gellner (Julian Levinson Research Foundation, Chicago) saw mental retardation as a condition resulting from a number of different learning handicaps. "This recognition of different basic abilities, underlying the different manifestations of Mental Defect is however, not yet shared by the great mass of professionals working in the field of mental deficiency." For her, the role of medicine in prevention, "and therefore in seeking out causes" had not encouraged pathogenetic research. She urged the need for diagnosis of the cerebral roots of behaviour disorders in a manner which might guide educational treatment. For her a central objective was to find compensatory methods, as had been done with brain-injured soldiers, using the intact systems.

She urged that whilst "in former times, children born blind or deaf or acquiring these sense defects were condemned to become imbeciles", the situation had now changed. "Today, educators can develop the intelligence of these children by special compensatory training methods."

Sensory Losses

There was certainly by this time a much wider awareness of formerly unsuspected slight sensory losses. Professor Sir Alexander Ewing, for example, remarked that: "at a very early stage in the history of audiology, we found that many school children, rated as low in intelligence and both socially and educationally difficult, were in fact handicapped by deafness. Their problem was fundamentally one of communication with sensory deprivation as a secondary factor." In the survey conducted by his audiology department, with the Cheshire School Health Service and Education Department (1962), it was already clear "that the children admitted to special schools for the deaf constitute only a part, although a very important part, of the total problem".

Noting Sir Alexander Ewing's stress upon the vital importance of auditory training in the early years of childhood, Dr. J. Kershaw observed that this period was a "natural" one for the development of auditory perception, and if training did not occur at this time a unique opportunity would be missed "and will not occur again". There was in Kershaw's view, "growing evidence that in other faculties of body and mind there are similar ideal times for training to start and that these also are in the early years".

There was by this time appropriate treatment for hearing loss which was most successful "if begun within the first four months of life".

The Association of Educational Psychologists drew attention to a "special educational treatment selection" test devised for children in the 7-plus age group. With this technique

> some differential scores are produced which indicates that a minority of children are handicapped for other than reasons of dull intelligence, for example, subtle difference of hearing and sight are hinted at and may lead to a fuller investigation. . . . More generally, the S.E.T.S. result combined with the schools' assessments can provide a sound basis for placing underachieving 7–8 year olds in several categories of need.

The Soviet Approach

The Soviet emphasis upon physical causes and their practice of considering mentally handicapped children to be "invalids", made them distinguish in their thinking and provision between children who had suffered early damage (before, during, or in the early years after birth) and other children who were school failures.

In 1965 just under 1 per cent of the school population in the USSR were in special schools. A USA delegation, however, thought that the Russians strained to find "organicity" in certain doubtful cases, and included in their special school population many children who would have been similarly placed in the USA but without any assumptions of the causes.

Professor Pevzner, however, replied to questions about the Russian concept of "oligophrenia" this way:

> After some twenty-five years of dealing with this problem we have defined a reasonably exact concept. We consider to be oligophrenic those children who have brain injury, and we agree that the causes are multiple. Certain causes have been generally agreed, such as chromosomal abnormality, intra-uterine and perinatal infection, birth injury and so on, but we do not now class as oligophrenic children whose handicap seems to be mainly attributable to hereditary factors. We restrict the term to those whose defect appears to result from circumstances arising during the process of birth, the impairment being a residual effect arising from these circumstances. In fact, brain injuries arising from hereditary causes comprise the smaller group and metabolic disfunctions the larger. We certainly do not regard as oligophrenics children who need to repeat a class in ordinary school, or who are backward because of poor speech development or visuo-spatial disorder or because they are in delicate health or are socially retarded. Our definition appears to be more narrow than that in your country, and this enables us to work out a more precise approach.

For the Russians, responsibility for children who were backward for reasons which excluded them from the oligophrenic category or from that of any other category of handicap, was the responsibility of a research institute other than the Institute of Defectology. Treatment for such backward pupils might include repeating a class, additional homework, a change of teachers or outside help, and, if still unable to catch up with the grade, transfer to vocational schools which offered a different kind of course.

Dr. Lubovsky (1964), in an article on "Some results of physiological researches in defectology", revealed some further aspects of the work of a special department in the Institute of Defectology. He made the salutary observation that until this department was set up "all physiological studies in cases of vision, hearing and speech disorders as well as in cases of mental retardation had been carried out mostly on adults", the tests in use being either clinical or tests of job adjustment only. He considered that the development of objective techniques was of great importance in investigating problems of "auditory threshold, the characteristics of hearing sensitivity when deranged, higher nervous activity in oligophrenia, and those of physiological peculiarities of speech disturbances. . . ."

Until the setting up of this special department, the Institute had failed to contribute anything to special education because "the problems connected with compensation of defects did not arise in most of the studies". The new department, however, had the special task of studying children with abnormalities. It saw as of fundamental importance, the choice of its experimental technique. A physiological approach was decided upon, namely: "the technique of recording electrical activity in the cortex (EEG), the method of motor-conditioned reflexes accompanied by verbal reinforcement, of myographic tracing, the recording of eye-movement and other techniques. All these were analysed to find if they could be suitably applied to the study of abnormal children."

Results from the studies of EEGs of children suggested "for instance that the erroneous answers given by oligophrenic children when their tactile sensitivity was studied result from pathological peculiarities of their higher nervous activity rather than from derangements at a sensory level".

In particular, Lubovsky found that a number of the difficulties once found in the diagnosis of oligophrenia "were eliminated when the EEG was used". Brain electrical activity in such children apparently differed from that in both normal children of the same age and in children suffering from general under-development caused by auditory impairment.

Differential Diagnosis

Clearly, inside this interdisciplinary Institute various defects of a physical and sensory character (loss of vision or hearing, speech defects, and oligophrenia) were studied side by side, and forms of differential diagnosis were being evolved. If the use of the "intelligence test" had helped to develop provision of special schools for intellectually retarded children in our own country, the use of the EEG seemed to play a similar role in the USSR.

In practice, the USSR, the USA, and the UK were probably closer together than the statement of their theories suggested. As Dr. A. Kushlick, for example, pointed out, whilst some of the normal children with IQs within the 50–70 range might have "minimal brain damage" resulting from peri-natal complications which were more common amongst the lower working class children than other sections of the community, the social prognosis for these children was good.

CHAPTER 11

Nature or Nurture

The problems of allocating the cause or causes of mental defects either to inborn or acquired characteristics with scientific accuracy has been shown to be much more complex than formerly supposed.
(PROFESSOR L. S. PENROSE, *The Biology of Mental Defect*, p. 83.)

FOR educationalists, as for other disciplines, there could be no point in seeking out causes of handicap except with a view to prevention, treatment, or compensation. Professor Penrose, for example (1960), drawing attention to the many changes in the concept of mental deficiency during the previous 30 years, saw them as bound up with advances in three fields:

1. The psychology of education and training.
2. Biochemical genetics (which opened up new vistas of treatment as distinct from description).
3. Chromosome investigations (which had enabled exact studies of causation into such conditions as Down's syndrome to be undertaken with confidence). (London Conference on the Scientific Study of Mental Deficiency.)

Educationalists were certainly not alone, however, in their growing interest in the relationship between speech, language, and intelligence; and a number of disciplines converged to indicate the dynamics of this relationship.

Speech

Long before Dr. J. M. Itard sought to provide a support for the tongue in the belief that its debility played some part in speech disorder, attention had been attracted to speech disturbances and their treatment. During the first two decades of the twentieth century, Lancashire (1906) provided an official clinic for stammerers, and two London hospitals (St. Bartholomew's (1911) and St. Thomas's (1913)) established speech clinics. This latter was "the first to provide clinical training for the treatment of speech disorders, this training being subsidiary to training as teachers of speech and drama" (Morley, 1961).

With the 1944 Education Act—in fact in that very year—a College of Speech Therapists was formed, bringing together "persons engaged in the treatment of disorders of voice, language and speech". The study of disorders of speech and communication emerged as "a well defined academic field. . . . It also has close connections with psychology, acoustics in relation to hearing for speech, with education in respect of certain learning disabilities associated with language, such as reading, writing and spelling, and with medicine."

The increasing awareness of this interdisciplinary connection was underlined in 1962 when a questionnaire on the treatment of speech disorders in cerebral palsied children was distributed to speech therapists.

Language Development and Intelligence

Many authorities emphasized the existence of an area of learning before speech. This area was sharply delineated by Dr. Mesheriakov (USSR, 1965) who worked with children who were deaf, dumb, and blind. He protested that whilst such children were sub-human if left in the helpless condition in which they were born, and whilst they were too readily diagnosed everywhere as imbeciles, they could in fact be educated into intelligent human beings. He stressed that everything "had to be taught from outside, formed from outside". These children revealed for him the importance of all social experience in the education of the child, "from the use of trousers to the knife and fork". These children had to be "taught to love and hate" or even, as Dr. Mesheriakov humorously put it, "how to lie". Given this prolonged, pre-speech training, he could point to a number of such children who were then proceeding through a normal secondary school course in the USSR. In their interaction with teachers and other adults, in the view of Dr. Mesheriakov, "they developed human qualities" and became normal.

But such a happy development could not be ensured for all these children. Research on speech and language development in the USA (Harrison, *American Journal*, 1958) led to the conclusion that there should be an investigation of speech and language development during the pre-school period. A need for diagnostic scales and evaluation of therapeutic programmes was also pointed out. Professor M. M. Lewis (1963), began a study of "the relationship between linguistic development of children with impaired hearing and their social and ethical development". (This project included work on finger-spelling and communication by signs.) In the Isle of Wight a survey carried out by a senior medical officer, based on maternal memory of milestones in relation to 78 ESN pupils and 145 pupils in ordinary schools, revealed that late development of speech among the ESN group was six times more common than for ordinary children. He discussed the possible value of this finding for the earlier discovery of ESN children (Ashley-Miller, 1964). Professor Luria, in the USSR, devised a range of experiments which indicated the importance of language at each stage of a child's development. He stated that:

> In schools, not only do abilities which have already developed come to light, but also children's abilities are formed, further developed; all normal children, in acquiring methods and habits of learning in school, compensate for deficiencies and realize their potentialities for mental development. The school, like life itself, is a powerful formative factor; it is the greatest mistake ... to consider that "innate ability" inevitably determines the child's future and so assign difficulties in learning to a low level of innate ability.

Luria recognized, however, that there were children who "experience insurmountable difficulties in mastering the curriculum", and he sharply differentiated these from other school failures, claiming that in the former case some damage at an early stage was responsible for the abnormal development. He distinguished also between what animals acquire as a result of their interaction with the environment and what humans acquire through language—social-human experience. He considered the main function of speech to be generalization, but added that language was also a source of thought. In mastering words the child was mastering the outer world, analysing and synthesizing, classifying and remembering. Speech also became a means of regulating behaviour.

> It may be said that not a single act of behaviour is formed by the normal child without the participation of speech which systematises his previous experience and directs his active behaviour.

For Luria, disturbance of the part which speech played in the formation of complex mental processes, and defects of the function of speech as a generalizer and regulator, were "the traits which differentiate the intellectually backward child". (B. and J. Simon, 1963.)

Meanwhile, individual language instruction with a group of children in the USA, having Down's syndrome (mongols) revealed a small but significant increase in IQ on the Kuhlman test compared with another matched group which did not get this instruction (Kolstoe, 1958). Verbal instructions, in a simple learning situation, were shown to improve the performance of severely subnormal children (O'Connor and Hermalin, 1959). Whilst original instruction was found to improve the performance of both normal and severely subnormal persons, it only aided transfer with the former group, impeding it with the latter (Bryant, 1964). Dr. P. Bryant put forward the hypothesis that the severely subnormal person transferred negative rather than positive learning. However, there was evidence from several research workers with severely subnormal subjects of considerable transfer between tasks in which different material was being used (Clarke and Blackmore, 1961; Clarke and Cookson, 1962; and Tizard and Loos, 1954). Transfer was also seen to be related to age.

A hypothesis by D. O. Hebb that transfer of training would be inversely correlated with age was strongly supported by Professor

A. D. B. Clarke and C. D. Blackmore who stated that: "early training enables the institutionalized imbecile to achieve levels more characteristic of older imbecile children or adults, and who show greater relative profit from experience." Professor Clarke found that "the traditional clinical opinion which has emphasised what the imbecile cannot do is correct only so far as short term observations or very short periods of training are concerned. Limitations on learning, though considerable, are by no means as profound as have hitherto been supposed".

How it is that a Child does not learn

In the USA one differential diagnostic test was constructed in order to reveal specific weaknesses in the communication process and thereby suggest the best lines of treatment. The Illinois test of psycho-linguistic ability was designed for children aged from 2 to 9. The test recognized two channels (receptive and expressive) by means of which the children could engage in three processes, "decoding", "encoding", and "association". It also recognized two levels of organization, the "representational" and the "automatic-sequential". On the receptive side there was the visual and auditory channel. On the expressive side was the vocal and motor channel. The test sought to find defects or deficits in this pattern as a prelude to devising a remedial programme for each defect or deficit. A case study was made of each child with a view to finding his specific learning disabilities in these areas, to organize a programme of a remedial kind and then to re-examine the child. By using the child as his own "contrast", the investigators hoped to define more clearly the patterns of disability found, how these correlated with other characteristics, and "to determine the extent and rate at which one can ameliorate these deficits". (Kirk, 1963.)

Summarizing several ways of explaining how it is that a severely subnormal child does not learn, Dr. N. O'Connor suggested the following:

1. there could be an interruption of an elementary process at the physiological level;
2. a deficiency of an attentional capacity;
3. a poverty of associative skills; or
4. some localized cortical malfunction which gave rise to a problem of linguistic expression.

He pointed out that Professor Luria considered that the properties of objects were pointed out to a child "historically" by parents and teachers. Active memorization, logical thinking, and similar faculties or abilities were not considered to be innate, but were developed. This was particularly true of the organization of perception. Disturbance of a function as a result of a localized lesion or cortical damage would have one effect upon a child and a totally different effect upon an adult.

> So, for example, Luria would disagree with Sir Cyril Burt, suggesting that Burt is wrong to assume that hearing loss is not *responsible* for backwardness. According to Luria it could easily *cause* backwardness. He would support this view by saying that aggrammatism is much more common in deaf schools in the USSR than in other schools. In other words, a relatively inconsiderable particular defect may evoke essential changes in the general mental development of a child.   [O'Connor, 1965.]

Changes of this kind might give grounds for an incorrect assessment of the child as having an inborn mental deficiency.

Dr. O'Connor cautioned, however, that there were children who could not read or who could not write but who were otherwise able. Deficiencies did occur which did not have a general effect. He accordingly guarded against some current as well as some traditional trends, favouring those who moved toward differential diagnosis or approaches which revealed specific defects, rather than those who like some disciples of Sir Cyril Burt or, in a new sense, of Professor Piaget, saw a more general pattern of mental development with fairly uniform stages in mentally handicapped or dull children.

CHAPTER 12

Some Social or Environmental Factors

The commonly existing procedure of having children with learning
difficulties enter school, experience academic failure and then be
identified as mentally retarded, has concerned educators in the
United States for a number of years. The very connotation of mental
retardation as a non-obvious, non-remediable disability until it
becomes an academic learning handicap has served to defeat efforts
towards early identification.

(PROFESSOR IGNACY GOLDBERG, 1963.)

The Post-war Climate

The upsurge of interest in the mentally handicapped was inseparable from the new social climate following upon the Second
World War. In the USA Professor J. H. Rothstein attributed the
phenomenal growth and development of concern there for mentally retarded persons to four events:

1. A thorough revulsion towards the Nazi mass slaughter of retarded persons;
2. An adamant, unashamed, and well-organized parent movement;
3. A reawakening of interest on the part of biological and social scientists;
   and
4. Public awareness of how little had been done for these "forgotten people".

The Minister of Health (1960) stated: "Scientific research and
medical treatment is really mainly a very modern plant, and a
modern plant of an intensely vigorous and rapid growth. I put
this scientific and medical advance first among the reasons for our
progress. . . ." But this is "not the only advance. Complementary
with it, and in no small degree due to it, there has been a parallel
and a most welcome advance in the public's attitude to mental
disorder." Clearly the new trends in Britain were inseparable
from the national efforts to create a welfare state.

Awareness of a heritage of social neglect and disadvantage was reflected in the national campaign for the "Advancement of State Education", in the trend towards comprehensive schools, and in the spreading hostility towards "streaming" in schools.

That progressive intent could create some unwanted by-products was underlined by the fact that Dr. J. Daniels, in an article on "Research on streaming in the primary school", saw a need to emphasize that

> the abandonment of streaming should be regarded not so much as a negative act of renunciation, but as a positive affirmation of how junior school education can most effectively be organized. Non-streaming to be successful implies that the staff believe wholeheartedly in the great potentialities for educational enterprise in all their pupils, and a willingness to organize their teaching in accordance with that belief. . . .

Some of the intricacies of the developing challenge were highlighted by Dr. Douglas (1964). Addressing a meeting of the National Union of Teachers (1965), Dr. Douglas drew attention to the fact that whilst those working-class students who entered the universities did at least as well as other students, social differences in educational opportunity still remained as great as they were 30 years previously. The aspirations of parents affected progress, being closely related to the type of education the parents themselves had received. Size of family was another factor. Middle-class children tended to read earlier—and reading played an important part in the placement and progress of a child at school. When asked how the balance might be restored, Dr. Douglas suggested that the social structure was too complex for an easy answer but that the development of nursery schools was an important step forward.

In evidence submitted to the Central Advisory Council for Education, the Association of Educational Psychologists drew attention to (amongst other things) the effect of an educational structure which was based on chronological age—which again had an adverse effect on those most in need of help. There was increasing evidence that "lack of flexibility is particularly harmful to children at entry and promotion stages, particularly that

children born in the Spring and Summer are at a disadvantage.
. . . These children not only have less time in infants' school, but
their introduction to it is difficult as they enter when school rolls
are at their peak."

The Association of Education Psychologists found a serious lack
of contact and consistency between nursery schools, infant schools,
and junior schools in a considerable number of areas.

But apart from such general factors which occasioned concern,
it was increasingly appreciated that "equality of educational
opportunity" for handicapped children could only have meaning in terms of the personal, social, and vocational development of each pupil. This called for different or differential
provision rather than the same provision for all. It called
for separate consideration of the needs of each category of
handicap.

The Educationally Subnormal

One category of handicap—the largest—aroused complex emotional reactions and appeared to have far-reaching social con-
notations. The Department of Education and Science had carefully defined this category as "educationally subnormal" and
estimated it to comprise 10 per cent of the entire school population. The majority of these children were expected to receive their
special educational treatment within the ordinary school. On the
generally accepted positive side, this new classification did away
with the label "mental defective" for any pupil retained within
the school system. The concept of educational rather than mental
subnormality was expected to help remove the stigma formerly
attached to "defectives" and to reveal these pupils as a part of a
more substantial group of backward pupils none of whom had
attainments beyond the levels reached by children 20 per cent
younger.

At first the Department of Education and Science estimated
that about 12 in every 100 ESN children in urban areas would
require special schools. In rural areas, where the problems of

distance complicated the possibilities of provision, residential provision was thought necessary but only for 4 in every 100.

All these estimates, however, were based upon "past experience" which had suggested that "children cannot be educated at school when their intelligence quotient is below 55". Similarly, "a child with an intelligence quotient of more than 75 should rarely find his way there" (i.e. to a special school) "as his recuperative powers are so much greater than those of the majority of pupils in special schools".

Yet past experience had been extremely limited—and the IQ had never been the sole guide. At the time when Sir Cyril Burt had estimated that more than 100,000 children should be in special (MD) schools, there were never more than 15,000 children in such schools, nor had more than a total of 33,000 children ever been ascertained as in need of such schooling. When the Department of Education and Science published its pamphlet *Special Educational Treatment* (1946), there were only 11,000 in special ESN schools and 10,000 awaiting placement. Twenty years later the number on the waiting list remained almost unchanged although the number in special schools had quadrupled.

In an effort to obtain realistic estimates of the need, the Minister circularized all local education authorities and on the basis of empirical returns concluded that a total of 54,000 places were required.

At first glance the new estimates suggested that social changes might not only have helped to quadruple provision but to halve the need. Sir Cyril Burt had estimated $1\frac{1}{2}$ per cent of the school population to need special ESN schools, not the figure slightly more than half this ($0 \cdot 8$ per cent) now proposed by the Minister. If the returns from the LEAs could have been accepted as a result of scientific surveys, there might have been relevance in such questions as: Has there been a reduction in the number of children with IQs between 50 and 70?

A more relevant question proved to be: Why was the IQ not always proving the most relevant factor in the selection of children for special schools?

Doctors and Psychological Testing

The Association of Educational Psychologists (1965) pointed out that:

> Too many very dull children crawl apathetically through primary school to the secondary stage before special placement is affected. In some areas referrals are made direct to the School Psychological Service but in others the procedure is wasteful and disruptive of fruitful relationships between the schools and the School Health Services.
>
> A not uncommon pattern is that of a very backward child being referred for ascertainment, and a lengthy interview and examination by a school medical officer ending, in eight cases out of ten, in a brief one-line report to the school that the child is educationally subnormal (already known) but that he is not seriously enough handicapped mentally for placement in a special school. This is a meagre contribution after a one or two hour interview. When challenged or encouraged to provide more information for the sake of the child and the school, the school medical officer is modest enough to indicate that his role is simply one of "ascertainment", not to give advice to educationalists. In these circumstances schools often feel it is a waste of time to refer such children and subsequently they may do so—at a late day—only because the child's problem is now grossly obtruding.

The evidence continued:

> . . . standards of attainment are clearly unsatisfactory in many areas, particularly in the poor socio-economic neighbourhoods of urban areas. But there is remediable backwardness at all cultural levels. The slow learner is particularly susceptible. Causes are many but apart from the usual causes given we would emphasize instability of staffing in many city areas, over-large classes and lack of harmony on infant school and junior school methods. It is a corollary to promotion by age that we should provide, as of necessity, specialist help in basic skills. To ignore these is to ignore the wide individual differences of children existing in any age group.

There were other complications. Where former MD schools were merely renamed ESN, they could not easily shake off the inherited stigma and approach of pre-war "dotty schools" or "silly schools" as these were called locally. Teachers recognized only too well how parental hostility to children being selected for special schools could distort the need by obstructing or discouraging the necessary referral and placement. There were other factors, too, which distorted the need. From one locality to another and even within the same locality, special schools differed in the range of ability they would accept. The results of one questionnaire on "ascertainment", for example, revealed that a quarter of the pupils in special schools for the ESN had IQs outside the 55–75 range. If low measured general ability was clearly not the only relevant factor with at least a quarter of these pupils, what other factors determined selection for special schools or retention in ordinary schools? How far could ordinary schools cope with children in the 55–75 IQ range, and how far did such children prove able to hold their own and even to progress personally, socially, and vocationally via the normal school?

Problem Pupils

There was evidence that problem pupils, disturbing the classes in ordinary schools, were amongst the first pressed forward for ascertainment as educationally subnormal, and these were outstandingly evident amongst the pupils with higher IQs in special ESN schools. The part played by social or cultural factors in selection, also worried educationalists. Research by the Department of Social Science and Preventive Medicine (Manchester University) focused upon an element of "social selection" at each stage in the selection process from (a) the rate of referral from schools of various kinds, and (b) the decisions of school medical officers to (c) children subsequently admitted into institutions. Dr. Susser found from a follow-up study of ESN children that it was possible to show that cultural characteristics of the family were "very significant in determining whether or not they would be selected as part of a sample of ascertained educationally subnormal". Dr. Bernstein, 1963, showed that the children of unskilled working-class parents had a language structure which lacked certain components found in middle-class language structure. Dr. Kushlick, in a summary of research, found that

> although there is evidence that the social and intellectual capacity may to some extent be determined by additive effect of multiple genes, the cultural factors, i.e. the social and material way of life, appears to be crucial in

determining the extent to which the child's genetic potential will be realized. The lower working class subculture appears to be the main factor responsible for the occurrence of clinically normal individuals with IQs in the mildly subnormal range, 50–70.

A parent (Constance Hughes) remarked:

> When parents are talking about education and I say I have a son at a special school they either show surprise or embarrassment, looking at me a little oddly, or they are sympathetic and say "I am sorry". When I am with parents of severely handicapped children and my son is mentioned they invariably ask me if he goes to school and when I answer that he does they always say "You're lucky". And indeed we are, very blessed by comparison, but we have our special problems because our children stand between the two worlds, that of the normal and that of the severely handicapped. What training and employment are available are questions which bedevil the parents and their child.

Meanwhile, outside the school system entirely, amongst a section of the population considered to be "ineducable", changes took place in the form as well as the content of training. As Dr. L. T. Hilliard put it in a new textbook, *Mental Deficiency*, "mental deficiency practice is tied to outdated procedures whose aim is to separate the defective from the community rather than integrate him with it". The new direction was pioneered by such work as that of Dr. N. O'Connor and Professor J. Tizard who demonstrated that with suitable motivation and training, it was possible "in a period of full employment", to employ imbeciles and to make such employment of economic as well as therapeutic value.

At each level of mental and educational handicap, then, new insight into the nature of the problems and a new direction or expansion of provision was being urged.

And to the forces to which Professor Rothstein attributed the changes, might be added:

1. The research undertaken by disciplines outside the education system (but having educational implications).
2. The influence of a number of voluntary, semi-professional, and statutory facilities and organizations (some of which are described in a later section of this book).
3. The activities of teachers themselves (notably through the National Union of Teachers and its Advisory Committee on

Special Education, the former Special Schools Association and its successor the Association for Special Education, and the post-war Guild of Teachers of Backward Children, a professional, interdisciplinary organization concerned with the entire field of "backwardness" from the severely subnormal excluded from schools to the "bright but backward" in ordinary schools. It is also noteworthy that the National Association of Schoolmasters offered practical help, alongside other educational bodies, in furthering some of the Guild's initiatives).

CHAPTER 13

Interdisciplinary Research

The need for facilities and support to train research workers is now urgent, even more so perhaps than finance, for large scale projects. On the whole there is a reasonable supply of newly graduated young men and women with a background in psychology or sociology, but without research or educational experience.
(*National Foundation for Educational Research Eighteenth Annual Report*, 1964.)

Difficulties in Practice

Understandably, teachers have frequently approached research findings with a certain scepticism. The National Foundation for Educational Research was keenly aware of this fact when it noted that the "acute shortage of men and women with a wide knowledge of the schools, a thorough training in the relevant discipline and good research experience" was leading to "the promulgation of the doctrine that research in education can most profitably and practically be carried on by psychologists, sociologists, economists, statisticians and even medical men with no knowledge or experience of teaching in the day to day hurly burly of schools".

Although there was a place in research teams for members of several disciplines, research in education generally would suffer

in practice and in its public relations with the schools, unless it is manifestly directed by men and women whose practical insights into the uncodified but real problems of the classroom can be respected by serving teachers. To use teachers as mere auxiliaries to so called experts, who were unaware of the realities of the classroom was to court disaster and a distortion of truth.

Whilst England and Wales lacked a centre specifically devoted to research on handicapped children, both the USA and the

USSR had set up such research centres, although they differed in size, direction, and the composition of their interdisciplinary teams.

Although it has only been possible to indicate the composition and emphasis of these two research institutes, there is no question but that both have already had an influence far beyond their own countries. Grace (1963), commented that the Institute for Research on Exceptional Children "was a pioneer development in American education". Established in 1952, Grace stated that "this Institute was the first active research and graduate training department in this country [USA] or abroad. Its base was the cooperative relationship of State agencies and interdisciplinary relationships of the department within the University, utilizing the theories and personnel from research areas from other behavioural sciences."

In Dr. Grace's view, the first 10 years of the Institute had already demonstrated the wisdom of its organization by (a) its research, (b) its training of leaders for development of services as well as research, and (c) its overall contribution to the development of other centres in the USA and abroad. At this time the Institute had a full time staff of thirteen.

Certainly some contributions from this Institute have had some impact in Britain. Reference is made elsewhere to some of the relevant textbooks for teachers of retarded children (Kirk and Johnson, 1950) and to a significant *Curriculum Guide* (H. Goldstein and D. Seigle).

To these might be added two less well-known textbooks (because of the different pattern of teacher training and services), *Educating Exceptional Children* (Kirk, 1962), and *Exceptional Children in Schools* (edited by Dunn, 1963, Holt Rinehart & Winston). Both these books cover the entire range of handicaps recognized in the USA.

The failure of research to keep pace with the expanding services in the USA was attributed by Kirk and Spalding in 1953 to such factors as (a) a lack of highly trained researchers within the field, (b) the isolated and fragmentary nature of the research that had been conducted, (c) the concentration upon medical and psychological diagnostic research to the exclusion of educational and remedial programmes, and (d) the failure to attack the complex problems of handicapped children from the required inter-disciplinary approach.

It is significant, however (revealing the major challenge) that the majority of the seventy pages of the report have reference to "the mentally retarded". A chapter on "Children with sensory disabilities" occupies two pages. The report is divided into the following sections, most of them relevant to schooling.

1. Prevalence studies.
2. The development of diagnostic instruments (i.e. the Illinois test of psycholinguistic abilities, to which reference has already been made, a test of basic information, and analysis of classroom verbal interaction).
3. Characteristics of the mentally retarded (including reading abilities, arithmetical abilities, incidental learning, and vocational interests).
4. School programmes for the mentally retarded (i.e. for severely subnormal (trainable) children as well as ESN children).
5. The effects of training the mentally retarded.
6. The effects of handicapped children on families (mainly retarded children, but one study is of "the cerebral palsied child in the family").
7. Programmed instruction.
8. Gifted children.
9. Children with sensory disabilities.

As Kirk points out in the Epilogue, "the research was generated primarily from the theories of education, psychology, sociology, and related behavioural disciplines. Although biological data and theories were used in some of the research projects, the major emphasis has been on behavioural research. The paucity of biologically orientated research has been partially due to the particular backgrounds of the staff . . ." and partially to "the lack of biological laboratories and clinical materials on the campus".

There were, however, plans for expansion to include a residential centre for sixty emotionally disturbed and mentally retarded children. Apart from an outpatient's clinic, residential cottages, etc., this centre will include a research facilities building, housing research workers "in recreational therapy, social service, speech pathology, and psychology, psychophysiological laboratories, child psychiatry and child development". The Institute would be under the same roof with all sharing a common aim.

President's Panel on Mental Retardation

One of the most imaginative steps taken to stimulate interest in mental retardation internationally was taken by President J. F. Kennedy in October 1961, the setting up of a President's Panel on Mental Retardation. This panel of experts, charged with preparing a national plan, reported in 1962 with a 200-page document containing nearly a hundred recommendations.

The Panel saw mental retardation as "a major national health, social and economic problem affecting some $5 \cdot 4$ million children and adults and involving some 15 to 20 million family members in this country".

It employed four main methods in obtaining the required information. Advisers were appointed to help members working on specific subjects. Public hearings were held in seven major cities. Facilities and programmes were studied along with literature and research. And panel members were sent on a fact-finding mission to England, Sweden, Denmark, Holland, and the USSR to study methods, provision, and research.

The Panel's recommendations were summarized by its chairman, Leonard W. Mayo, under the following headings:

1. Research.
2. Prevention.
3. Clinical and medical services.

4. Education.
5. Vocational rehabilitation.
6. Residential care.
7. The law and the mentally retarded.
8. Local, state, and federal organization.

Whilst most of the recommendations have significance far beyond the borders of the USA, it is useful to select a few here which are of particular relevance to this book.

On research, for example, the Panel recommended amongst other things; that

1. ten research centres affiliated with universities should be set up "to insure continuing progress in research relevant to mental retardation in both the behavioural and biological sciences and to provide additional facilities for training research personnel";
2. a Federal Institute of Learning be established under the general auspices of the Department of Health, Education, and Welfare;
3. programmes to train research educators, sociologists, and psychologists in mental retardation be initiated.

For prevention, the Panel recommended programmes keyed to culturally deprived groups in certain areas; a domestic Peace Corps to meet the personnel shortage and special needs in deprived areas where the prematurity rate is high and the hazards to infants greatest; and genetic counselling, review of drug-testing procedures, regulations regarding registration, inspection, etc., of X-ray and fluoroscope machines and other ionizing radiation sources. Hospitals were to adopt every known procedure to ensure "the prevention of pre-natal and neonatal defect and brain damage" and to apply modern child-rearing knowledge and practices in "dealing with infants who may have suffered from trauma resulting from maternal separation".

On education, there was a need for the extension and improvement of specialized educational services to "provide appropriate educational opportunities for all retarded children". This included pre-school education. "Most retarded children live in city slums or depressed rural environments. Research suggests that deprivation of adequate opportunities for learning contributes to and complicates the degree of mental retardation. . . . Formal pre-school programmes of increased learning opportunities may accelerate development of these children. . . " Early detection and the training of 55,000 special educators were also recommended.

On vocational rehabilitation the needs were for the following services:

> vocational evaluation, counselling, and job placement; training courses in appropriate vocational areas; joint school work experience programmes co-sponsored by schools and vocational rehabilitation agencies; clearly defined and adequately supervised programmes for on the job training; employment training facilities; sheltered workshops; vocational rehabilitation services in conjunction with residential institutions; and counselling services to parents.

The Research Institute of Defectology

In the USSR a rather different interdisciplinary team, or a team with a bias and background different from that in the USA Institute, was set up in 1929. The language barrier, amongst other things, has not made the findings of this substantial centre, with its numerous publications, as well-known in the West as they should be. Translations have been made available from time to time of specific lectures, occasional publications, and even some books, but the need for an effective translation service is now being pressed in both the USA and the UK. There is no report of the kind published by the Illinois University, available in English.

However, it is interesting to note the nature and direction of this research institute as reported by a British delegation from the Guild of Teachers of Backward Children in 1965. (For the full report see *Backward Pupils in the USSR*, Ed. S. S. Segal, E. J. Arnold.) At the same time the Institute had a staff of more than sixty scientists and a hundred ancillary workers. Its close link with schools was underlined by the fact that it published the curriculum for special schools, used certain schools as "experimental schools" where research workers could plan the programme and try out experimental approaches, and gave advice to teachers who brought children to the Institute's attention as presenting specific problems.

This Institute had close links with the Faculty of Defectology in Moscow, which was the centre for training teachers of handicapped children (defectologists). The two bodies were independent but the staffs worked closely together on research problems, training of teachers, organization of conferences, and design of the school curricula. Textbooks used in special schools had to be approved by the Institute staff.

Professor Pevzner, who headed the Department of Clinical and Pathophysiological Studies, said that research there covered all aspects of special education and was carried out according to a planned programme.

In the department which studied the deaf, much of the research was devoted to improving the accuracy of early diagnosis. And since hearing loss before a child could speak had different effects from hearing loss after a child could speak, "different methods of teaching the two" had to be evolved.

Impressive results had demonstrably been obtained from work on the curricula and techniques of teaching the blind. Professor Pevzner stated that blind children were now able to follow at the secondary stage the same courses as children in ordinary schools. "For blind people a wider range of skills is offered in the USSR than in most other countries; it is not unusual for instance, for blind persons to be trained as skilled electronic technicians." A special school for gifted blind mathematicians was to be opened shortly.

The delegation saw some ingenious equipment used in teaching blind children. These included audio-equipment for (a) determining the levels of liquids, (b) the positions of indicators on instruments, and (c) responding different light tones. The latter could be used to interpret maps, for example.

One remarkable machine with immense possibilities "read" a book line by line, translating it into something like a Morse code which pupils could learn after some 40–60 hours of preliminary tuition. This machine opened up the whole of literature to the blind. A teaching machine with braille keys and a branching technique was also demonstrated; this enabled the learner to select from multi-choice responses and place in order eight sequential items to complete a logical answer.

As was noted in an earlier chapter, one small department was focused upon children who were blind, deaf and dumb.

A "simple" arresting aid seen in this department was a "telephone" for the blind and deaf. Since the child could neither see nor hear, the "bell" was a fan. The pupil would feel the movement of the air and place his finger above a braille key which would thrust up in relief the braille letters of the message.

Great attention was paid to speech with all handicapped children, its importance as a "second signalling system" along Pavlovian lines, guiding practice. Speech was seen to enable children to reorganize perceptions, to generalize and to draw conclusions from such generalizations. The Research Institute also dealt with defects of speech and hearing of children in ordinary schools.

Apart from treatment given to children with faults in the speech mechanism (e.g. with defective palate) or with nervous malfunctions (e.g. dysalia or dyspraxia), specially trained "logopeds" gave remedial instruction in kindergartens.

The importance attached to speech is seen in the remarkable size of this category. About 8 per cent of the children in ordinary schools in the USSR were thought to have speech defects requiring treatment which did not necessitate placement in special schools. About a half of one per cent had hearing loss.

Teachers could refer children to the Institute where advice would follow to the teacher.

The impression gained by the delegation was of "a well planned, efficient organization whose members were deeply involved in their work and concerned with its human implications".

Educational Researches in England and Wales

Whilst it is plain that each nation grows its own way and evolves its own instruments—research in education seems to have been particularly handicapped. Twenty-one years after the 1944 Education Act, J. G. Wallace could write:

> It is a sad commentary on the effectiveness of our methods of enquiry that after some eighty years of physiological investigation and a discontinuous history of forty years of laboratory experiment, our fund of accepted knowledge on the subject of conceptualization comprises so little of consequence that it is hardly worth compiling.

He assigned the major responsibility for this to factors which were not inevitable.

> The chronic lack of adequate research funds to finance the large scale enquiries essential to explore the basic problems in sufficient depth to yield authoritative findings has produced an endless series of small research projects often claiming to be dealing with the same topic and producing contradictory results. Any conclusions reached are of extremely limited value due to their narrow, numerical, temporal, socio-economic and cultural basis, and to the common practice of leaving major variables out of the reckoning by controlling, rather than evaluating them.

There were small, scattered, if respected, centres of research in mental deficiency hospitals and a few universities.

Whilst the Department of Education and Science financed some research, and the National Foundation for Educational Research provided a national stimulus, there was little inside the educational system to compare in size and direction with the research institutes in the USSR or the USA.

Not until 1965 was a Chair of Child Development set up in London with Professor Tizard responsible for five departments which included courses for teachers of four categories of handicapped children.

The National Bureau for Co-operation in Child Care, due to its happy choice as Director of the well-known psychologist and educationalist Dr. M. Kellmer Pringle, reflected in part the general awareness of the need for a research centre specifically devoted to handicapped children.

Dr. Kellmer Pringle had already provided reviews of research and cautioned against the practice of training teachers in intelligence testing as such. She urged that such tests should be used for the qualities of mind they revealed, i.e. for diagnosis rather than prognosis, such diagnosis being coupled with practical suggestions to the teacher from an educational diagnosis and techniques. It might lead also to a generalizing of improvement in IQ reflecting a general improvement in intellectual functioning.

Through *Educational Research*, the journal of the NFER which carried a series of articles on different handicaps (February 1964), Dr. Kellmer Pringle provided teachers with their first reviews of the scattered literature on "the emotional and social adjustment of blind children". In this, as in her subsequent review of the literature on "the emotional and social adjustment of physically handicapped children", she came to the same conclusion, amongst others, that "more and better research is needed".

She divided the literature into six groups for the blind.

1. General, descriptive studies.
2. Rehabilitation and therapy.
3. Case studies.
4. Tests and other techniques for assessment.
5. Retrolental fibroplasia.
6. The relationship between adjustment and maternal parental attitudes.

For the physically handicapped 4 and 5 above were replaced by (a) comparative studies, and (b) education and achievement.

The reportedly small personality disturbance which seemed to accompany blindness, prompted many queries for teachers. Dr. Kellmer Pringle posed, too, the need "for adequate conceptualization to account for the many discrepant findings" and for a "theoretical structure . . . which can be tested experimentally". Whilst comparative studies of the physically handicapped revealed in the main that such children were less mature and more disturbed than the control groups, the evidence was against any suggestion that handicapped children were inevitably maladjusted. She found widespread agreement, however, that parental attitudes towards the child and his handicap were of paramount importance.

Since teachers of handicapped children were increasingly aware of the whole child, and the whole child as a member of a number of groups, "emotional and social adjustment" pointers were of great importance. Studies of handicapped children, like the current inadequacies of differential diagnosis, generated conflicting estimates of the educational needs, facilities, and possibilities. For example, the relationship between "motivation" and "maturation" was of particular interest and required exploration in depth. Stott's findings that motivational impairment might be made good at puberty provided a typical challenge. (Stott found that boys who were ineducable "until say, 14, acquired the confidence and wish to learn". The provision of a suitable and stimulating environment "has transformed a lot of children once diagnosed as feebleminded into reasonably capable adults".)

What relation had this, for example, to Professor Elkonin's discovery in the USSR that following a specialized teaching programme in various subjects, children did not respond to Professor Piaget's experiments in the manner revealed by Piaget. (Piaget's stages of development according to Elkonin could not be viewed as laws of development. Teaching could influence the kind of development that took place.)

Longitudinal studies of handicapped children—qualitative as well as quantitative—and of the effects of educational procedures required finance, planning, trained personnel to carry them through, and the transmission of the result in digestible form to teachers and others involved. Forms of differential diagnosis, more refined with the less able children, required to be developed so that differential forms of treatment might evolve to replace hit-or-miss approaches.

In certain respects the prospects appear brighter. One major, longitudinal study of a complete age group (born during a week in March 1958) is under way, directed by Dr. Kellmer Pringle and Dr. N. Butler, and under the general guidance of a scientific planning and steering committee chaired by Mr. H. Elvin and Dr. W. D. Wall.

This began with a thorough ante-perinatal and post-natal study of 17,000 children born in 1958 (3–8 March). The perinatal study was financed and sponsored by the National Birthday Trust Fund and directed by Dr. Neville Butler, lecturer in Paediatrics at the Institute of Child Health. The Department of Education and Science provided funds for a first follow-up study, and the Home Office for the study of some special groups. A continued, interdisciplinary study is sponsored by four bodies, the National Birthday Trust Fund, the National Bureau for Co-operation in Child Care, the Institute of Child Health, and the National Foundation for Educational Research.*

Similarly, Professor Tizard's longitudinal study of "the medical, psychological and social factors contributing to the educational retardation of children of junior school age" has begun with a pilot scheme in the Isle of Wight.

This survey is particularly concerned with the prevalence and interrelationship of a number of rather ill-defined syndromes of educational importance. These behaviour problems include study of movement, dyspraxia, disorders of language, specific disabilities of reading, writing, and arithmetic, and autism. Special attention is being paid to the problems of multiple handicaps among such children.

A Research Institute of Special Education

Currently efforts by voluntary organizations to set up a Research Institute of Special Education have almost reached fruition. The National Association for Mental Health has accepted responsibility for leadership in this direction, advised by a steering committee which includes representatives of the Department of Education and Science, the Guild of Teachers of Backward Children, the National Society for Mentally Handicapped Children, the Spastics Society, and individual specialists.*

* See Postscript.

CHAPTER 14

The Training of Teachers

It is axiomatic that the success of a school programme for the mentally retarded is in direct proportion to the ability of the teacher.
(J. H. ROTHSTEIN, *Mental Retardation: Readings and Resources*, 1961, Holt, Reinhart & Winston.)

The Views of the NUT

Teachers' organizations and publications have increasingly drawn attention to work with handicapped children. The philosophy and activities of the National Union of Teachers played a particularly significant role in this area. It had built into its constitution an Advisory Committee on Special Education which had representatives of every kind of special school, of some other forms of special provision, and of the NUT Executive. Its views, developing with the developing knowledge in this entire area, were published in several pamphlets.

It took the opportunity provided by a Royal Commission to urge that the responsibility for the education and welfare of "the ineducable child" should rest with the education authority instead of being passed to the health authority. (In its evidence to the Scott Committee it referred back to these views and to others it had shared with those who sought to bring training centres under the education authorities.)

In suggesting this, it gave amongst its reasons

the failure under the present arrangements, to provide for the education, as distinct from the care, of such children. Quite obviously, where there is no place available in a special school and the child is attending a normal school and is having a deleterious effect on the education of children in that school, there is a greater danger that the child may be reported prematurely.

In its view the advantages offered by the suggested change were that parents would suffer less distress as their children would not require to be "reported" as "ineducable", and transfer back to a special school or from the special school would be simpler.

Whilst the NUT now conceded to the Royal Commission that local authorities were accustomed "to the formation of joint committees or subcommittees for the administration of joint services" and concluded that they could be left free to work out their own methods of co-ordination, the vital need for co-ordination and co-operation was underlined. The Union pointed out that the section of the 1944 Education Act under which children were excluded (57) referred to "a disability of mind of such a nature and to such an extent as to make them incapable of receiving education at school", and that this did not suggest that these children were incapable of receiving education elsewhere. The Union's view was that it should never be taken for granted that any child was incapable of being taught the three Rs "because much successful work had been and is being done with seemingly hopeless children from the educational viewpoint. Children attending training centres are often anxious to attempt work in the Three R's, and it has been found that some children make little progress until they are about 14 years of age . . .".

The Union believed that children in training centres should be under expert educational supervision and that transfer to a special school should be a simple matter. More specifically, it urged that the person in charge of the training centre should be a trained, qualified (that is recognized by the Ministry of Education) teacher, and the staff of any training centre attended by young people and adults should include at least one trained, qualified teacher in the above sense.

The training of teachers for special schools was of particular concern to the NUT Advisory Committee. In 1965, 21 years after the 1944 Act, only the special schools for the blind and for the deaf could expect their staff to be specially qualified for their work. In other special schools training could not yet be a condition of entry to new staff. In one document, produced 5 years after the report published by the Ministry's Advisory Council on the *Training and Supply of Teachers of Handicapped Pupils* (1954), the Union referred back to the recommendation that: "as from an appropriate date" which has still to be decided, "new teachers in special schools . . . should be required to have satisfactorily completed an approved one-year course of training under the supervision of an area training organization qualifying them as teachers in special schools . . .". The NUT also pointed out that there was still no course which teachers in special schools recognized as being of the general character indicated by the National Advisory Council. Remarking that teacher training was essentially "a forward looking area of social organization", the NUT itself, in a document to encourage the setting up of special courses, made the suggestions which took note of the changing picture or handicap and the numerical strength of the various categories defined. The document stressed that the changing pattern would leave the mentally handicapped as the largest category, followed by the emotionally handicapped as a close second. It pointed out that "80% of the educable spastics are in the ESN category which at present contains a whole multitude of physical handicaps of all types".

The Basic Educational Problem

Accordingly throughout the entire range of handicaps, the basic educational problem was seen as that of "the slow learner" irrespective of the origins of this backwardness. As a result of the handicap, learning difficulties could be quite subtle, requiring the teacher to have "deep insight into a number of areas of knowledge" which could be utilized to help the individual handicapped child.

Documents published by the Union as a result of the work of it Advisory Committee on Special Education included the evidence it gave to the Newsom Committee on *The Average and Below Average Child*; and to the Working Party of the British Council for Rehabilitation on *The Employment and Welfare of the Handicapped*

School Leaver. It sent out questionnaires and published the results on *The Day School for Delicate Children* and *Day Schools for ESN pupils.* Its pamphlets considered:

1. "Conditions of service of teachers in residential schools" (1961).
2. "The ascertainment of ESN children" (1962).
3. "The education of maladjusted children" (1962).

Following upon the failure to develop a 1-year diploma course of the general kind indicated by the 1954 report of National Advisory Council on the Training and Supply of Teachers, the NUT Advisory Committee itself produced a suggested syllabus and outline course.

The Content of a One-year Course Leading to a Diploma in Special Education

Proposed by the National Union of Teachers (1960).

A basic course for breadth would be taken by all students and would cover the whole field of special education.

The needs and interests of individual students could be met by alternative lecture courses, visits, and seminars.

This emphasis could develop in the final term into a concentration on one category, or a group of related types of handicapped children, and could involve attendance at lectures, carefully planned visits, and practical work with seminars to follow, and the preparation of a thesis on a practical investigation or critical study.

As an alternative, opportunities could be provided for the specialist teachers, e.g. art and handwork, to develop personal skills and practical knowledge of the teaching of the specialist subject to handicapped children.

The choice of a training centre was considered important. Many advantages were held to accrue from meeting other groups of students and sharing their lectures.

Suggested Syllabus

(a) *Child health*

A revision course in health education.
Physical abnormalities, disabilities, and handicaps.
Psycho-somatic illness.

(b) *Normal development of children*

A study of the wide variations in growth and behaviour within the normal range of development.

(c) *Recent developments in psychological thought*

The dynamics of human behaviour with particular reference to the deeper levels of emotional development in children.
Some appreciation of the psychiatric orientation in regard to children.
The teacher's personality and the adjustment of children in the classroom.

(d) *Psychology of the handicapped child*

The application of (a), (b), and (c) to the basic needs of children.
The effects on learning and personality of physical defect, frequent illness, hospitalization, epilepsy, school failure, parental and family attitudes, emotional deprivation.
The special needs of the backward (both retarded and ESN), the maladjusted (emotionally, socially, and educationally), and the delinquent child.

(e) *Educational method in the special school*

The implications of recent research. The therapeutic value of play. Interest and activity methods.
Individual differences.
The psychology and methods of teaching reading and arithmetic to children of all ages.
The causes and treatment of backwardness.
Teaching problems in particular types of school.

(f) *Individual records*

Their importance in assessing and guiding physical, social, emotional, and educational progress.

(g) *Attainment and diagnostic testing*

The interpretation of results and application to the devising and preparation of methods and apparatus, and the grading and grouping of children and material.

(h) *A knowledge of a wide range of practical activities and their importance and therapeutic value in the education of the handicapped*

Music, movement, and drama.

Painting and modelling.

Crafts—puppetry, weaving, needlework, and work in wood and metal.

Nature study, gardening, pet and livestock keeping, youth hostelling, lightweight camping and canoeing, and useful hobbies.

(i) *Special school routines and problems, day and residential*

Diet, rest, supervision, clothing, recreational activities, and home and school co-operation.

Religious education.

The layout, buildings, and equipment and apparatus of different types of special school.

(j) *The handicapped child's entry into employment and community life*

After-care and further education.

(k) *Legal procedures relevant to the care of the handicapped*

A study of other agencies concerned with the treatment and care of the handicapped child—hospitals, clinics, child guidance clinics, children's homes, hostels, welfare centres, and remand homes.

The organization of the above, their terminologies and etiquette.

Visits to some of the above.

(1) *Visits to representative schools for normal children*

> Visits to special schools with short periods of teaching practice in one or two schools of a type other than the one chosen for special study.

Care or Special Education?

Growing interest in special education led to some attempts to examine the value of special school provision. But not all the researchers who sought to do this were aware of the many variables which required consideration.

Nevertheless, at a time when no more than 42 per cent of the special ESN schools could claim to have one or more members of staff who had been on one of the special courses, one researcher (Stein) found that: "special school education had made a significant contribution to literacy in children with intelligence quotients under 70." Those with IQs over 70 "had usually attained literacy whether or not they had special education". In arithmetic "children with IQs over 65 who are yet within the educationally subnormal range are helped to attain numeracy by special education which they may not attain if they do not have such education".

In the USA an effort was made by Professor H. Goldstein to answer the question whether "special classes for educable retarded children" in the schools were "more effective educationally than *ordinary* classes". At the end of a 4-year study, 1964, he found that:

1. There was no difference in intellectual development, but
2. the special class children were significantly superior to the ordinary class "educable mentally retarded" children in all areas of academic achievement with one exception (the subtest; word recognition in the Metropolitan achievement test).
3. The special class children *more nearly resembled normal children of the same chronological age* than did the ordinary class control group. The latter were less secure, less flexible, less creative, and more needful of recognition and approval.

The possibilities for the happiness and the attainments of such pupils, if all were given suitably trained teachers of the right type, can only be guessed.

Yet apart from some inspiring experiments, the general recognition of the need for teacher training was insufficient to arouse a national confrontation of the problem.

Two Approaches

A century after "payment by results" had been introduced, its echoes were to be found in the attitude towards the training of teachers for the severely subnormal child.

At this time, for the majority of staff in training centres for such children, there could be no expectation of any kind of training other than experience. For a fraction of them the only courses that had ever been available were the 1-year diploma courses provided by a voluntary, pioneering body, the National Association for Mental Health. But following upon the Scott Committee's recommendations, and the setting up of a Central Training Council by the Health Ministry, some 2-year courses were introduced for the selected new entrants with at least three GCE O-level passes.

The health authorities in seeking to recruit and train personnel for such centres, looked to suitable young people. The salary scales offered, however, were far below those of teachers. Meanwhile the education authorities, in seeking recruits for special schools, looked to experienced teachers in ordinary schools, and the philosophy underlying this approach was stated clearly by the NUT (1960):

> Certain personal qualifications are required for successful teaching of handicapped children. Such teachers obviously need the qualities and skills desirable in all teachers, therefore normal teacher-training should be a pre-requisite, and it is desirable that such training should be followed by a period which will allow basic teacher skills to develop and mature and which will allow a body of normal experience to accumulate as a touchstone against which the handicapped child can be assessed.

Since 1950 at least, this had been generally accepted practice. In that year the first two diploma courses in the education of handicapped pupils (one for teachers of ESN pupils, and one for maladjusted) had been introduced in London's Institute of Education. By 1965 there were about a dozen such courses in addition to the already existing ones for teachers of the blind and the deaf. A further eighteen courses known as supplementary courses and probably intended as more practical in nature than the diploma courses, were introduced in colleges of education. All these courses were full-time and of a year's duration.

But even in 1965, only 372 teachers in all were released for all the courses put together—for all categories of handicap including the blind and the deaf. This number included fifty on courses for the deaf.

At this same time the Minister of Education was drawing attention to a new obstacle—the fact that insufficient teachers had come forward to fill existing places on the courses—and the teachers were protesting that insufficient of them could obtain release from their schools to attend such courses.

It seemed incredible that even the limited facilities in this area could be threatened with a breakdown. There was clearly no relationship between the need and the rate of teacher training.

A conference organized by the Guild of Teachers of Backward Children, to discuss a proposed College of Special Education, was given the following indication of the need by the General Secretary, 1965:

> If we accept the estimate of educational subnormality provided by the Department of Education and Science, there will be a million ESN pupils in our schools by 1970. Almost a similar number of pupils will require some form of special treatment during some part of their school lives. If we omit the latter from our thinking for a moment—if we forget the need for pre-school education for deprived and slow children and continue to ignore what happens to children excluded from the school system altogether—and if we assumed that the one million ESN pupils were going to be placed in classes of 20, we would require a minimum of 50,000 suitable trained teachers for this category of handicap alone and this would involve neglecting many inspiring developments, such as the new diagnostic units new kinds of special entry classes, child guidance clinic teams, peripatetic

teachers, and so on. Moreover these figures assume that none of the 50,000 teachers will fall sick, retire, be promoted out of the class-room, or enter a related discipline.

To this required to be added the fact that all kinds of special schools were now remarking on their changing composition. Dual and multiple handicaps were more in evidence in schools for the blind, the deaf, the partially sighted, the partially hearing, the physically handicapped, and the educationally subnormal. Ever-greater or more complex skills were being required of such teachers.

Teachers for Other Handicaps

Retardation was clearly a problem extending to all categories of handicap. But the changing pattern of handicaps, the deeper insight into the nature of each handicap, and the extension of education to the pre- and post-school stages, created an increasing need for more specialized training and study in depth in each area. If there was an acute shortage of places in special ESN schools, other types of special schools were returning children to ordinary schools. Some special schools for epileptics, for example, had by 1962 closed down, whilst others found "that a substantial number of their pupils can be made fit to go to and do well in ordinary schools after two or three years of special schooling". Heart surgery had turned many children with congenital heart defects into virtually normal youngsters. Newly devised operations for spina bifida and hydrocephalus offered "hope of a tolerable life, if not of normality, to some children with these tragic deformities". Dual and multiple handicapped children were therefore increasingly to be found remaining or entering in special schools.

The challenge to teacher skills was perhaps highlighted in the treatment of the children with sensory defects, notably the visually handicapped and the partially hearing. Sir Alexander Ewing pointed out that "retardation problems, with defective hearing as a major factor amongst pupils in ordinary schools" provided much of the case load in audiology clinics. Verbal intelligence quotients were "inevitably affected in many cases of previously undiscovered cases of partial deafness". In 1965 a special school for maladjusted deaf children was opened at Larchmore by the RNID. "Its purpose is to cater for a class of deaf children for whom at present there is no form of education and training." Mr. M. Reed, chairman of the RNID Children's Committee, said that much depended upon the staff and it would not be easy to find the right type of person. There was no adequate precedent and much of the work would be experimental.

The education of the visually handicapped had undergone a considerable change. Many of the old causes of blindness had disappeared. Modern ante-natal methods, better drugs, and a wiser attitude towards certain diseases had helped. "Blindness due to retrolental fibroplasia in premature babies, which was responsible for a number of children being in special classes, could now be avoided. Many children suffering from this disease would not have survived before the Second World War. Other children, saved by surgical treatment which removed a cerebral tumour, lost their sight."

Premature children often suffered other ailments. Emotional problems and the differing background of experience of those who had once seen, compared with those born blind, had to be considered. In special schools places "were now given to partially sighted pupils of low intelligence". The tendency had become "for those partially sighted pupils who are maintaining a fair standard in the sighted school to remain with their sighted fellows. Their less gifted class-mates are transferred to the special school when it is seen they cannot keep up this standard."

If special schools offered smaller classes and individual attention, they were also offering the teachers a new kind of situation: "late diagnosis quite often means transfer at the onset of adolescence" with all that this could mean. G. Exley and D. R. Gray emphasized that few of their children had single handicaps. Teachers, they said, sought long- and short-term courses in the methods of dealing with other handicaps. But "general feeling among candidates is that they can expect to be last in line for these courses. The reason is mainly one of priorities, but it is hoped that as more courses are planned, the teachers in the existing special schools are given the opportunities they need to better themselves for the job they do."

The Courses Available

In 1965 the Department of Education and Science published a list in alphabetical order of the 1-year courses available for qualified teachers. Each 1-year course for handicapped children was described individually. Apart from three courses for teachers of the deaf (two in Manchester and one commencing in London), there were thirty other courses providing for all other handicaps.

Seven of these courses led to diplomas in the education of ESN children (Birmingham, Durham, Kingston upon Hull, Leeds, Liverpool, and London). Four were diploma courses in the teaching of handicapped children (Liverpool, Manchester, Newcastle upon Tyne, and Southampton). Two offered diplomas in the education of backward children (Leeds and Swansea). Bangor had a diploma in remedial education, and London, in the education of maladjusted children. Apart from the centres already named, there were courses available in Middlesex, Berkshire, Derbyshire, Sussex, and Lancashire, and in Bristol, Coventry, and Sheffield. Diploma courses, being held in university institutes of education, were intended to encourage a rather different kind of specialist study to the certificate courses organized in colleges of education.

Some Practical Considerations

The apparent obstacle to the flow of experienced teachers into the 1-year courses (diploma or certificate) contrasted with the apparent success of the new courses for teachers of severely subnormal children in attracting able young applicants. None of the three or four 2-year courses for such students appeared to be having difficulty in obtaining applicants of suitable quality.

F

The beginnings of a movement to train students for work with severely subnormal children—yet to be recognizable as fully qualified teachers by the Department of Education and by the National Union of Teachers—was seen in the initiative of another voluntary organization, the National Society for Mentally Handicapped Children. In 1965 its project to set up a new kind of college in Birmingham was widely publicized.

Meanwhile some practical factors began to encourage further experiment or some rethinking with regard to special training at least for special schools.

1. The teacher shortage in general did not encourage the existing profession to be a ready contributor to supplementary courses. Some dedicated teachers feared what might happen at the school if they went away for a year, and not all local education authorities were prepared to release teachers for full-time training.

By 1965 the Department of Education was drawing attention to the fact that many places on existing courses for experienced teachers of handicapped children were not being taken up—this at a time when such places were still too few to meet the need.

2. A further factor discouraging experienced teachers who might otherwise have been attracted by this work, was the distance of the university or college centres, where the few courses were held, from their homes. Older teachers tended to have domestic commitments which were more restrictive than was the case with students. As a result there was a pressure for part-time courses, correspondence courses, and other approaches which might save a proportion of these teachers for "special education".

3. There was also a questioning of the nature and value of "experience". Whilst certain qualities were necessary, and a certain maturity, there were different kinds of experience in teaching. Not all kinds of experience in teaching were found to be helpful in encouraging a "child-centred" individualized resourceful approach to the handicapped child. Criticisms of some of the habits acquired by teachers in ordinary schools in both the USA and the USSR had been voiced, both countries having

had experience of both forms of teacher training of "special educators".

Amongst possible advantages in training some teachers from the beginning as "special educators" were:

1. Opportunity to select suitable keen, young, idealistic students who might go beyond the usual course to advanced study. A parallel with medical students might be made, and an awareness of the need for a multi-disciplinary approach to the multiple handicapped child encouraged in this way.

2. Easier cultivation of the kinds of skills and habits required of a teacher of more severely handicapped children might be possible.

No one expected a secondary school teacher first to have had experience of infant teaching; nor was the infant teacher expected to teach first in a secondary school. Was there a parallel here in special education? Would special education be raised this way to the status at least of "infant education" or "secondary education".

The similar problems or successes in other countries, notably the USA and the USSR in training inexperienced teachers for this work, also encouraged some rethinking. The USA delegation to the USSR drew attention on their return to the 4-year course offered to selected students in the USSR which led to a qualification as a special educator (defectologist) and a 25 per cent increase in salary.

Such a course seemed to overcome practical difficulties balancing the advantages gained from having experienced teachers with the advantages of training new teachers in a manner which discouraged certain habits from forming.

But clearly, such was the overall need that arguments of the above kind seemed merely academic. A substantial advance on every possible front was called for, and the maximum efforts so far offered had done little more than paddle at the shallow end of the possibilities.

A vast programme was required to help the existing generation of teachers, and through them, the children. Every possible kind of course (short, correspondence, sandwich, etc.) leading to some

recognized qualification and further study required encouragement and substantial expansion. Teachers, themselves more
keenly aware than most of the needs, set up their own College of
Special Education in 1966.

CHAPTER 15

Towards International Co-operation

One might well speculate about the driving force behind this spontaneous (parents) movement which occurred in widely separated countries with widely different cultures. It took root alike in countries with little or no organized service and in countries where schooling, residential care, and supervision of the retarded adult in the community had been the concern of public agencies and voluntary associations for many years. It was started by no visible force; there were not then, nor were there to be for another decade, any international professional or voluntary organizations specifically active in the field of mental retardation.

(ROSEMARY DYBWAD, *Challenges in Mental Retardation*, 1963.)

UNESCO

Considerable encouragement must have been given to many struggling parents' organizations and professional workers by the discovery of similar groups in other countries. Moves towards exchange of information, co-operation within small groups of countries, and, where possible, actual international co-operation, reinforced and inspired developments within every category of handicap.

A general concern with child welfare was apparent soon after the First World War with the formation of the Save the Children International Union (created in Geneva) and the International Association for the Promotion of Child Welfare (set up in Brussels). The two merged in 1946 to form the International Union for Child Welfare and, from the beginning, included an active concern for the physically or mentally handicapped child.

In 1964 this International Union for Child Welfare established a Mental Retardation Project to assist its member associations in developing support for services for the mentally retarded in their countries. Dr. Gunnar Dybwad and his wife Rosemary, whose work had helped build the remarkable parents' association in the USA (the National Association for Retarded Children) left the USA to participate in the work at Geneva. (The headquarters of the Union in Geneva is at 1 rue de Varembe, and the Secretary General is Mr. D. G. R. Mulock-Houwer.)

In the same year as the Mental Retardation Project was established, four countries put forward the following resolution on handicapped children which was carried at the UNESCO General Conference, 13th session.

> Reaffirming the belief, contained in the Constitution of UNESCO in the Universal Declaration of Human Rights, in full and equal opportunities for all,
>
> Considering that these opportunities must also be available to handicapped children and youth,
>
> Noting that in many countries the provisions made for this purpose are unsatisfactory or non-existent,
>
> Realizing the need for planning in the education of deaf, blind, cerebral palsy, mentally retarded and similarly handicapped persons,
>
> Concurring in the view expressed by the Executive Board "that highest priority in the education programme should be given to those areas of education, deficiencies in which constitute the greatest bottlenecks to economic and social development",
>
> Invited Member States to take appropriate measures to safeguard the rights of education for deaf, blind, cerebral palsied, mentally retarded and similarly handicapped persons;
>
> Requests the Director General:
>
> (a) to give increased attention, within the framework of overall educational planning, to the education of handicapped persons by engaging in research study of the problems;
>
> (b) to seek the co-operation of institutions already actively engaged in the education of handicapped persons in order to achieve optimal results in efforts to assist this category;
>
> (c) to give due consideration to the problems of handicapped persons in UNESCO-sponsored projects for teacher-training and free and compulsory education of (ordinary) children of primary school age, and to the article in the "International Code of Education" concerning the rights to education of handicapped persons;
>
> Recommends that the Director General bring to the attention of the International Institute of Educational Planning that the planning of the handicapped persons should be an integral part of all educational planning.

International Society for Rehabilitation
of the Disabled

Active international interest in "crippled children" was stirred too and given expression between the two world wars as a result of voluntary initiative. Edgar F. Allen, an active member of the Rotary International, formed an International Society for Crippled Children in 1922. The first world conference organized by this society took place in Geneva in 1922. With its Fourth World Conference of Workers for the Crippled, 1939, the Society changed its name to reflect its concern for adults as well as children. By 1960, instead of limiting itself to the orthopaedically handicapped, the organization had become The International Society for the Rehabilitation of the Disabled and had expanded to include all major areas of disability.

> Older organizations were frequently known as societies for "the care of" crippled or disabled. The obsolete concept of passive, custodial care for the handicapped person has now evolved into the dynamic idea of enabling him to become a useful and functioning member of society. The work of the International Society will not be completed until all the world's handicapped population are restored to the fullest measure of their abilities.

This magnificent declaration reflected the changing climate internationally—without hiding the desperate needs. By 1965 the society had become a world federation of voluntary organizations in no less than sixty-one countries. Its programme included the exchange of information concerning new developments in the medical, educational, social and vocational aspects of rehabilitation. It sought to improve rehabilitation services in all parts of the world and to assist professional workers as well as laymen to a better understanding of the needs of the disabled. Expert commissions and committees were established to deal with problems in particular areas of disability. Active specialized groups now exist in arthritis, cerebral palsy, leprosy rehabilitation, prosthenics and orthnotics, research, technical aids, social aspects, special education, speech and hearing, spinal cord injury, vocational rehabilitation, and volunteers. (Address is 219 East 44th Street, New York, N.Y. 10017, USA. The society also maintains an international rehabilitation film library of approximately 195 titles, which are available to members on a rental basis.)

The Mentally Handicapped

Significant moves towards international exchange and co-operation as regards work with mentally handicapped persons was concerned, sprang from at least three separate forces in the post-1945 period: parents' organizations, organizations of special educators, and professional organizations belonging to other (notably medical) disciplines.

Considerable impetus towards international interest in the mentally handicapped was provided by two parents' organizations, one in the USA (to which reference has already been made in this chapter) and one from Britain. The former grew from well under 100 members in 1950 to well over 50,000 members by 1960. Although a national association, it formed an International Relations Committee which by 1955 distributed a twenty-page bulletin on mental retardation programmes in twenty-two countries. "By 1957 the Committee had active contacts with some forty countries, and two years later with sixty, twenty of which had national associations; in another twenty-four, one or more local groups were active" (Rosemary Dybwad, *Mobilizing for Action* CEC, 1963).

In 1960 the General Secretary of the National Association for Mentally Handicapped Children in the UK was helping to found the European League of Societies for the Mentally Handicapped which later expanded into an International League of such societies and had membership in twenty-six countries. (The secretariat is at 12 rue Forestiere, Brussels, 5. The General Secretary is Dr. R. Portray. The League holds an international congress every three years and issues a news-letter.)

International Association for the Scientific
Study of Mental Deficiency

At this same time (1960), a teacher organization held its first International Conference on the Backward Child (Guild of Teachers of Backward Children) whilst two international conferences on mental deficiency were held by two different groups, one in the USA (Portland, Maine) and the other in the UK (the London Conference on the Scientific Study of Mental Deficiency). In 1961 the two groups met at the Vienna Congress and amalgamated to form an International Association for the Scientific Study of Mental Deficiency. This represented an historic move forward towards fostering research and disseminating knowledge. The international committee elected under the chairmanship of Dr. A. Shapiro of Harperbury Hospital prepared the Copenhagen Conference (1964)* at which the draft constitution was ratified. The first international conference arranged following upon this ratification, was to take place in Montpelier in 1967.

The officers of this new international association were distinguished authorities, well-known inside and outside their own countries. In addition to Dr. A. Shapiro there was Professor A. D. B. Clarke from Britain (Secretary), Dr. H. A. Stevens, and Dr. Clemens E. Benda from the USA, and Dr. Giovanni Bollea from Italy.

The association set out to promote the scientific study of mental deficiency, through a multi-disciplinary approach, throughout the world. To this end it sought to serve as a medium for the exchange of "ideas, knowledge, skills, and experience, and for compilation and dissemination of information". It organized conferences, encouraged research into "causes, prevention, diagnosis, evaluation, therapy, management, education and social rehabilitation of the mentally deficient". It sought, too, to encourage membership in the various professional disciplines and national

* In 1966 the Association for Special Education drew more than 700 colleagues to its first international conference.

organizations concerned with mental deficiency, assist in the creation of national organizations, and provide any other services and develop other functions as were compatible with these purposes.

Here was a significant positive contribution towards changing the situation in a number of countries. It was significant that education was represented in both the USA and the UK branches of this organization.

Other international organizations which have some place in the context of this book include the World Union of Organizations for Safeguarding Children and Youth (28 Place St. George, Paris, 9) and the International Union of Workers for Maladapted Children, which has a branch in the UK.

National Co-ordination

Meanwhile, within many countries, stimulated by forces within as well as developments outside, moves towards developing separate disciplines and creating interdisciplinary co-operation were taking place.

The Council for Exceptional Children

In the USA a Council for Exceptional Children, which had its origins in 1922, became in 1950 a department of the National Educational Association, a national teachers' organization. Autonomous within this organization, the CEC had a membership open to "special educators and other interested persons". It published a journal, *Exceptional Children*, which covered the range of handicaps from the viewpoint of special educators and allied disciplines. The CEC was divided into a number of associations, including one for *The Gifted*, an Association of Educators of Homebound and Hospitalized Children, a Council for the Education of the Partially Seeing, the Council of Administrators of Special Education, and the Division on Teacher Education. It published Research Monographs and the CEC Special Publication Series.

More recently it set up a section specifically devoted to the mentally handicapped. (Address: 1201 Sixteenth Street, N.W., Washington 36, D.C.)

In several other countries there were developments of a parallel kind of which that in Italy was perhaps least known in the UK yet of considerable interest.

The Italian Society for Handicapped Children

The SIAME in Italy was constituted in 1948. Its members were drawn from a number of disciplines (paediatrics, neuro-psychiatry, education, welfare, administration, and related areas). Amongst its sections was an association working on behalf of abnormal infants (Pro Infanzia Annormale).

The SIAME held national congresses and aimed "to propagate scientific study, researches and experiences within the medico-psychological-pedagogical field", for all forms of physical, sensory, and psychological handicaps which were revealed during a child's development. It sought to influence legislation, co-ordinate initiatives, and collaborate on the international plane towards these objectives. (Address: SIAME, Roma, Piazza Lovatelli, 36.)

Western Europe

Despite the language barriers which discouraged communication even with nearby countries, a number of developments have taken place which are helping improve communication. More and more teachers, for example (as well as parents' organizations), have become familiar with some of the pioneering contributions to special education made in several neighbouring countries. For example, the Scandinavian countries provided the first organized international activity in the field of mental retardation, and a Nordic Association for Special Education held congresses at four-year intervals. There are "Heilpedagogic" associations in

Germany, Austria, and Switzerland. And reference has been made to the Italian organization.

Each country has experiences to offer and a need for contacts. In Holland it became obligatory as long ago as 1910 for school authorities to provide classes for children whom we, at the time, considered "ineducable".

> Experience in some countries, especially in the Dutch sheltered workshops, has also shown that even seriously mentally handicapped men and women are able to perform useful work and that intelligence has no positive correlation with working fitness. . . . The higher classes in Dutch day-special-schools, consisting of children who are then 15 to 18, receive preparation for employment in the sheltered workshop. These classes often have instruction in working techniques to enable them to earn a living in the future, or at least to contribute to it. The earlier this education begins, the better are the prospects for future successful employment. In view of this, in recent years, nursery schools have been established for pre-school children in the age group 3 to 6. These nursery schools mean an early commencement of speech development, social and emotional behaviour and co-ordination of motor activity. . . .
>
> In Germany the nursery school also features in our overall programme. Before the war a promising system was beginning to develop of community care, special classes and some workshops. However the Nazi government practically annihilated what had been achieved necessitating a new start from the bottom again. *Personal contact with the parent's organization in the USA and in the UK, encouraged us to start a similar movement in Germany. . . .*
>
> [Mutters, 1960]

Eastern Europe

More information is also available about similar developments in eastern Europe, where all forms of provision are a state responsibility.

In 1962, for the first time, delegates from eastern Europe participated in an International Conference on the Backward Child in London. In return, representatives of the Guild of Teachers of Backward Children and of the National Society for Mentally Handicapped Children were invited to a conference on the Scientific Selection of Children for Special Schools. The delegates were clearly surprised and delighted to find representatives of a number of countries participating in a crowded conference filled with teachers and workers from allied disciplines who were actively involved with special education. In Budapest itself there was a training college devoted entirely to special education which had survived several different regimes and was headed by Dr. Barczi, who had been there for more than 30 years. The head of the special education department at the Ministry of Education was a Mrs. Etelke Vinze, who stated: "all children and juveniles who, in consequence of some abnormality or damage to their nervous system, their physical development, or any deficiency of their senses cannot be educated and taught in the ordinary school, benefit from our special education scheme."

From Eastern Germany, where the Humboldt University was devoted to the training of specialists for handicapped children, to the USSR, where considerable attention was devoted to this area, it was plain that there was here an area of common endeavour where each country might contribute to all and where countless handicapped children stood to gain from freer and fuller exchanges.

PART II

Professional and Voluntary Organizations:
Facilities; Publications; Films

CHAPTER 16

Mental Handicaps and Disorders

The National Society for Mentally Handicapped Children

Address: 5 Bulstrode St., London, W 1.

The initiative of a mother of a handicapped child led to the formation of a National Association of Parents of Backward Children in 1946. This published its first news-letter in 1947, and the Association grew, with local groups being formed in many parts of the country.

It is not possible to exaggerate the importance to parents of the local societies which come face to face with the problem of mental handicap. They provide special care units, clubs, nursery schools, residential hostels, summer camps, holiday homes, and raise funds in connection with these projects in addition to performing such tasks as baby sitting. They help parents to overcome their feeling of isolation by arranging social gatherings and discussions. They provide amenities for those at present outside the mental health and welfare schemes, and they are, in many cases, represented on the local government health committees.

The first short-stay home, where children could be looked after by trained staff for a few weeks, was opened near Liverpool. The Association was reconstructed under its present style in 1955 and has since grown remarkably. There are 345 local societies in England and Wales and Northern Ireland, and 12 regional groups affiliated with the National Society.

The National Society exists to:

1. Help mentally handicapped children and their families

through welfare and counselling services and facilities to care for the children.

2. Promote and finance research into the causes, prevention, and treatment of mental handicap in order to improve existing medical treatment and training facilities, and set up pilot schemes such as the National Hostels and Training Centre.

3. Stimulate public awareness, professional understanding of the problem, and local authority action by publicizing the needs of these children and the latest information and statistics on all aspects of the problems through publication and news-sheets, a *Journal of Mental Deficiency Research*, films, and tapes, and a lending library.

4. Urge the integration of mentally handicapped children in the open community.

One of the many problems confronting the parents of mentally handicapped children is providing both themselves and the children with holidays, sometimes separately, thus giving the parents a much-needed break. Pirates Spring is a holiday and short-stay home opened at St. Mary's Bay, on the coast road between Dymchurch and New Romney. It consists of the home Pirates Spring, where groups of children can be accommodated a bungalow unit used for short-stay care in the summer, and "Coastways", a small house providing holidays for the whole family. The home is also used for pilot schemes and short-stay care in the winter. Over a thousand children spend holiday annually at Pirates Spring.

Research projects financed by the National Society include:

(a) The University of Manchester's study of the epidemiology of mental subnormality and of the role of hypoglycaemia in the new-born period and the part it plays in the causation of mental defect and cerebral palsy;

(b) the inquiry by the University of Essex into hospital conditions;

(c) the extension of Guy's Hospital cytogenic research facilities;

(d) studies at Great Ormond Street Hospital of neurolipidosis, Hirschsprun's disease, cerebral gliosis, metachromatic, and other leucodystrophies;

(e) Queen Mary Hospital's survey of the incidence, natural psychology, and aetiology of hydrocephalus and meningoceole with special reference to mental retardation;

(f) the Borough of West Ham's study of personality development in mentally handicapped children against a home and training centre background with special reference to the services needed to integrate them into the community.

In 1965 the National Society inaugurated a Five Year Development Programme which included a Welfare and Counselling Service; a Teacher-training College to train teachers of the severely subnormal, a Rural Training Centre (similar to Slough but run along agricultural rather than industrial lines), a Residential School for Autistic Children, an Institute of Mental Defect; and a holiday and short-stay home at Winterton, Norfolk.

The National Society also operates a Trusteeship Scheme to look after mentally handicapped children after their parents have died.

PUBLICATIONS

JOURNALS

Journal of Mental Deficiency Research. A quarterly technical journal (12s. 6d.), annual subscription £2 10s.

Parents' Voice. The Society's quarterly magazine (1s. 3d.), annual subscription 5s.

REPORTS

Community Care of the Mentally Handicapped. Report of NSMHC Conference, 1960. 3s. 6d.

The Psychotic Child. Report of NSMHC Conference, 1961. 1s. 9d.

The Needs of Mentally Handicapped Children. Report of a Working Party set up by the Paediatric Society of the SE Metropolitan Region, 1960–1. 2s. 6d.

A Study of the Mentally Handicapped Child. Report of a study group at the London School of Hygiene and Tropical Medicine, 1960–2. 1s.

Training and Employment of the Mentally Handicapped. Report of NSMHC Conference, 1962. 3s.

Communication and the Withdrawn Child. Papers presented at the Annual Conference of the Guild of Teachers of Backward Children, Leicester, 1963. 1s. 9d.

International Congress on the Education and Social Integration of the Mentally Handicapped, Brussels, 21–25 October 1963. Report. 7s. 6d.

Booklets and Leaflets

The Mentally Handicapped Child. Information on education, a reprint from *Where?*, journal of the Advisory Centre for Education. 3d.

The Mongol Child. A reprint from the magazine *Parents*, outlining the potentials and limitations of these children. 3d.

The Psychotic (Autistic) Child. A leaflet to inform the general public about these children and ways in which they and their parents can be helped. 6d.

The NSMHC National Hostel and Sheltered Workshop. An illustrated leaflet describing the purpose of the Slough Project. 3d.

Technical Details on Hostel and Workshop Training Centre, Slough. 4d

Home Care of the Backward Child. An informative article for parents on training and care, feeding, etc. 6d.

You have Friends you are not Alone. A leaflet designed to tell parents of mentally handicapped children about the Society 4s. per 100.

Lonely Child. Appeal leaflet outlining aims of the Society. 6s. per 100.

Johnny Leaflet. Publicity leaflet giving information about the National Society. 2d.

Not Physically Handicapped, etc. Publicity leaflet similar to above with emphasis on the regions. 1½d.

National Society News-letter. Published quarterly. 2d.

OTHER PUBLICATIONS OBTAINABLE FROM NSMHC

BIOGRAPHIES

This is Stevie's Story, by DOROTHY G. MURRAY. An American parent writes of adjustments of family and community. 9s. 3d.

Bartje my Son, by NEL VAN HOUTEN. A mother's practical and sensitive approach to her problems. 10s. 6d.

Karen, by MARIE KILLIEA. The story of a family whose daughter Karen was born suffering from cerebral palsy. 3s. 6d.

GENERAL

Caring for the Intellectually Handicapped Child, by RALPH WINTERBOURNE. This deals with problems encountered by parents in an extremely lucid and thorough way. 4s. 6d.

Reading Methods and Games for Teaching the Retarded Child. A handbook for parents and teachers. An American publication. 12s.

Play Activities for the Retarded Child, by B. W. CARLSON and D. R. GINGLEND. An American publication designed to show how to "help him grow and learn through music, games, handicraft and other play activities". 27s. 6d.

Teaching Backward Pupils, by S. S. SEGAL. 12s. 6d.

Mental Subnormality, by ALAN HEATON-WARD. 7s. 6d.

The Retarded Child, by HERTA LOEWY. A guide for parents. 3s. 6d.

Educating the Sub-normal Child, by FRANCI LLOYD. Aspects of the work of a junior school for ESN children. 12s. 6d.

Teaching the Severely Subnormal, E. B. McDowall (Editor). 20s.

Unwillingly to School, by John J. H. Kahn. 15s.

The Handicapped School Leaver. Report by the British Council for the Rehabilitation of the Disabled. 15s.

Public Health and Hygiene Journal (February 1965). Special Issue—"The Mentally Subnormal". 3s. 6d.

Simple Readers

"The Fountain Picture Book" (a series of 3 books), specially compiled for mentally handicapped children illustrating situations within his experience and using a vocabulary that is most likely to be understood. 3s. 8d.

"Space Age Readers", Books 1, 2, 3, and 4, by S. S. Segal. 7s. 6d.

The Cat in the Hat, by Dr. Seuss. 8s. 6d.

Hop on Pop, by Dr. Seuss. 8s. 6d.

Snow, by Roy McKie and P. D. Eastman. 8s. 6d.

"Trouble Series", Edited by H. C. Gunzburg, with the assistance of R. Londt.

Book One: *Trouble with the Landlady*. 2s. 6d.

Book Two: *Trouble at Work*. 2s. 6d.

Book Three: *Trouble with the Wages*. 2s. 6d.

Book Four: *Trouble on Saturday*. 2s. 6d.

Technical Publications and Textbooks

Subnormal Personalities, by C. J. C. Earl. 30s.

Clinical Child Psychiatry, by Kenneth Soddy. 42s.

Social Rehabilitation of the Subnormal, by H. C. Gunzburg. 27s. 6d.

The Mentally Handicapped and their Families, by J. Tizard and J. C. Grad. 30s.

The Social Problem of Mental Deficiency, by N. O'Connor and J. Tizard. 30s.

Community Services for the Mentally Subnormal, by J. Tizard. 28s.

Educating Exceptional Children, by SAMUEL A. KIRK (Institute of Research into the Exceptional Child at Illinois). 37s. 6d.

Mental Retardation (Readings and Resources), by JEROME H. ROTHSTEIN. 54s.

Education and the Handicapped 1760–1960, by D. G. PRITCHARD. 28s.

The Education of Slow Learning Children, by A. E. TANSLEY and R. GULLIFORD. 28s.

The Biology of Mental Defect, by L. S. PENROSE. 42s.

Mental Deficiency, by R. F. TREDGOLD and K. SODDY. 40s.

Stoke Park Studies Mental Subnormality, edited by J. JANCAR. 30s.

Remedial Reading (Teaching and Treatment), by MAURICE D. WOOLFE. Edited by D. and JEANNE A. WOOLF. $5.75.

The Child and the Family, by D. W. WINNICOT. 16s.

Child, Family and Outside World, by D. W. WINNICOT (Penguin). 4s. 6d.

The Normal Child and some of his Abnormalities, by C. W. VALENTINE. 4s.

Educational Rhythmics for Mentally Handicapped Children, by FERRIS and JENNET ROBINS. 63s.

London Government and the Welfare Services, by F. K. RUCK. An inquiry by the London School of Economics on Political Science. 25s.

Brain Damage in Children. The biological and social aspects. Edited by HERBERT C. BIRCH. $5.95.

CURATIVE EDUCATION (THE WORK OF RUDOLF STEINER)

The Education of the Child, by RUDOLF STEINER. 2s. 3d.

The Task of the Curative Teacher, by CATHERINE D. GRACE. 2s.

Practical Activities. Details of schools and homes using curative education methods. 1s.

Adventure in Curative Education, by ISABEL GEUTER. 13s. 6d.

Rudolf Steiner Education (The Waldorf Impulse), by FRANCIS EDMUNDS. 10s. 6d.

The National Association for Mental Health

Address: Maurice Craig House, 39 Queen Anne St., London, W 1

The National Association for Mental Health was constituted in 1946 by the amalgamation of three pioneering voluntary mental welfare bodies—the Central Association for Mental Welfare, the Child Guidance Council, and the National Council for Mental Hygiene. Its activities are a direct continuation of the work of these bodies with additional enterprises to meet new needs and opportunities.

MEMBERSHIP

Membership is open to all. Over fifty local mental health associations in different parts of the country are affiliated to the National Association for Mental Health.

Local associations work in close co-operation with the national body, and their members are automatically enrolled as associate members of the National Association for Mental Health.

SERVICES PROVIDED

CONFERENCES, COURSES, AND GENERAL LECTURES

The Association organizes an annual conference on mental health which is attended by members, by delegates from local authorities and government departments, and is also open to the general public. Other conferences are arranged for staffs of child guidance clinics, staffs in the adult mental health services, and on specialized subjects. Short courses for professional and voluntary workers include:

Courses for local authority officers in the health and welfare service; special short courses for teachers, for general practitioners, for parish clergy, and chaplains in hospitals for the mentally disordered.

At present a special interest is being taken in the training of staffs of hostels for the mentally disordered, and a number of short courses in this connection are in preparation.

Lectures can be arranged for organized groups, including parents, teachers, local mental health associations, etc. (Case study seminars can also be arranged on request for groups of professional case-workers.)

TRAINING COURSE ON MENTAL SUBNORMALITY

The Association organizes full-time training courses, approved by the Central Training Council for Teachers of the Mentally Handicapped, to qualify men and women who wish to specialize in the teaching of mentally subnormal children. Courses of 1 year's duration are held in London, Manchester, and Sheffield for mature and experienced students, and a course of 2 years' duration in Bristol for new and young entrants to the work. A full-time training course of 1 year's duration, also approved by the Training Council, is held in Birmingham for men and women who wish to specialize in the training of mentally subnormal adults.

An annual residential refresher course is held for those already engaged in both these aspects of work with the mentally subnormal.

There are short courses for school medical officers on mentally subnormal children (in conjunction with the University of London Extra-mural Department).

The Association's specialist staff are also available for consultation by local health authorities, hospital management committees, and others, in connection with the training of the mentally subnormal.

The Association administers:

> A short-stay home for mentally subnormal children between the ages of 2 and 12 years.
>
> Two holiday homes by the sea for parties of the mentally subnormal from hospitals.
>
> Two hostels for ESN school-leavers and one hostel for boys leaving schools for the maladjusted and working in the Greater London area.

The Association is Trustee for:

Two approved schools for delinquent adolescent girls in need of psychiatric treatment.

A special boarding school for maladjusted boys.

All three schools are administered by independent boards of governors appointed by the Association.

ADVISORY CASE-WORK SERVICE

The Association provided an advisory case-work service to help patients, their families, and others with problems arising from mental illness or subnormality. The case-workers can also offer information and guidance about statutory and voluntary services, and give information about homes and schools which seem likely to be suitable for the individual concerned.

An educational psychologist is available to give reports on individual children and advice on their needs.

PUBLIC INFORMATION AND PUBLICATIONS

The Public Information Department maintains liaison with the press, radio, television, and the cinema: it provides advisory services in these fields and on the use of mental health films.

Booklets are published on mental health subjects: e.g. on child care, subnormality, mental breakdown. Reports are issued of the Annual Conference and the Inter-clinic Conference. A list of current publications is available on request.

MENTAL HEALTH JOURNAL

The Association's *Mental Health Journal* is published six times a year to full members. The *NAMH News* containing the General Secretary's letter, and news of local associations is published separately.

INTERNATIONAL WORK

In the international field as well as in the national, co-operation in promoting mental health is sought by the Association from other bodies and individuals. It is in touch with mental health organizations in many different countries as well as with British organizations whose work has international aspects.

The Association is a member body of the World Federation for Mental Health, which has consultative status with the World Health Organization. It acts as convenor of the United Kingdom Committee of the World Federation for Mental Health, which arranges national delegations to the Federation's annual meetings.

Students from overseas and foreign visitors interested in mental health work are given information and introductions, and programmes of visits can be arranged for them.

PUBLICATIONS

CHILDREN

Can I Leave My Baby?, by DR. J. BOWLBY. Discussion of the harm which may be done to a baby or very young child by being parted from the mother. 1*s*. 6*d*.

Child Guidance and Child Psychiatry as an Integral Part of Community Services (with special reference to the training of child psychiatrists as members of the profession team). 1*s*. 3*d*.

Directory of Child Guidance Services and School Psychological Services, 1962. 10*s*.

Discipline and the Child, by Dr. T. A. RATCLIFF. 1*s*. 6*d*.

Do Babies have Worries? Questions and answers on child care with cartoon illustrations. 1*s*. 6*d*.

Do Teenagers have Wisdom? Deals with problems of adolescence. 2*s*.

Room for More, by KENNETH BRILL. A booklet to help prospective foster parents. 1*s*. 6*d*.

A Survey Based on Adoption Case Records, 1955. 3*s*. 6*d*.

Why Special Schools? A leaflet for parents of children recommended to attend an ESN school; revised edition. 6*d*.

CHILD GUIDANCE INTER-CLINIC CONFERENCE REPORTS

Evaluation with a View to Action, 1956. 5s.
Truancy—or School Phobia?, 1959. 3s. 6d.
Child Guidance at Home and Abroad, 1960. 3s. 6d.
The Child Guidance Clinic and Delinquency, 1961. 3s. 6d.
Adolescence, 1964. 4s.
Child Guidance: Function and Social Rule, 1965. 4s. 6d.

FAMILY HEALTH PUBLICATIONS. Illustrated booklets for mothers of young children

Children and Sleep, by PROF. R. S. ILLINGWORTH. 1s. 3d.
Children who wet their Beds, by DR. PORTIA HOLMAN. 1s. 6d.
Children's Fears, by RUTH THOMAS. 1s. 6d.
Children's Jealousies, by RUTH THOMAS. 1s. 6d.
Children who Dislike their Food, by RUTH THOMAS. 1s. 6d.
Habit Training, by RUTH THOMAS. 1s. 6d.
Temper Tantrums, by RUTH THOMAS. 1s. 6d.
Young Children and Play, by JOSEPHINE GUY. 1s. 6d.

MENTAL HANDICAP

Another Kind of School. A leaflet for parents of children who are not accepted for school. 6d.
Autistic Children, by DR. LORNA WING. Written for the guidance of parents who have an autistic child. 5s.
Letter to Parents of a Mongol Baby: from a Children's Specialist. 1s. 3d.
Services for the Mentally Subnormal. A brief survey of community and residential facilities. 1s. 6d.
Special Care Units. Mental Subnormality Series No. 1. 3s. 6d.
Junior Training Centres. Mental Subnormality Series No. 2. 3s. 6d.
Senior Training Centres. Mental Subnormality Series No. 3. 3s. 6d.

Your Mentally Handicapped Child. Written to help parents to understand a little about the nature of mental handicap. 5*s*.

EPILEPSY

An Epileptic Clinic as a Community Service, by B. S. McFIE. 6*d*.
Social Aspects of Epilepsy, by J. TYLOR FOX. 9*d*.

GENERAL

Directory of Adult Psychiatric Out-Patient Facilities, 1964–5. 10*s*.

Do Cows Have Neuroses? A simple explanation of the way in which neurotic or psychotic behaviour differs from the normal. 2*s*.

Everybody's Business, The Mental Health Act and the Community, by NESTA ROBERTS. 1*s*. 6*d*.

From After-care to Community Services, by PAULINE SHAPIRO. Describes some cases dealt with under the NAMH Psychiatric Community Care Scheme. 9*d*.

A Guide to Making and Using Mental Health Films, by Dr. T. L. PILKINGTON. 2*s*. 6*d*.

Mental Breakdown. A guide for families of those in hospital. 2*s*.

The NAMH Guide to the Mental Health Act, 1959, by APHRA L. HARGROVE. Revised edition. 2*s*. 6*d*.

Not in my Perfect Mind by NESTA ROBERTS. Describes problems of caring for mentally frail old people and gives practical advice. 1*s*. 6*d*.

Patterns of Care, by KENNETH ROBINSON, MP. A study of provisions for the mentally disordered in France, Holland, the USA and the USSR. 2*s*. 6*d*.

Questions on our Minds. Facts and guidance for the layman on some questions concerning mental disorder. 2*s*. 6*d*.

Serving the Mentally Handicapped, by APHRA L. HARGROVE. A record of the work of the Central Association for Mental Welfare. 15*s*.

The Sociological Review, Monograph No. 6. The Canford families, a study in social case-work. 25*s*.

Time for Yourself, by Dr. ANNIS GILLIE. A new look for the middle-aged family woman. 1*s*.

NAMH CONFERENCE REPORTS

Mental Health at Home and Abroad, 1960. 5*s*.

Emerging Patterns for the Mental Health Services and the Public, 1961. 5*s*.

Hostels and the Mental Health Act. Papers given at Conferences, 1960–1. 3*s*. 6*d*.

The Distant Goal, 1963. About community care services. 6*s*.

The Whole Truth, 1964. About mental health services. 6*s*.

The Price of Mental Health, 1965. 7*s*.

MENTAL HEALTH JOURNAL

Single copy: 2*s*. 6*d*. (postage 6*d*.).

Annual subscription (including postage): 15*s*.

Published six times a year: February, April, June, August, October, December.

The Society for Autistic Children

Address: 100 Wise Lane, Mill Hill, London, NW 7.

The Society for Autistic Children began in May of 1962 on the initiative of parents of these children. The parents were soon joined by professionally interested people, doctors, teachers, and social workers who now form over half the membership of the Society.

MEMBERSHIP

Membership of the Society is for parents whose children have been diagnosed as psychotic, autistic, schizophrenic, severely obsessional, asphasic, or non-communicating, and doctors, teachers, social workers, and others interested in the problems of these children.

AIMS

To provide and promote day and residential centres for the treatment and education of autistic or psychotic children. To help parents, particularly by arranging meetings between them where they can exchange information. To encourage research into the problems of these children. To stimulate more understanding among the lay and medical public of these children's problems.

ACTIVITIES

Advisory service for parents, specifically to help them with educational or hospital placement. Information service for professionally interested people on the nature of childhood autism, the type of service needed, and teaching methods. Publication and distribution of leaflets and booklets on management and education of autistic children.

EDUCATIONAL SERVICES

The Society's school provides approximately twenty places for autistic children up to school-leaving age. This serves as a pilot scheme to demonstrate how specialized remedial teaching can bring about an improvement in the condition of autistic children. The Society's Head Office also gives advice to parents or teachers who are setting up their own tuition units or classes for autistic children.

PUBLICATIONS

Autistic Children in a Day Nursery, by MARGARET LOVATT. From *Children*, May–June 1962, US Department of Health Education and Welfare. 1s. This describes a nursery centre in

Toronto which admits autistic children, and how the problems of socializing and educating these children are approached.

Diagnostic Memorandum. Supplied to doctors and professional workers only. 6*d*. Compiled by DRS. JOHN and LORNA WING and based on the "9 points" described in the article entitled Schizophrenic syndrome in Childhood, *BMJ*, 30 September 1962, **ii,** 889–90, this memorandum gives concrete examples of the symptoms associated with this condition.

Services Memorandum. 1*s*. 6*d*. Compiled by DRS. JOHN and LORNA WING, this memorandum outlines a pattern of services which should be developed for the care and education of autistic children using a metropolitan borough as the basic unit. The necessity for flexibility in the operation of these services is emphasized, so that children manifesting varying degrees of disturbance can be cared for throughout their lives.

Children in Chains, by COLIN FRAME. 6*d*. This article, reprinted by permission of the *Evening News and Star*, first appeared 9 November 1962 and was instrumental in arousing public sympathy for autistic children. An excellent simple statement of what autistic children are and accompanied by two photographs, this article stresses the urgent needs of parents and their children in such a way as to make a vivid and lasting impression on readers' minds.

Society for Autistic Children—Memorandum to Ministers of Health and Education. 1*s*. Based on the experience of parents in their efforts to find diagnosis, care, and education for their children, this memorandum outlines certain failings of present services and points out where co-ordination and expansion of these services are necessary. Tables of statistical information on school and hospital provision based on a survey of children represented by the Society are included.

Teachers' Memorandum. No charge. In response to frequent inquiries this memorandum was drawn up indicating, in the absence of training courses specifically designed for teachers of autistic children, what courses of study might be helpful for teachers wishing to enter this field of work and where experience with autistic children might usefully be acquired.

Costs of Running a Day School for Five Autistic Children. No charge. This is a tentative estimate which parents or teachers might find helpful if they are considering the foundation of a nursery school with the high staffing ratio essential if these children are to respond to an educational approach.

Teaching the Autistic Child. Talk given by MRS. S. ELGAR. 9*d*. Mrs. Elgar, a Montessori trained teacher, gave this talk at a conference on the Education of Autistic Children in March 1964. In it she demonstrates how, with individual and specialized teaching, even very severely autistic children can be taught. The success of her method is proved by the fact that many people visiting the school several terms after it started have found it difficult to believe that the children originally had all the typical symptoms of childhood autism.

Autistic Behaviour in Children, by LORNA WING, Reprinted by kind permission of *Mother and Child,* Journal of the National Baby Welfare Council, June 1963. 1*s*. A very practical definition of autism—these children seem not to be able to make use of information about the world that comes to them through their senses—accompanied by specific examples of the symptoms, is followed by an outline of ways in which parents can be helped. The acute shortage of educational provision is mentioned, and attention is called to the marked difference between children who have had individual tuition and family love, and those who have been relegated to unsuitable institutions.

Who will Educate our Psychotic Children?, by PAULA DAVIES. 9*d*. Reprinted by permission of the *Daily Telegraph,* where it first appeared on 6 September 1963, this article is based on interviews Miss Davies had with the doctor who is studying these children at the Eveline Hospital, with Mrs. Elgar, the teacher of a small nursery group, and with parent members of the Society. The importance of education, preferably

G

alongside normal children, is emphasized, and the author
gives encouraging praise to those professionals and parents
who are trying to ensure that autistic children have this
opportunity.

The Mental After-care Association

Address: Eagle House, 110 Jermyn St., London, SW 1.

ORIGIN

The Association was founded in 1879 by the Rev. H. Hawkins
Chaplain to the Middlesex Asylum, Colney Hatch, London, now
Friern Hospital. Mr. Hawkins was distressed by the number of
patients who were returned to the Asylum soon after having been
discharged "recovered", and he attributed this in large measure
to the fact that, on discharge, patients had to go back im
mediately to a cold and unsympathetic world in which organized
social services were practically unknown. Discharged patients
were usually looked upon with doubt and suspicion by their
families and former friends, and rarely possessed enough resources
in money, clothes, or tools to enable them to obtain suitable work
and earn a living.

Mr. Hawkins succeeded in interesting some of the leading
psychiatrists of the day, and the result was the formation of a
small, informal Association of which Mr. Hawkins became the
honorary treasurer and secretary. When the Association was only
1 year old, the Earl of Shaftesbury became its President. The
Association was the first organized psychiatric social service in
Great Britain, and for the greater part of its 80 years it remained
the only one.

ACTIVITIES

The first object of the founder and his colleagues was to provide
convalescent homes in which discharged patients could be re
habilitated ("befriended" was the word used by Mr. Hawkins

and prepared for the struggle with the outside world in every way possible. The number of these homes grew rapidly, and changes in the law made it possible to accept not only "recovered" patients, but patients on probation or trial who could be taken back to hospital without formality if they proved insufficiently recovered to remain away from it.

Next, the Association extended its activities to patients who, though well enough to leave hospital, were not fit to return to their homes and would always require some degree of supervision and care. Such patients often remain in the Association's care for many years.

Then, as a natural development, came pre-care, and the Association received numerous requests to take patients into its homes, not to rehabilitate them after residence in a mental hospital, but to avert nervous and mental breakdown, if by rest, quiet, friendliness, and good counsel, it were possible to do so.

Lastly, the Association set aside some of its homes during the summer months specially for patients who, though too mentally ill to remain permanently away from hospital care, could yet enjoy a summer holiday at the seaside or in the country, and were able to respond satisfactory, for the time, to the slight supervision and simple everyday medical care provided. This branch of the Association's work continues to be, perhaps, more appreciated than any other by the patients, and it is remarkable how few of those selected fail to adapt themselves to the rules and methods of the homes, and have to be returned to hospital before the holiday is complete.

ORGANIZATION

Psychiatry has always been strongly represented on the Council, and although the chairman is not necessarily a psychiatrist, many of the leading psychiatrists in the country have been chairmen of the Council during the last half-century.

METHODS

The great majority of the patients are received from mental hospitals or outpatients clinics. The selection is made by the hospital or clinic doctors who fill up the Association's application forms but do not send the detailed medical notes from the hospital or clinics. The application forms have to be signed by a psychiatrist who states therein that the patient is, to the best of his knowledge, safe to live under very mild supervision, able to conform to the simple rules of the homes, and likely to benefit from their atmosphere.

The Association has the right to decline to accept a case on any grounds, and it is always understood than an unsuitable patient is taken back without question to the hospital or clinic from which he came.

The Association does not limit its admissions to cases of schizophrenia or any other type of psychosis or neurosis. It does not continue organized occupational therapy in its homes, because patients prefer to think that they have left that behind in the hospitals, and also separate workshops affording training in new occupations are now provided by the Government.

It has been found that the optimum size for the homes is somewhere between twenty and forty patients. A lower figure than twenty is uneconomic, and a higher figure makes it hard to maintain the friendly, homelike atmosphere, and the personal contact with individual patients which it was the original object of the Association to provide, and which still remains its central aim, despite the enormous changes in method and outlook which have taken place.

There is no visiting psychiatrist to the homes, but patients in each home are registered with a local general practitioner who visits the home. The homes are in the charge of a trained nurse and assistant, qualified and experienced in mental illness. No uniform is worn by the staff. The patients are visited frequently and regularly by a social worker from the Head Office of the Association, and progress reports are made monthly or quarterly on each patient, these being sent to the authority through whom the patient was admitted.

No active psychiatric treatment is given, and no patient is admitted until the Association receives authoritative psychiatric opinion that no active modern treatment of any kind is indicated.

There are no rules other than those of an ordinary household. The patients partake of outside activities, such as church and its social life, concerts, cinema-going, shopping, and visiting friends and relatives who may also visit them and take them out or away for week-ends or holidays, on permission being given by the matron in charge. Some younger patients go to evening classes or refresher courses in such subjects as shorthand-typing, and to social clubs.

Patients are encouraged to help in the house, but those going to work only make their beds. Games, television, and radio are provided, and in those homes where there is a large garden, patients are encouraged to take an interest in it, and games such as croquet, clock golf, etc., are provided.

The Association maintains close contact with all other social service organizations, voluntary or state-supported, and in particular it co-operates fully with local authorities, labour exchanges, and the appropriate government departments and officials in obtaining suitable employment for discharged patients.

The Guild of Teachers of Backward Children

Address: Minster Chambers, Southwell, Notts.

The first two diploma courses for teachers of handicapped children (ESN and maladjusted) were begun at London's Institute of Education in 1950 and 1953. The two courses gave rise to two new organizations—one for teachers of backward pupils and the other for teachers of maladjusted children.

The Guild of Teachers of Backward Children began as a Guild of Diploma Teachers of Backward Children, but soon realized that this limitation to diploma holders was not in keeping with the need. Reconstructed in 1955 and subsequently incorporated, the Guild became a more far-reaching organization open to all professionally concerned with backward children, whether such children were excluded from school as "ineducable", were included in the school system but thought to require special schools, or were "school failures", with learning difficulties in the ordinary schools.

In 1956 the Guild launched its journal *Forward Trends in the Treatment of the Backward Child* which has been published quarterly since and is read in many countries.

In 1957 the Guild initiated the first of its national conferences on the backward child which have since taken place annually.

The aims of the Guild were to bring together all those working on behalf of such children so that the experience of the different disciplines might be available to all. It sought to act as a clearing house for ideas and to raise the knowledge, skills, and status of all teachers working with backward or mentally handicapped children. To this end it published bibliographies, teachers' guides, special editions of *Forward Trends*, and organized lectures and short courses. Membership is open to all *professionally* concerned in some way. Branches have been formed in many parts of the country.

In 1960 the Guild organized the first international conference on the backward child to be held in London. Delegates were invited from every country in the world, and those present included representatives from eastern Europe. Guild representatives were, as a result, invited to an international conference in Hungary on the Scientific Selection of Pupils for Special Schools (1963). The British Council also arranged for a delegation from the Guild to visit the USSR (1965) under the 1965–7 Cultural Exchange Agreement.

In addition to sub-committees set up for specific purposes (e.g. for the Severely Subnormal, for Ordinary Schools, for After-care, a Library and Publications Committee, etc.), the Guild's branches frequently had their own study groups and issue reports.

PUBLICATIONS

Forward Trends in the Treatment of the Backward Child. Quarterly.
A journal for the teaching profession but also read by other
disciplines.

Evidence to the Plowden Committee.

Communication and the Withdrawn Child.

Backward Children in the USSR.

Bibliographies.

Film list.

SERVICES

Advisory service for teachers.

Library, books, and films.

Panel of lecturers.

In addition to the film library which the Guild is building, it is
proposed to record important speeches. One by Sir Cyril Burt is
available on loan. Inquiries should be sent in all cases to the
Librarian, the Guild of Teachers of Backward Children, Minster
Chambers, Southwell, Notts.

REPRESENTATIVES OF THE GUILD SERVE ON THE FOLLOWING
BODIES

The Elfrida Rathbone Association.

The Education Advisory Committee of the National Society for
Mentally Handicapped Children.

The Advisory Committee for the Research Institute of Special
Education, National Association for Mental Health.

The British Committee for the Scientific Study of Mental
Deficiency.

Joint Council for the Education of Handicapped Children.

Liaison is maintained with other organizations concerned with
handicapped children, including the Association for Special
Education. Efforts are being made by the Guild to bring together
all organizations in any way concerned with the education of

handicapped children. One aim of the Guild is to see a National Council for Handicapped Children emerge, inside or alongside the National Bureau for Co-operation in Child Care.

The Guild gave evidence, oral and/or written to the following bodies:

The Working Party of the South-east Metropolitan Paediatric Society: *The Needs of the Mentally Handicapped Child.*

The Scott Committee (on the Supply and Training of Staff for Training Centres).

The Plowden Committee (on Primary Education).

The Royal Commission on Penal Reform.

A COLLEGE OF SPECIAL EDUCATION

Address: Minster Chambers, Southwell, Notts.

In 1965 the Guild launched an appeal for £200,000 and proclaimed its intention of setting up a College of Special Education to begin in September 1965 as an advisory and information centre in its first stage.

This College of Special Education was set up in 1966 by the Guild of Teachers of Backward Children. Its governing body includes representatives of various educational and professional organizations. Initially it serves as an out-going advisory and information centre, providing information, bibliographies, books and other forms of help to teachers and others concerned with pupils who are backward or have learning handicaps.

It also provides panels of lecturers, individual speakers, short courses, and exhibitions for professional and lay persons interested in the problem.

Association of Workers for Maladjusted Children

The Association of Workers for Maladjusted Children was formed in 1951 in response to a widespread demand (1) to bring together those doing the same work to compare their experiences and exchange ideas, (2) to make a closer contact between staffs of schools and hostels, on the one hand, and child guidance clinics on the other, and (3) to give workers such as probation officers, teachers in ordinary schools, administrative officers, and others in frequent contact with maladjusted children or their families, an opportunity to contribute from their special experience.

Workers of all these types have belonged to the Association from the start, and the discussions have thus covered a wide field from many points of view. The meetings and visits to schools and clinics have been very well attended and valued as an opportunity for social intercourse as well as for gaining a wider perspective and fuller understanding of the complexities of the problems being tackled by our members.

The activities through which the Association endeavours to achieve its purpose include social gatherings, which give opportunities for members to get to know each other, and visits to institutions where some of the members work. The Association is often able to act as a channel for giving public expression to the views of its members and thus of spreading its knowledge about enlightened methods of therapy to the promotion of a sympathetic and understanding attitude towards the maladjustments of childhood.

Activities of a more specialized kind include written and oral evidence to the Ministry of Education Committee on Maladjusted Children. The Association has also been consulted in such matters as training and conditions of staff. It holds meetings and conferences addressed by experts from among its membership. In the practical field it is able to bring together those requiring staff and those seeking appointments. It is also interested in research and has completed an analysis of some significant features of schools for maladjusted children.

Membership may be individual or corporate. Among corporate members who have joined are hostels and schools, professional organizations, clinics, and kindred associations.

Some of the lectures and meetings are open to non-members.

The Association is always willing to suggest to other organizations speakers on any aspect.

MEETINGS

Meetings are held in London and in provincial centres every 3 months and include lectures by specialists in different fields of the work, psychiatrists, school medical officers, headmasters and mistresses of schools for maladjusted children, magistrates, psychoanalysts, psychologists, psychiatric social workers, and university lecturers. These lecturers are carefully selected and always deal with the discussions after meetings in a most valuable manner.

REGIONAL ORGANIZATION

The need for more compact grouping became apparent, and there are regional branches for the south-eastern, south-western, Scottish, Midland, London, Home Counties, and northern areas.

COURSES

Easter courses of a week's duration have been held in Oxford, Broadstairs, Henley in Arden, Bournemouth, Cambridge, Nottingham, and Bristol. These courses have been well attended and are a most important aspect of the activities of the Association.

MEMBERSHIP

Membership is open, subject to committee approval, to those whose work is concerned in any way with the problems of maladjusted children.

1. *Individual membership.* Applicants require to be proposed and seconded by members of the Association and to be elected by the Committee.

2. *Corporate membership.* Hostels, schools, clinics, and other interested bodies working for maladjusted children may be elected by the Committee as corporate members if proposed by members of the Association who are personally acquainted with the work of the association or institution.

PUBLICATIONS

The following publications have been issued by the Association and are obtainable from the Hon. Secretary:

Report of the Association.

Evidence submitted to the Ministry of Education Committee on Maladjusted Children. Out of print. 3s.

Qualities of Staff of Schools and Hostels for Maladjusted Children and Problems of Selection. 2s.

Research reports on the Differences between Schools for the Maladjusted and Ordinary Boarding Schools.

List of Independent and Local Authority Schools taking Maladjusted Children. 3s.

The Incidence of Some Supposedly Adverse Conditions and of Left-handedness in Schools for Maladjusted Children. 2s. 6d.

The Association of Teachers of Maladjusted Children

Secretary: Mrs. Irene M. Bowman, Flat 1, Cedar Court, Churchfields, South Woodford, London, E 18.

The Association was formed by past members of the course leading to the Diploma in the Education of Maladjusted Children at the University of London Institute of Education. Membership is now open to all teachers interested in maladjusted children, whether or not they have taken a special course of training, provided they are nominated by a diploma-holder member and approved by the Council of the Association.

Three meetings are held each year in London and a *Newsletter* is published twice yearly. Members speak at meetings of non-specialist teachers and at courses, e.g. two members organized and lectured at a course in the Educational Development Association's Summer School, for teachers who wished to know more about emotional disturbance in childhood. A north-eastern branch of the Association is about to be formed.

These activities are designed to further the aims of the Association which are:

1. The dissemination of information on the latest developments in the education of maladjusted children and child development generally.
2. To provide a means for an exchange of views. Membership is 10s. per year.

The Midland Society for the Study of Mental Subnormality

Address: Monyhull Hospital, Kings Heath, Birmingham, 14.

The Society was founded in 1952 to mobilize, foster, and encourage interest in any of the problems of the mentally subnormal by meetings, publications, or by any other means. Membership is open to persons and corporate bodies having an interest, whether professional or otherwise, in any aspect of mental subnormality. At present the membership is predominantly made up of people working in some professional capacity in the field—social workers, teachers, nurses, psychologists, and doctors.

The Society holds meetings approximately every 2 months at various hospitals or training centres in the Midlands when papers are read by well-known authorities and discussions take place about all aspects of the speciality.

The *Journal of Mental Subnormality* is published by the Midland Society for the Study of Mental Subnormality.

The *Journal* originated in the proceedings of these meetings, but it was very soon found that the papers given were of sufficient interest to attract attention outside the Society. The *Journal* has, therefore, replaced the proceedings, and publishes nowadays not only the most important papers given by the Society but also many articles written specially for the *Journal*.

The policy of the Editor (Dr. H. C. Gunzburg) has been right from the beginning to emphasize the practical aspects of applied research in mental deficiency. The *Journal* publishes only occasionally articles connected with the rehabilitation, training, and education of the subnormal. A constant feature of the publications in recent years has been symposia dealing with aspects like language development of the subnormal, training and education of the severely subnormal, the hospital services for the mentally subnormal, social training, nomenclature in mental subnormality.

The *Journal* has now an international circulation and is taken regularly by most specialized libraries. The annual subscription to the Society of £1 includes free copies of the *Journal*. *Journal* subscription alone is 15*s*. per annum for two issues a year (June and December). American subscription is $4.50 for two copies including air mail dispatch.

Rudolf Steiner Schools and Provision

General information regarding the varied provision for handicapped children, teacher training, and remedial education courses under the Rudolf Steiner umbrella can be obtained from the Anthroposophical Society in Great Britain, Rudolf Steiner House, 35 Park Road, London, NW 1.

A range of provision is available for children who are severely subnormal or suffering from childhood psychosis, emotional disorders, behaviour disorders, sensory defects, motor handicaps, convulsive disorders, etc., between the ages of 6 and 16. The Camphill–Rudolf Steiner schools (Central Office, Murtle House, Bieldside, Aberdeen) is perhaps best known to members of the public. St. Christopher's School (Kenwith Lodge, Westbury Park, Bristol, 6) accepts mentally handicapped children aged from 5 to 18. The Sunfield Working Training Course (Clent Grove, Clent,

Stourbridge, Worcestershire) offers a 2-year course for young school-leavers who wish to make a career of social service, child care, and possibly teaching. Sunfield is a home for mentally handicapped children. A training course in remedial education is held at the Camphill–Rudolf Steiner Schools. Students are required to have spent a preliminary practical year at one of the centres of the Camphill Movement.

The Society of St. Bernadette

Address: 19 Stanley Park Road, Wallington, Surrey.

The Society of St. Bernadette aims to provide "family group" care and training with education where this is relevant for mentally handicapped and emotionally disturbed children who may also be physically handicapped. The Society was founded in 1960 and now runs three homes besides doing a great deal of social work in the south-east. It is registered as a national charity, and its members train and dedicate themselves to the service of the handicapped for life. The Society also gives assistance to small groups who wish to run their own homes, and specializes in liaison work with these groups and local authorities.

SERVICES

Family group residential training in homes or small schools on a local basis; general social work, including holiday placement of children and emergency placement. The Society of St. Bernadette is primarily concerned in providing residential care and training for mentally handicapped or emotionally handicapped children. Many of these children are also physically handicapped.

PUBLICATIONS

A regular magazine is published three to four times a year, and various other publications are produced *ad hoc*.

The Poplars Special School

Incorporating Abbotswood Hostel, Buckshaft Rd., Cinderford, Gloucestershire.

This small independent venture concentrates upon the adolescent age ranges 15–19 years:

(a) the former ESN pupil who does not secure a job on leaving;
(b) the former maladjusted pupil who does not secure a job on leaving;
(c) the "work shy" secondary modern school-leaver who presents an employment problem to the youth employment officer.

It offers to youth employment officers and school and county medical officers who are after-care agents, vacancies in vocational training units, and gives 3–6 months' training, followed by 12 months' work hostelling.

The Ravenswood Foundation

Address: 18 Seymour Place, London, W 1.

Provision includes a village settlement, special care unit, junior school, and training centre for mentally handicapped children. Sheltered employment of various kinds is also provided.

The Elfrida Rathbone Association

Address: Toynbee Hall, Commercial St., London, E 1.

The Elfrida Rathbone Association was formed in 1963. It is a voluntary body formed for the purpose of promoting the welfare of children attending or having left schools for the educationally subnormal and their families in whatever way seems most necessary (e.g. case-work, clubs, group work, and so on).

At the time of its inauguration, there were three local Elfrida Rathbone committees in existence (all in London). As a result of the new Association, a preliminary survey was carried out of any work already being undertaken and to estimate the need for starting new work in new areas.

The survey, undertaken by Mrs. A. Piper, was completed in 1964. A sub-committee of the Association was set up to consider the recommendations, but first examined the structure of the Association as a result of which various organizations were invited to be represented on the committee (i.e. the National Association for Mental Health, the National Society for Mentally Handicapped Children and the Guild of Teachers of Backward Children).

A recommendation that a national development officer should be appointed to spread clubs, groups, case-work, and after-care work already being undertaken and to initiate new projects, took effect from January 1966 when the national development officer began his work. The national development officer is helped by a small sub-committee.

Ex-Services Mental Welfare Society

Address: 37–39 Thurloe St., London, SW 7. *Scottish Office*: 3 Cadogan St., Glasgow, C 2.

The above Society exists to assist ex-members of the forces, including the merchant navy, suffering from nervous or mental disabilities and more particularly those with active or long regular service.

Apart from its other activities the Society offers residential facilities either of a temporary or permanent nature:

CONVALESCENT CENTRE

Tyrwhitt House, Leatherhead, Surrey.

This is a small comfortably furnished home, which retains a country house atmosphere. No active treatment is given, but the

PLATE 1. At the hostel provided by the National Society for Mentally Handicapped Children at Slough. Playtime.

PLATE 2. Doing light hand work at the National Hostels and Training Centre (NSMHC) at Slough.

Plate 3. A break for parents as well as children at Pirates Spring (NSMHC).

PLATE 4. Mentally handicapped youths preparing for the working world (NSMHC).

PLATE 5. An exhibition for teachers of retarded children organized by Somerset's remedial teachers. The service is provided under the guidance of the Schools Psychological Service. *(Photo by Harold C. Tilzey.)*

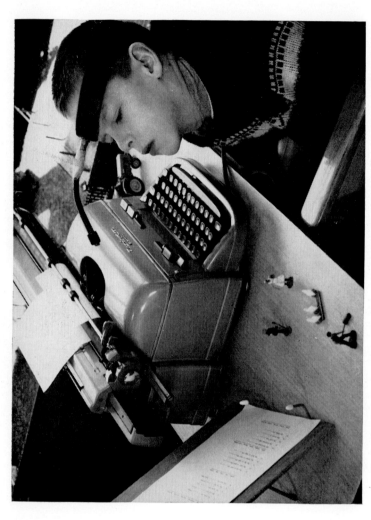

PLATE 6. Where a spastic child cannot use his hands and has speech impediments, electric typewriters provide an aid

PLATE 7. Small classes make individual teaching possible. There is an average of one teacher to every eight children in the special boarding schools provided by the Spastics Society.

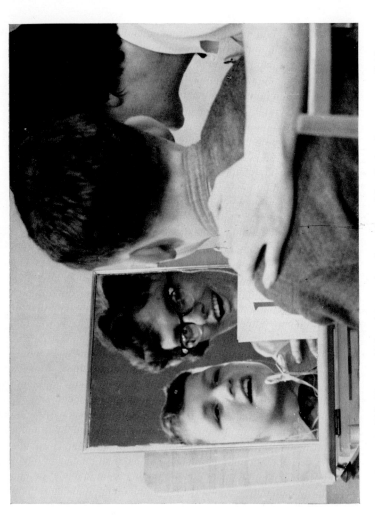

PLATE 8. This 13-year-old boy has two hearing aids and has had to learn to use all his speech muscles with the help of the speech therapist.

PLATE 9 a, b, c. d. A purpose-built school for the physically handicapped child. The Franklin Delano Roosevelt School, provided by the Inner London Education Authority for pupils aged 2–16. This school has a multi-disciplinary staff (including part-time teachers for children with hearing loss or partial sight). An outstanding feature is the specially constructed hydrotherapy pool, with its highly qualified personnel.

(a)

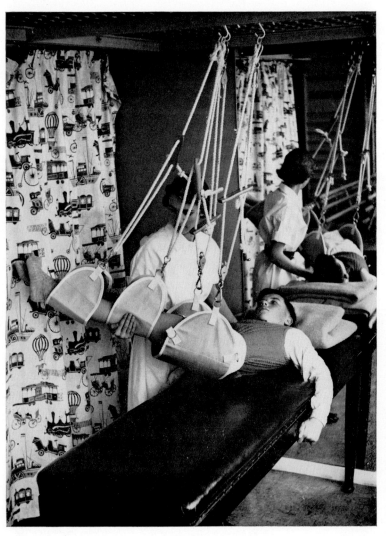

(b)

(c)

(d)

PLATE 10. A purpose-built training centre for mentally handicapped children. The John F. Kennedy Training Centre, West Ham, London.

PLATE 11. Social training at a training centre.

routine and surroundings are designed to benefit neurotic or psychotic patients.

SHELTERED INDUSTRY

Thermega Ltd., Leatherhead.

The Society also has an industry, Thermega Ltd., where recovered patients, who are unable to hold their own in the ordinary competitive world, are employed on the manufacture of electrically heated blankets and pads in a sheltered environment.

INDUSTRIAL HOSTEL

Milner House, Leatherhead.

This is a hostel attached to the factory, and after 3 months, if found suitable, the trainee receives full-scale wages and contributes to his keep or, in certain cases, lives outside in the district or in one of the cottages for married men on the estate.

HOME FOR AGED EX-SERVICE MEN

Kingswood Grange, Lower Kingswood, Surrey.

This is a permanent residence for elderly ex-service men who are mildly neurotic or psychotic and are now incapable of working. It has the same country house atmosphere as the other establishments.

Before a case for any of the homes can be considered, a full psychiatric report is necessary for the information of the Society's Chief Consultant, Dr. C. P. Blacker. Where distance permits, it may be necessary for the applicant to be examined by Dr. Blacker at the Society's London Offices.

Applications should be made to: The Administrative Secretary, Ex-Services Mental Welfare Society, 37–39 Thurloe St., London, SW 7.

Or, for cases in northern counties or Scotland, to the Manchester or Scottish Office as appropriate.

Church of England Board of Education

Address: 69 Great Peter St., London, SW 1.

The Church of England Board of Education is a part of the National Assembly of the Church of England. Its task is to promote and co-ordinate the educational work of the Church. It has six constituent councils and committees to which are delegated the main areas of the Church's educational work. Among these are the Schools Council and the Council of Church Colleges of Education. The Children's Council is concerned chiefly with the voluntary side of religious education, the fostering of junior club and group work, house groups and holiday courses for school-age children, and the care of deprived and handicapped children of all sorts. In 1963 the Children's Council embarked upon a series of working groups and publications concerned with handicapped children, of which the first was *Number Unknown* (1965), dealing with the needs and problems of the mentally subnormal child and his family. The second publication was concerned with the care and religious education of the ESN child, and a symposium was prepared concerned with the near delinquent child of school age. In addition to these publications, duplicated material is issued from time to time to keep teachers, clergy, and others in touch with recent developments in the care and education of handicapped children and to help with their religious needs.

A considerable amount of work is done by individual members of the Church and by religious orders, among which might be mentioned the Franciscans who have a school for maladjusted boys at Hooke, Dorset, and the Community of the Sisters of the Church who are responsible for homes for deprived children.

PUBLICATIONS

Number Unknown, ed. A. H. DENNEY, CIO. 7s. 6d.

DUPLICATED PUBLICATIONS

Today's Child. Issued quarterly. 2*s.*

The Church and the Backward Child. A report of a conference held in 1964. 1*s.*

Notes on Worship with Severely Sub-Normal Children. 1*s.*

The above are available from the Church of England Children's Council, 69 Great Peter St., SW 1.

An Australian Journal
"The Slow Learning Child"

Reference has already been made to the role of Sir F. J. Schonell in encouraging remedial work in special education in the UK. Schonell was subsequently to become Chancellor of the University of Queensland where he was also one of the three editors of the Australian journal on the Education of Backward Children, *The Slow Learning Child.*

This journal developed advisory boards in Australasia and other continents, and contained many articles of interest outside Australia. The journal is published by the University of Queensland, Australia. See also, next chapter: the Association for Special Education, Invalid Children's Aid Association, the National Bureau for Co-operation in Child Care, the Spastics Society.

CHAPTER 17

The Physically Handicapped

The Association for Special Education

(Formerly the Special Schools Association, Est. 1903.)

Hon. General Secretary: Mr. L. J. McDonald, Headmaster, Stanley School, Liverpool (and 19 Hamilton Road, Wallasey).

The Association was founded in 1903. It includes among its members those who work with all kinds of handicapped children, ranging from the mildly backward who can be educated in ordinary schools to those with severe mental or physical handicaps who need very special care and education.

The Association gains strength from including all kinds of professional interest, and numbers among its members administrators, doctors, employment officers, members of education authorities, nurses, parents of handicapped children, psychologists, teachers, therapists, and welfare workers. All mingle at its meetings and conferences and in its committees. These informal contacts help to promote teamwork from which grows an increasing understanding of the many aspects of the problems on which we are engaged, to the ultimate benefit of the children with whom we are concerned.

Membership of the Association is spread through thirty-seven branches in Great Britain and abroad. Each branch has its regular meetings and visits and organizes local conferences: in addition, biennial conferences are held and information on the latest developments in the field of special education is available.

Members receive the Association journal, *Special Education*, which is published quarterly. This contains articles both of an immediate practical value and of a more theoretical interest. It contains reviews of current books, and information about new school material and teaching aids. A *News-letter* is also distributed to members three times yearly, helping them to keep abreast of new developments.

The Association is able, through its information officer, to give advice about books, pamphlets, films, and speakers. It has a Research Committee, with members representing all areas of Great Britain, to encourage and co-ordinate research in all aspects of work with the handicapped.

The Association is called upon to give evidence to important committees, e.g.:

The training and supply of teachers of handicapped pupils.
The training of staffs of training centres for the mentally subnormal.
The training of child care workers in boarding special schools.
The Newsom and Plowden committees.
The Royal Commission on the Penal System in England and Wales.

Dr. Barnardo's Homes

Address: Stepney Causeway, London, E 1.

Dr. Barnardo, a medical missionary, was born in Dublin in 1845. The poverty in which he found many children, and the circumstances which motivated him to open the first of the Dr. Barnardo's Homes, are movingly described in a short pamphlet, *One Man's Vision*, obtainable from this organization. In 1964, nearly 100 years after the first boy was admitted into their care, Barnardo's Homes were accepting more than five children a day— nearly 2000 a year. More than 3000 children are in branch homes and cottages provided by the organization. A further 1500 are fostered out. A family assistance scheme aims to help unsupported mothers care for their children. Amongst the children in the care of Dr. Barnardo's Homes are 500 physically handicapped child-ren. In 1964 a technical booklet, *Barnardo's and the Handicapped*, was printed by boys in training at the press of Dr. Barnardo's Homes in Hertford. This report described provision made by this organization for physically handicapped, educationally sub-normal, maladjusted, and mentally handicapped children. Films of the work of the Dr. Barnardo's Homes are available without charge.

The Industrial Society

(Formerly the Industrial Welfare Society.)

Address: Robert Hyde House, 48 Bryanston Square, London, W 1.

The Industrial Society provides practical aids and sources of information available for schools, employers, and other organizations arranging courses for young people.

Since its formation in 1919, the Industrial Society has been concerned with questions affecting young people at work. Thus the Society has always given willing help to youth employment officers, church organizations, schools, parents and industry and commerce in any efforts that have been made to help smooth the transition from school to work.

The Industrial Society receives inquiries and requests for help and information on running so-called "bridging the gap" courses, and its first active help was to plan experimental courses in two comprehensive schools—one for girls and the other for boys—designed to broaden their view of the world outside school and give them an idea of the different opportunities that were open to them.

As a result of this work and recent developments, including the publication of the report by Mr. Leslie Paul on *The Transition from School to Work*, the Society felt that there was a need to collect and publish information which would assist all those who are anxious that young boys and girls should be successfully launched on their working lives and be spared the disappointments and frustrations that false starts can so easily lead to.

They have provided a publication on *The Transition from School to Work*.

The Standing Conference for Amateur Music

Address: 26 Bedford Square, London, WC 1.

The Standing Conference for Amateur Music was founded in 1946 to provide the means for the then existing county music committees to come together annually to discuss their problems. It has developed into an association of county and county borough music committees, county and county borough education authorities, and practically all national statutory and voluntary organizations concerned with the development of musical education and amateur musicians.

Although primarily a consultative and co-ordinating organization, the Conference initiates experimental work. It has concerned itself with initiating practical courses in music for teachers of ESN children, whether musicians or not. It is represented on the new Music Panel convened by the Disabled Living Activities Group of the Central Council for the Disabled. It arranged a conference in February 1966, of organizations concerned with the physically handicapped with a view to determining its next activity in this field.

PUBLICATIONS

The Training of Music Teachers, 1954. 1s.
Youth Makes Music, 1957. 2s. 6d.
The Scope of Instrumental Music in Schools, 1960. 4s. 6d.

IN DUPLICATED FORM:

Specimen Planning Notes on Musical Requirements in School Buildings. 1s.
Specimen Planning Notes on Musical Requirements in Further Education Colleges. 1s.
List of Recommended Contemporary Choral Works. 1s.
List of Contemporary Choral Music Suitable for Schools. 1s.

List of Contemporary Orchestral Music. 1s.
A Policy for Pianos. 1s.

IN PREPARATION:

Music Centres and Talented Children—A survey.
Comments on the Newsom Report.

Society for Music Therapy and Remedial Music

Address: 48 Lanchester Road, London, N 6.

The Society for Music Therapy and Remedial Music was founded in 1958 with the object of promoting the use and development of music therapy and remedial music in the treatment, education, training, and rehabilitation of children and adults suffering from emotional, physical, or mental handicaps.

Its membership is open to all whose vocational activities enable them to further the objects of the Society, and there is an associate membership for others who are in sympathy with these objects. There is also a student membership with a reduced subscription. The activities of the Society are many and various.

MEETINGS

The Society holds frequent meetings with talks and discussions about different aspects of music therapy.

Among the medical, educational and general topics considered have been "Music in a Psychiatric Social Club", "Child Development, Sense Perception, and Music", "Music in the History of Psychiatry", and "Music and the Disturbed Person".

COURSES

The Society is now offering courses specially planned for musicians. They present music therapy as a function of music and approach it through its psychological, physiological, and social aspects.

A more extensive scheme now prepared by the Society aims at promoting the practice of music therapy on a sound professional basis with a comprehensive full training course, a recognized qualification, and an accepted status.

Association of Occupational Therapists

Address: 251 Brompton Road, London, SW 3.

The value of treatment by occupation has been recognized from the earliest days of medicine. It was not until the end of the last century, however, that it was prescribed regularly for the mentally ill. Development in the physical field came later when, during the First World War, its value in the restoration of function after physical injury was appreciated. The first school of occupational therapy was started in 1930, and the Association of Occupational Therapists was formed in 1936. The Association of Occupational Therapists is responsible for the recruitment and training of occupational therapists and the conduct of examinations which lead to the award of the Association's diploma in England. Occupational therapy is one of the registered professions supplementary to medicine and only state-registered occupational therapists may practise within the National Health Service. The Association of Occupational Therapists' diploma is accepted for purposes of state registration.

AIMS OF OCCUPATIONAL THERAPY

Occupational therapy may take the form of any activity, work, or recreation chosen specifically for the individual patient to aid his recovery and resettlement or to minimize the effects of a permanent disability and to help him live with this. The immediate aims of treatment by occupational therapy can be summarized as:

1. The development of function, physical and mental, to the fullest possible degree for the re-establishment of the patient in his former life and work.
2. Where this is not possible, the maintenance of existing function and the use of residual abilities in the re-establishment of the patient in his former work or in a new occupation.
3. Where this is not possible, the use of activities to help in a happier adjustment to limitations, personal and in the home, with perhaps the possibility of occasional earnings.

AREA OF WORK

Occupational therapists may only work under medical direction. Patients are referred by a doctor who indicates the diagnosis and aim of treatment. The occupational therapist is then responsible for determining the treatment in detail. Occupational therapists work in general, orthopaedic, and psychiatric hospitals, and day centres, rehabilitation units, many specialized units dealing with varied complaints, and in domiciliary work and sheltered workshops. The employing authority is usually the Hospital Medical Director or the local medical officer of health.

SPECIALIZED WORK WITH CHILDREN

This is carried out in:

1. Children's wards of general hospitals and children's hospitals.
2. Cerebral palsy units.
3. Hospitals and day centres for subnormal children.
4. Units for children with congenital deformities, particularly in connection with training children in the use of prostheses.
5. Child guidance clinics and play therapy centres for emotionally disturbed children.
6. Special psychiatric children's units dealing with traumatic conditions and autistic children.
7. In prisons and hospitals such as Rampton, Broadmoor, and Moss-Side.

8. Domiciliary work, where occupational therapists may visit a child with any disability in the home.

The National Bureau for Co-operation in Child Care

In 1959 the National Council for Social Service was invited by a number of leaders in the child care services to lend its support to a proposal for the establishment of a national centre or institute, the purpose of which would be to improve the lines of communication over a wide variety of relevant services for children and to develop understanding among workers and improve the quality of the services they provide. Its purposes were convincingly presented to the Council by individuals of great experience, holding responsible positions in statutory and voluntary work, whose views were based on first-hand study of the problems involved.

The need for such an organization arose not so much from a general neglect of children's needs as from the very multiplicity of agencies and services which existed for their welfare. For this reason its sphere of interest embraced a wide range of children's needs. Its purpose was to help many different kinds of workers, professional and lay, paid and voluntary; those working in residential homes, in special schools, approved schools, and remand homes; those working for illegitimate children, undertaking child adoption, or providing for children with mental and physical handicaps. They include child care officers, health visitors, moral welfare workers, psychiatric and other case-workers, paediatricians, and practitioners in the child guidance services.

A wide variety of skills was necessary: what was urgently required was a better all-round understanding of the different contributions which were being made by the many workers involved.

> The Bureau fulfils a valuable purpose if the various disciplines and activities can be better focused. This is the basic aim of the project.
> It will not, however, be an executive body itself; neither will it provide training nor seek recognition as the co-ordinator of the policies of its

corporate members. It will have full regard to the official and other machinery which already exists for this purpose.

In December 1960 a large and representative conference of some 100 organizations agreed to ask the National Council to appoint an Organizing Committee to establish the centre under some such title as the National Bureau for Co-operation in Child Care. The Committee was appointed in May 1961 under the chairmanship of Sir John Wolfenden, and carefully reviewed the purposes of the Bureau, its constitution and membership, its methods of work, and its financial requirements.

The Bureau was established in 1962 as a legal charity. The following is a formal summary of its purposes:

(a) To promote the benefit of children or young persons who are in need of special care or support for the maintenance and improvement of their social, mental, physical, or emotional well being.

(b) To promote and organize co-operation in the achievement of the above object and to that end to bring together representatives of statutory authorities and of voluntary organizations and individuals who are concerned with the furtherance of the above object.

(c) To promote the study of and research into the welfare of children and young people: to collect and disseminate information.

(d) To increase knowledge and understanding in matters affecting the welfare of children and young people.

While the intention of the Bureau was to concern itself with the needs of children in need of special care, it was recognized that this can only be done effectively if those responsible for these services can relate their activities to the normal needs of children and young people generally.

Membership of the Bureau is open to corporate bodies, including local authorities, professional associations, universities, and voluntary organizations which are concerned in some general or special ways with children in need of care. It will also be open to individuals who are practitioners and to others with special knowledge and experience.

Initial activities of the Bureau include the collection of information about research and the establishment of a reference centre where relevant information about the work done in this country and abroad can be indexed and kept up to date. Close contacts will be developed with universities, professional associations (social, educational, and medical); new projects for research and inquiry will be studied, and means of consultation established with the appropriate bodies for the furtherance of relevant inquiries.

An important part of the Bureau's equipment will be the establishment of a special library which will assemble and keep up to date a collection of books, journals, reports, surveys, etc., which can be regarded as basic documentation for the child care services. In the initial period its main use may be for committees, groups, and staff as a reference library, perhaps developing later on as a lending library for its members and as a partner collaborating with other special libraries.

An integral part of the Bureau's activities will be the establishment of regional and local groups of professional and lay people actively engaged in various child welfare services. The Bureau will provide guidance on the methods of organization of these local groups and supply them with information and, in return, receive suggestions and views on practical problems which require study. It will arrange conferences and seminars to provide opportunities for individuals working in different services to meet together for joint study and discussion of common problems.

Handicapped Guides and Scouts

In both the Scouts and the Guides there is a section specifically for handicapped young people. The Girl Guides Association (17–19 Buckingham Palace Road, London, SW 1) has an extension service which caters for handicapped girls who are capable of grasping the implications of the promise and wish to join. This service extends to hospitals, homes and schools for the physically handicapped, epileptics, the blind, the deaf, the educationally subnormal, and the mentally handicapped.

PUBLICATIONS

Guiding for the Handicapped. 5s.

HANDICAPPED SCOUTS

Handicapped Scouts are Scouts who are prevented by physical or mental handicap from joining completely in the activities of normal Scouts. Boys who are blind, crippled, deaf, epileptic, invalid, may become Scouts in this branch.

A boy with a handicap may become a member of the Scout Movement by:

(1) joining an ordinary group;
(2) joining a handicapped group in a hospital or school;
(3) registering as a lone scout.

THE EDUCATIONALLY SUBNORMAL BOY

Special tests are not provided for the mentally handicapped boy.

The mentally handicapped boy presents a different problem from the physically handicapped who, however limited in movement, can still comprehend and act on the Scout Law and Promise.

For many educationally subnormal boys, the degree of subnormality is not such as to prevent them from taking part in and understanding scouting. By scouting is meant:

(1) The fundamental basis of the Scout Law and Promise which must be understood (even if simply) and practised.
(2) The programme of training of mind and body by aiming at established goals and achieving set standards.

"Where a boy is ineducable, he is incapable of understanding the Scout Law and Promise and therefore he cannot be a Scout."

THE BOY WITH A HANDICAP

The handicapped boy's desire is to be as normal as possible therefore he benefits by associating with normal boys.

Scouting can provide him with a great opportunity to enjoy the company and engage in some of the pursuits of normal boys.

Groups can do a great service to a boy by welcoming him into the Group. The Group also gains greatly by including a handicapped boy.

The danger is not that the boy will be neglected, but that he will receive too much kindly attention, thus undermining the self-reliance and personal effort the boy must make. Overindulgence will draw attention to his handicap.

PLs and Sixers should be told before his arrival what help he must have and how best to integrate him into the Pack or Troop.

It is doubly necessary to maintain a close contact with the parents of the handicapped boy.

In any difficulty your ACC (Scouts) Handicapped will be able to help, or failing that, your District Commissioner.

The Spastics Society

For a time after the 1944 Education Act children suffering from cerebral palsy—spastics—were not only classed as ineducable but, in the majority of cases, were regarded as being mentally deficient. It was considered, generally, that the degree of physical handicap was closely correlated with the degree of intellectual potential.

In Croydon in 1952 three parents of spastic children and a social worker refused to accept this assumption. With a capital of £5 they formed the Spastics Society. By the middle of the same year eighteen parent groups were present in London at a meeting of this newly formed society. The initial intentions were to provide education and therapy for spastics and to get authorities to accept that spastic children (i.e., children in whom part of the brain has been damaged or has failed to develop) justified educating.

There are three main forms of spasticity. Damage to the cortex of the brain may affect the limbs of one side of the body, both the lower limbs, or all four limbs: it may also affect movement, thought, and sensation. If the basal ganglia (the inner brain) is affected, the subject suffers from athetosis resulting in slow, writhing, involuntary movements of the distal parts of the affected limbs, particularly the fingers and hands: speech may also be affected. When the subject has ataxia, which means that the cerebellum at the base of the brain is damaged, there is weakness and inco-ordination of movement, unsteady gait, and difficulty in balancing. Unfortunately the damage is not necessarily confined to one area but may spill over into the other areas, resulting in multiple handicaps.

Because of the complexity of the affliction it was not easy for doctors to diagnose children as spastics. A child who was an athetoid with jerky, involuntary movements of the body and who was also deaf was frequently regarded as an imbecile. In fact, in the present state of knowledge, of every twenty children with cerebral palsy, fifteen will be able to attend school, three will need other training provisions, and two will need special care.

The decision to tackle this enormous problem was realistically backed by the concerted efforts of the four founder members in Croydon. In a short while the initial £5 became £600 and from then it grew. In the first 5 years £1 million was raised; in the second 5 years another £5 million; this was achieved by voluntary contributions from appeals, door-to-door collecting, Christmas seals, Christmas cards, and collateral donations from members of a football pool.

With money it was possible to implement the original ideas and plans. In 1954 £45,000 was allocated for medical research and there is now a medical research unit at Guy's Hospital financed by an endowment from the Society of over £2 million.

Since the brain and central nervous system are intricate and finely balanced, research, as always, is slow and difficult to measure. Professor Polani, head of the Research Unit, was confident, however, that some forms of spasticity would be controlled by drugs in the very near future. It has already been discovered that lack of oxygen in newborn babies, which can occur in premature and delayed births, is one of the major causes of spasticity, and in this field the research scientists are now working to over-come possible damage by supplying the essential oxygen at birth. In the special assessment centre at the Research Unit the doctor and his assistants are trying to formulate a pattern for the early discovery of spasticity which will act as a guide and basis for doctors everywhere; babies of a few months are being assessed so that early therapy can prevent deformities.

In 1955 the Society opened its first school at Craig-y-Parc in Wales, where spastic children from 6 to 16 receive formal primary and secondary modern education. The first comprehensive school, the Thomas Delarue School at Tonbridge, which includes grammar and secondary modern streams, was opened in the same year. It was followed shortly by another secondary and primary school, the Wilfred Pickles School at Duddington, near Stamford, Lincs. A few years later came Irton Hall, the first school for spastic children with special learning difficulties whose assessed capabili-ties appear to be lower than those demanded for primary and secondary modern schools.

In 1961 a second similar school, Ingfield Manor, was opened at Billinghurst in Sussex. All five schools are recognized by the Ministry of Education. In the very near future Meldreth Manor, near Melbourn, Cambridgeshire will accommodate 120 severely subnormal spastic children who would not otherwise have any educational opportunity.

In 1958 Hawksworth Hall, near Leeds, was opened as a resi-dential assessment centre. Here children between 5 and 13 years of age spend from 6 months to a year on an assessment course. In the majority of cases this is the first time the children have been away from home. They are taught to dress and feed themselves where physically possible, to become continent, and to develop independence. During the period of assessment other physical handicaps that are not immediately apparent become known. Many children have only partial hearing, a disability sometimes difficult to detect in spastics, and often hearing aids increase their awareness, permit them to hear sounds for the first time, and from this educational advancement is often possible. Some spastic

H

children have difficulty in spatial perception so that they are not fully aware of position or direction and can make only very slow progress in drawing and writing, reading, and number.

From Hawksworth Hall suitable children go to one of the Society's schools. The fees during the assessment period and at the Society's schools are paid by local authorities, and cover between a third and a half of the actual cost.

In the two schools for children between 6 and 16 with special learning difficulties, Irton Hall and Ingfield Manor—the latter has a high percentage of partially deaf children—children learn the three Rs at their own speed and in individual ways. Because of the limited life their handicaps have forced them to lead, many slow-learning spastic children have no desire to learn and everything is done to arouse their active interest in life. There is one teacher to every six children in the units for the partially deaf and one teacher to every eight in other classes. The progress that has been achieved is shown by the fact that two children who were certified as mentally deficient are now known to have IQs of over 80 and read well.

As with many spastics there is social and educational immaturity because of deprivation. The schools are geared to the special needs of the children which, because no two spastics have exactly the same handicaps, are completely individual. The more advanced children work towards the equivalent of the 11-plus, and those academically minded can gain places at the Thomas Delarue School at Tonbridge. For children who are partially blind, books have been photographed and enlarged to speed up reading, and enlarged magnifying glasses are also in use. All normal subjects are studied during the day and the evening sessions—according to age—include woodwork, domestic craft, pottery, art, and needlework.

In all the Society's schools, individual time-tables have to be arranged to allow for physiotherapy and speech therapy, which forms a very important part in the training and education of spastics. A child who is given physiotherapy early in life has less likelihood of deformity of the limbs because the body is kept more supple by special exercises instead of being inert. Speech defects can often be improved, and deterioration prevented by early speech therapy. The speech therapists play an important part in the feeding of spastics whose vocal muscles and lips are incapable of or unaccustomed to being used. The physiotherapists and speech therapists work closely together, complementing each other's work so that the spastic child obtains the maximum benefit. Independence and working towards becoming socially acceptable when they leave the environment of their special school is the keynote for educating spastics, so that their inability to move about freely or their initial lack of awareness and their physical handicaps will not prevent them from fitting into society.

For children whose hands are affected, the use of typewriters is being increasingly encouraged, and although tremendous effort is often needed by spastics, the ability to type even with one finger of one hand has speeded up written work and is often a welcome means of communication where there is a serious speech defect.

As in all boarding schools, out-of-school activities play an important part in the curriculum: these include visits to places of interest, scouts, guides, chess, swimming—which is also of therapeutic value—riding, television, parties, pantomimes, and concerts. Pupils train for the Duke of Edinburgh bronze medal awards as part of their Red Cross activities, and local clubs and groups visit the schools.

House parents play a very important part in the children's lives, particularly in the aim towards making the children socially acceptable. A spastic's physical handicap may mean that he can only partially dress himself or that he needs help with his toiletting. Table manners and general courtesy receive particular attention, and it is very interesting to observe the way the children behave towards each other: there seems to be a greater courtesy and thoughtfulness than is normal in young children, and spontaneous laughter and general cheerfulness is very apparent.

In the Thomas Delarue School at Tonbridge an increasing proportion of the pupils are in the grammar school stream. Pupils go to the school either from one of the Society's special schools, from physically handicapped schools, or occasionally from normal schools: in the latter some intelligent young spastics have found that their physical handicaps have caused emotional disturbances and consequently lower academic results than anticipated. In the special environment of the Thomas Delarue School, late-developing children are often able to justify their early expectations. With a largely graduate staff the academic achievement is high although, because the physical handicap has meant that written work is frequently an arduous task, examinations tend to be taken later than at normal schools.

Success is achieved in the O- and A-level examinations of the General Certificate of Education as well as in the Royal Society of Arts, the Institute of Languages, and the College of Preceptors. Subjects include English language and literature, geography, history, mathematics, physics, languages (Latin, French, German, Spanish), mechanical drawing, art, Bible knowledge, and commercial subjects. This is the only major concession made by the examiners for the Cambridge University Local Examinations. A school day, which must include the whole curriculum, physical education, physiotherapy, and speech therapy, as well as arts and crafts, is very full. Pupils often have class lessons in the evening prep. period, doing their preparation during the day in order to overcome the absences necessary for treatment. In the A-level classes the work is inevitably more concentrated, and lessons are tutorials rather than classes.

Typing is being increasingly used in the school, and plays an important part for the students in their means of communication. For those who are unable to use their hands at all, amanuenses are available who give their time either without charge or for a small fee. To save time the amanuenses, who may write a number of foreign languages as well as mathematics, also take notes in class for reference purposes and these are distributed, after duplication, to the students. Amanuenses are also used by students for examination work.

Since students at the Thomas Delarue School take longer for their studies than normal students, there may be pupils at the school who have passed their nineteenth and sometimes twentieth birthdays.

From the school places have been gained to universities and the London College of Printing.

Students from Craig-y-Parc, the Wilfred Pickles School, and the Thomas Delarue School who have no definite vocational bent, attend assessment courses which are held by the Spastics Society. From these courses they may go straight into open employment or be trained at one of the Society's industrial or office training centres: Sherrards at Welwyn Garden City, Herts., has training courses for light engineering and assembly work as well as woodwork, and office training is available at the Stockport and Chester office training centres. Young men and women who have not attended the Society's schools also take part in the assessment courses and may receive training at an industrial or an office training centre or go to one of the many sheltered workshops that are being built all over the country by the Spastics Society in conjunction with local Spastics groups.

For spastics living away from home who are capable of working in outside employment but need special care and attention out of working hours, hostels are being built by the Society all over the country.

Some of the young people who attend assessment courses, however, are in need of further education. Those between 16 and 18 years of age may go to the Dene Park Further Education Centre at Tonbridge, where they can complete education which has been hindered either by late development caused through handicaps or because handicaps have made it impossible for them to keep up with pupils in ordinary schools.

For young men and women with higher intellects whose severe handicaps prevent them from taking part in university life, there is yet another centre. At Oakwood, in Kelvedon, Essex, students enjoy the atmosphere and amenities of a small modern college with the physical facilities necessary for heavily handicapped spastics.

Side by side with the growth of schools and facilities for education and training, have been built residential centres where spastics who cannot live and work in the outside world find interest, occupation, companionship, and physical care. An increasing number of adult residential centres will be built as the need arises. With the acceptance of spasticity, brought about by the initial efforts of four people in Croydon, parents are looking to the Society to help them with their burden. Added to this is the fact that a need for such residential centres will increase as students leave the Society's schools and, because of their physical handicaps, are unable to take their place in society.

Residential adult centres have, in the past, catered mainly for spastics who have been denied education because of their handicaps. Now that many more young spastics are receiving some education and are growing up with a knowledge and awareness of the world they live in, the pattern of the residential centres must inevitably slowly change.

Over 5 years ago the Society began to consider the possibility of establishing an Educational Research Unit to discover how teachers should be trained for the special task of teaching spastics so that they could fit into the national educational pattern. In 1964 it was decided that the Society should provide funds, amounting over a period of 10 years to £600,000, to the University of London which has undertaken to set up and maintain a Department of Child Development under a Professor of Child Development. This Department is divided into five sections and co-ordinated by the Professor. One section dealing with special training for teachers of spastic children, and associated research activities is headed by a senior lecturer, a lecturer, and junior staff. The Society's contribution will meet the cost of this section and the professorship. The remaining four sections will cover research and teacher training for deaf children, maladjusted children, educationally subnormal children, and the study of the normal development of children.

In 1965 there were 320 spastic children in the Society's national schools, 140 on the waiting list, and 1600 receiving education through the Society, including those in affiliated schools. A further 1500 were receiving education in other private and physically handicapped schools. There are about 6000 spastics of school age about whom little is known at the present time.

It is not envisaged that more new schools will be built by the Society, at least for the time being. It is intended, however, that the schools already in existence will in the future be able to increase the number of places available. But for the rest, it is hoped that spastics will be absorbed either in normal schools, physically handicapped schools or physically handicapped schools with a cerebral palsy unit.

PUBLICATIONS

All publications are sent post free. The dollar prices include additional cost of overseas postage.

Spastics News. A monthly magazine giving particulars of the activities of the Society and its affiliated groups. 11*d*. 25 cents (USA). Annual subscription: 11*s*. $2.00 (USA).

Special Education (Incorporating *Spastics Quarterly*). The Journal of the Association for Special Education on the Educational Journal of the Spastics Society. A quarterly journal for those concerned with the teaching and training of the handicapped child. 5*s*. $0.75 (USA). Annual subscription: 20*s*. $3.00 (USA).

The Hemiplegic Child, by V. CULLOTY, No. 5 in the Parents Handbook Series. A booklet, with illustrations, for the parents of hemiplegic children. 2*s*. 6*d*. 50 cents (USA).

Learning Problems of the Cerebrally Palsied. A report of a study group held in Oxford 1964. Deals with various aspects of the education of the cerebrally palsied child. 1965. 12*s*. 6*d*.

Spastic School Leavers—A Survey. A survey of 54 London spastics who left school between the years 1957 and 1962. 1964. 5*s*.

Spastic School Leavers—Employment? Two addresses given at a conference held in London, December 1960. Contents: "Education for Life after School; "From School to Work".

Reviews some of the problems facing school-leavers and the help which should be given at school and later. June 1961. 1*s*. 6*d*. Six or more copies: 1*s*. 4*d*. each. 35 cents (USA).

Notes on the Assessment of Educational Needs of Children with Cerebral Palsy. 1958. 1*s*. 25 cents (USA).

Organization of Out Patient and Day Clinics, Diagnostic and Therapeutic, for Cerebral Palsied Children. 1958. 1*s*. 25 cents (USA).

After School What? Revised 1962. 1*s*. 25 cents (USA).

CONFERENCE REPORT

Mentally Subnormal Spastics. Four addresses given at a conference held in London, December 1960. Reviews the facts, describes two pioneer experiments in institution and community care and discusses the facilities which should be developed. 4*s*. 6*d*. Three or more copies: 4*s*. 4*d*. each. 75 cents (USA).

LEAFLET

Cerebral Palsy—an Introductory Bibliography. Designed for student teachers and other professional workers who may require general information on special aspects of cerebral palsy outside their field of work. Single copy sent free. Additional copies 2*d*. each.

THE FOLLOWING PUBLICATIONS CAN ALSO BE OBTAINED FROM THE SOCIETY

Born that Way, by DR. EARL R. CARLSON. An autobiography. First published in Great Britain by Arthur James, The Drift, Evesham, Worcestershire, in 1952. 8*s*. 6*d*. $1.45 (USA).

A Spastic Wins Through, by K. R. A. HART. An autobiography. The Bannisdale Press, London, 1955. 6*s*. $1.10 (USA).

Every Eight Hours. The story of the Spastics Society. 196. Hodder & Stoughton, London, EC 4. 2*s*. 6*d*.

POLYTHENE TUBING

This tubing can be used by spastic children and adults who cannot drink from a cup. It can be heated and then bent to obtain the angle required and can be sterilized in boiling water. 9*d.* per yard, post free.

FILMS

The following films may be borrowed free of charge (within the United Kingdom) from the Society on condition that borrowers undertake to pay for any damage which may occur while they are in use or being handled. Films are inspected before being sent out and are fully insured against loss or damage in transit. Borrowers are also responsible for payment of return postage.

Films are loaned on the understanding that they are returned promptly.

Although no fee is charged for hiring films, any collection made on behalf of spastics will be most gratefully received.

One of the Family. 16 mm sound monochrome film. Running time $28\frac{1}{2}$ minutes. Made in 1964. This film illustrates the work of the Society's Assessment Panel and its Parent Relief Centre at Nottingham.

What is a Spastic? 16 mm sound colour film. Running time 15 minutes. Made in 1964. This film explains in lay terms what cerebral palsy is.

Penny Parade. 16 mm sound colour film. Running time 15 minutes. Made in 1964. This film illustrates how the Society's funds are raised and why continued and increasing support is necessary.

A Gift for Love. 16 mm sound colour film. Running time 20 minutes. Made in 1964. Jewellery and Christmas cards made by spastics are the basis of a Christmas story.

The Contact. 16 mm sound colour film. Running time $12\frac{1}{2}$ minutes. Made in 1964. Normal teenagers meet a spastic— to their common benefit.

Cerebral Palsy—Early Recognition. 16 mm sound colour film. Running time 15 minutes. Made in 1952. Medical diagnostic film.

Special Equipment at Carlson House School for Spastics. 16 mm colour film with sound commentary. Running time 15 minutes. Made in 1956. This film illustrates some of the special educational equipment (including special furniture) made and used at Carlson House School for Spastics, Birmingham.

Pattern Movements in the Treatment of Cerebral Palsy. 16 mm silent monochrome film. English captions. Running time 25 minutes. Made in 1952 in Denmark under the supervision of Dr. Temple Fay. Technical instructional film illustrating Dr. Temple Fay's method of treatment. *Note*: distribution—medical, ancillary medical, and other professional personnel concerned with care, treatment, and education of spastics.

The Link. 16 mm silent monochrome film. Running time 25 minutes (approximately). Made in 1954. This film illustrates the work of the Welfare Department of the Midland Spastic Association with particular reference to the Association's work among young adult spastics.

Claremont. 16 mm colour film with sound commentary. Running time 12 minutes (approximately). Made in 1960. This film illustrates the education and treatment of children at Claremont School for Spastics, Bristol, and includes shots of the Cerebral Palsy Assessment Clinic at the Bristol Children's Hospital.

Right for the Job. 16 mm sound colour film. Running time 31 minutes. Made in 1961. A film illustrating the employment potential of spastics and their assessment and training for outside employment.

Jessy. 16 mm sound monochrome film. Running time 31 minutes. Made in 1959. This film illustrates a spastic girl's adjustment to life.

Door to Freedom. 16 mm sound colour film. Running time 25 minutes. Made in 1956, revised 1959. This film illustrates the work of the Society during its years of formation,

Includes scenes of Craig-y-Parc School, Wilfred Pickles School, Thomas Delarue School, and Prested Hall.

*Every Eight Hours.** 16 mm sound monochrome film. Running time 35 minutes. Made in 1960. This film illustrates the growth of the Society and the development of its special services for spastics throughout the country.

*The New School.** 16 mm sound monochrome film. Running time 5 minutes. This film illustrates the work of the Percy Hedley School at Newcastle.

Application for films on the above list should be made to: Film Secretary, The Spastics Society, 12 Park Crescent, London, W 1.

The following films may be borrowed from the Society's schools and centres on application direct to the school or centre concerned:

THOMAS DELARUE SCHOOL

A Letter from Anna. 16 mm silent monochrome film. Running time 30 minutes.

A Trip to France. 16 mm silent monochrome film. Running time 15 minutes.

Holiday in Holland. 16 mm sound colour film. Running time 30 minutes.

Application for the above should be made to: Headmaster, Thomas Delarue School, Starvecrow, Shipbourne Road, Tonbridge, Kent.

WILFRED PICKLES SCHOOL

And Forbid them Not. 16 mm sound colour film. Running time 35 minutes.

Application for this film should be made to: Headmaster, Wilfred Pickles School, Tixover Grange, Duddington, Nr. Stamford, Lincs.

* Films also available in 35 mm if required, but 16 mm films will be supplied unless the larger size is specified.

CRAIG-Y-PARC SCHOOL

The Craig-y-Parc School. (Only suitable for projector with magnetic head.) 16 mm. sound colour film. Running time 42 minutes.

Application for this film should be made to: Headmistress, Craig-y-Parc School, Pentyrch, Nr. Cardiff.

IRTON HALL SCHOOL

Arrival of the Steamroller. 16 mm silent monochrome film. Running time 4 minutes.

Arrival of the Lifeboat. 16 mm silent monochrome film. Running time 4 minutes.

Leisure Activities. 16 mm silent monochrome film. Running time 30 minutes.

Application for the above films should be made to: Headmaster, Irton Hall School, Holmrook, Cumberland.

PRESTED HALL

Life Anew. 16 mm partly sound colour film. (Only suitable for projector with magnetic head.) Running time 25 minutes.

Application for this film should be made to: Warden, Prested Hall, Feering, Kelvedon, Essex.

SOME FILMS ON CEREBRAL PALSY AVAILABLE FROM OTHER SOURCES

Inquiries must be addressed *direct to the distributor* of the films and *not to the Society*.

A Place in the Sun. 16 mm sound monochrome film. Running time 23 minutes. This film illustrates aspects of the State of California's cerebral palsy programme. Includes shots of cerebral palsy schools. *Distributor*: British Film Institute, 81, Dean Street, London, W 1. Telephone: REGent 0061.

First Steps (reference V.265). 16 mm sound monochrome film. Running time 10 minutes. Made in 1948. Portrays some of the essentials in establishing services for crippled children. Shows a typical centre in the USA and illustrates the general principles of rehabilitation of children suffering from spastic paraplegia. *Distributor*: Central Film Library, Central Office of Information, Government Buildings, Bromyard Avenue, London, W 3. Telephone: SHEpherds Bush 5555.

Hearing Tests in Cerebral Palsied Children. Silent monochrome 16 frames-a-second, 16 mm film. Running time 15 minutes. Made in 1956 by the Centre for Spastic Children in conjunction with the Audiology Unit of the Royal National Ear, Nose, and Throat Hospital. Is concerned largely with the conditioning technique developed by Dr. Fisch. *Note*: distribution to professional audiences only, e.g. doctors, teachers of the deaf, speech therapists. *Distributor*: The Centre for Spastic Children, 61 Cheyne Walk, London, SW 3. Telephone: FLAxman 8434.

Treatment of Cerebral Palsy in New Zealand. 16 mm sound monochrome film. Running time 69 minutes. Made by New Zealand National Film Unit for Department of Health. Illustrates management and treatment of cerebral palsy at the Cerebral Palsy Unit of the Queen Elizabeth Memorial Hospital, Rotorua. Main emphasis is on treatment of moderately handicapped children with normal intelligence. *Distributor*: Films Officer, New Zealand House, Haymarket, London, SW 1. Telephone: WHItehall 8422.

Towards a Brighter Horizon. 16 mm silent colour film. Running time 15 minutes. Made in 1955 at Westerlea School for Spastics, Edinburgh. Illustrates some of the equipment devised in the occupational therapy department, to meet individual difficulties. Includes adapted games. *Distributor*: Scottish Central Film Library, 16/17 Woodside Terrace, Glasgow, C 3. Telephone: Douglas 5143.

The Scientific Film Association, 55a Welbeck Street, London, W 1 (Telephone WELbeck 0758) publishes a catalogue of films on cerebral palsy, price 2s. 6d. This will be found particularly useful by those desiring information about medical films.

The Central Council for Rehabilitation, 34 Eccleston Square, London, SW 1 (Telephone VICtoria 0747) holds foreign films on temporary loan from the International Society for the Rehabilitation of the Disabled including, from time to time, films on cerebral palsy.

The Shaftesbury Society

Address: 112 Regency St., London, SW 1.

Founded 100 years before the 1944 Education Act, the Shaftesbury Society attracted many outstanding people, including the novelist Charles Dickens. A film *Shaftesbury's Children* is available, and describes work in the Society's residential schools for physically handicapped children. The Society pioneered work in the care of children with muscular dystrophy and has built hostels for young men with muscular dystrophy who have nowhere to go after leaving school "except the chronic wards of hospitals".

The Society has several residential schools for physically handicapped children, including one for children with a physical handicap resulting in incontinence. Holiday work and domiciliary case-work are amongst other services, further details of which can be obtained from the Society.

British Epilepsy Association

Address: 27 Nassau St., London, W 1.

This society was formed because there was no other society dealing specifically with the welfare of epileptics. As many people had wrong ideas about epilepsy, epileptics faced all sorts of social difficulties. Their greatest handicap was often "the fear and ignorance of those with whom they wish to work and play".

In 1938 Miss (later Dame) Evelyn Fox, a pioneer in the mental health field, invited Dr. T. Fox (for 30 years Medical Superintendent at Lingfield Colony) to join her in planning research into what happened to epileptics discharged as recovered from colonies. From this developed the scheme of after-care which was partly financed by local authorities.

Although the state and local authority welfare services were ready to aid all disabled people, the British Epilepsy Association found that the handicapped individual often did not come under these services or did not know about them. Moreover, in areas where the population was scattered it was not easy to provide specialist helpers. This Association therefore set out to provide services where they were lacking, to supplement existing provision, and to see that statutory provision was used or the services were used by people who needed them.

The aims of the British Epilepsy Association were listed as:

1. To assist all who suffer from epilepsy, both as individuals and as families.

2. To improve the understanding of epilepsy so that those who suffer from this disability shall not also suffer from the ignorance and prejudice of those around them.

3. To encourage and assist research into the causes and treatment of epilepsy.

4. To share our knowledge and experience with people in all parts of the world who wish to work for the welfare of the epileptic.

Membership and associate membership is open to all.

SERVICES

The Association offers a personal advice service, covering such problems as education, employment, marriage, children, housing, and available treatment. It organizes educational courses for teachers, social workers, welfare officers, and general practitioners. It also provides clubs for epileptic persons and their families, arranges holidays, acts as an international clearing house for information, and issues various publications.

PUBLICATIONS

Epilepsy? What to do. Free.

Prejudice. Free.

Employment Notes. Free.

Handbook for Parents. Free.

What the Minister should know about Epilepsy. 6d.

What the Nurse should know about Epilepsy. 6d.

What the Social Worker should know about Epilepsy. 1s.

A Teacher's Guide on Epilepsy. 3d.

Epileptics at Work. 6d.

The Patient's Situation. 6d.

Journal. (Quarterly) 1s. 6d.

Epilepsy, by LETITIA FAIRFIELD. 9s.

Review of the Social and Medical Services for the Epileptic Patient in

   (a) *England and Wales.* 1s. 6d.

   (b) *Scotland.* 9d.

   (c) *Belgium.* 1s. 6d.

   (d) *USSR.* 1s. 6d.

   (e) *Czechoslovakia.* 6d.

Some Studies in Epilepsy:

   Epilepsy and Employment. 2s. 6d.

   Epilepsy and Education. 2s. 6d.

The Adult Population of Epileptic Colonies. 2s. 6d.

Locked Out. 1s.

Epilepsy the World Over. 1s.

Symposium on Epilepsy. 1s.

Epileptic Colonies, Schools and Hospitals. 1s. 9d.

Candle Badge. 2s. 6d.

FILMS

Hiring fee of 30s. per film (except *People Apart* (£2) and *The Silent Factor* (10s.).

   People Apart. Black and white. 45 minutes. (No professional actors.) Includes a description of the EEG examination and simple explanation of the nature of epileptic attacks.

Blueprint for Epilepsy. Black and white. 25 minutes. Mainly about the Epi-Hap Workshop in Los Angeles.

L'Enfant Epileptique: Probleme Medico-social. Colour. English soundtrack. 18 minutes. Describes the situation in France of children who suffer from epilepsy.

I Want to Work. Black and white, 15 minutes. About a young girl seeking and eventually finding employment.

The Child with Epilepsy. Black and white. 30 minutes. A USA television film made by Syracuse University.

Modern Concepts about Epilepsy. Colour. 35 minutes. A medical film; not for general showing.

ATV Film on Epilepsy. Black and white. 25 minutes. From "About Religion" series.

The Dark Wave. Colour. 24 minutes. "Probably the best non-medical epilepsy film to be produced so far." An 11-year-old girl with petit mal is helped to feel wanted and kept from feeling *different*.

Seizures. Black and white. 21 minutes. USA, made for veterans administration.

Lifeline—Epilepsy. Black and white, 30 minutes. Telerecording of Dr. Stafford Clarke's programme featuring an interview with patients.

The Silent Factor. Colour. 10 minutes. Story of a holiday for children.

On the Go. Black and white. 25 minutes. Interviews in the USA with persons suffering from epilepsy.

The Muscular Dystrophy Group

Address: 26 Borough High St., London, SE 1.

The Muscular Dystrophy Group is a voluntary association of sufferers, parents or guardians of child sufferers, and other people interested in the well-being of all suffering from neuro-muscular diseases.

The aims of the Muscular Dystrophy Group are threefold:

1. to raise money for research into the cause and cure of muscular dystrophy and allied diseases;
2. to provide a friendly link between sufferers and those who care for them;
3. to utilize to the full the existing services for the physically handicapped, without unnecessary duplication. Much of the case-work undertaken is in an advisory capacity and the Group acts as a "clearing house" for information.

The first committee was formed in 1954, working under the aegis of the Central Council for the Care of Cripples until, in May 1959, it became a registered charity. Originally formed to provide a friendly exchange of information between sufferers, at the first general meeting, held in London, 1955, the members decided unanimously that the Group should have as its first objective the encouragement of research, and it was at this meeting the Group came into existence in its present form.

The Executive Committee works under the chairmanship of Professor F. J. Nattrass with Dr. J. N. Walton as vice-chairman, and is supported by a distinguished Research Committee and Medical Advisory Committee. An Appeals Committee, under the chairmanship of Mr. Haig Gudenian, Editor of *Ideal Home*, is responsible to the Executive Committee which conducts the Appeals policy of the Group. At the end of 1960, with grants from trusts, etc., and the efforts of the Group, £104,500 had been raised towards the vast sum required for research.

In November 1956 Mrs. John Vincent became the Organizer and is now the General Secretary.

Research projects are being carried out in London, Edinburgh, Newcastle upon Tyne, Smethwick, Oxford, and Glasgow. Many pieces of expensive equipment have been purchased, and the Group is wholly or partly responsible for the salaries of several doctors and technicians.

A tremendous amount of welfare work is done and where possible "cases" are passed to the statutory or voluntary organization best able to help. If all other sources fail, the Group will help

In April 1957 the *Muscular Dystrophy Journal* was begun, and is now a quarterly feature. It is issued to members and all interested people.

Invalid Children's Aid Association

Address: 4 Palace Gate, London, W 8.

ICAA was founded in 1888 by the Reverend Allen Graham, sometime curate of St. Paul's Church, Covent Garden. At the time he was working for the Charity Organization Society, and came to the conclusion that while something was being done for sick adults, there were no provisions for sick children. For some years he looked after 300 invalid children on his own, but by 1888 their numbers had grown too many for one man to look after. In its early years ICAA looked after mainly tubercular and crippled children.

Latterly it has extended its activities to include many of the psychological illnesses that attack children.

AIMS

To provide medical help and psychological support to handicapped children and their parents. No sick child, whatever his or her illness, is ever turned away.

SERVICES

(1) An extensive case-work service covering Greater London and the Home Counties.

(2) An information service available to parents, statutory bodies, and institutions throughout the world.

(3) Holiday camps during summer, on the south coast of England, for very severely handicapped children.

FACILITIES

(1) Four boarding special schools;

    (a) *Meath*: Ottershaw, Surrey, for asthmatic boys aged 7–11.

    (b) *Pilgrims*: Seaford, Sussex, for asthmatic boys aged 11–16.

    (c) *John Horniman School*: Park Road, Worthing, for children aged 5–9 with speech defects due to brain damage.

    (d) *Edith Edwards House*: Banstead, Surrey, for children with speech defects owing to emotional disturbance.

(2) Word Blind Centre for Dyslexic Children: Coram's Field, London, WC 1, for research and treatment (individual day classes) for dyslexic children.

PUBLICATIONS

A number of pamphlets and leaflets on various aspects of ICAA's work, available free on application.

FILMS

Two films: *Susan goes to Somptin* and *No Magic Cure*. Each is 16 mm sound, black and white, and runs for 15 minutes. The first is about one of ICAA camps on the south coast; the second about life in a school for asthmatic boys. No fee charged.

Lord Mayor Treloar Trust

Address: Froyle, Alton, Hampshire.

The Lord Mayor Treloar College was founded in 1908 by the Lord Mayor of London of 1906/7. Originally a Cripples' Hospital and College, the object of the College was the rehabilitation and technical training of crippled boys between the ages of 14 and 18 who, without such special training, could not hope to earn their own living.

In 1948 the Hospital passed into the control of the Ministry of Health but the College remained independent and moved in 1953 to its present home.

The Trust's decision to launch a 10-year development programme in 1965 coincided with the completion of the first boarding grammar school ever specifically designed and built in this country for physically handicapped girls. This marked a significant advance in the opportunities open to disabled girls both locally and nationally.

The total number of pupils who can be accommodated is now 235 of whom 135 are boys.

The aims are "to educate and train physically handicapped boys and girls, thus enabling them to lead a full and rewarding life as useful members of society".

SERVICES

Grammar and secondary modern courses and technical courses are provided for boys and girls between the ages of 11 and approximately 20 years. Provided there is a vacancy any physically handicapped child can be accepted. "The College cannot, however, take boys who are blind, deaf, dumb, mentally deficient or suffering from pulmonary tuberculosis."

THE COMMONWEALTH PLACES SCHEME

The Trust takes up to twelve boys or girls from developing countries at a time. These young people return to their countries after training.

CENTRE FOR HANDICAPPED ADULTS

A centre is proposed for sixty handicapped men and women in need of special accommodation, special work facilities, or both.

FILM

There's no Discouragement. Available on free loan to local organizations and schools. This film won a gold medal at the 2nd

234 NO CHILD IS INEDUCABLE

International Film Festival on Rehabilitation of the Disabled, Rome, 1964. It shows the day-to-day work of the Lord Mayor Treloar College and the way in which physically handicapped boys can be taught to live independent lives and follow productive careers.

The Jewish Association for the Physically Handicapped

Registered under the National Assistance Act, 1948.

Registered under War Charities Act, 1940.

The Association has been in existence since 1955, having started as a small group of people who wished to bring a little extra happiness to physically handicapped children. Today the Association provides for both children and adults, the membership of the Children's and Teenager's Groups being 45 and the membership of the Adult Group 250.

The work of the Association has been recognized by such organizations as the Jewish Board of Guardians, the London County Council, Middlesex County Council, and many hospital management committees who refer Jewish physically handicapped persons known to them to the Association for club amenities and welfare.

A children's club, the Merry Makers, meets on alternate Sunday afternoons, a teenage club every fourth Tuesday evening, and an Adults' club, the Walking Sticks, on alternate Tuesday evenings. All meet at the ILEA Welfare Centre, 131 St. Johns Way, N 1. At the clubs, members are able to participate in such activities as games, including table tennis, billiards, snooker, etc. In addition there are musical evenings, shows put on by professional and amateur artists, talks, and film shows.

The Welfare and Visiting Group ensures that members who cannot come along to the clubs, because they are home-bound or in hospital, are cared for by regular visits, and, where necessary, provided with comforts such as gramophones, television sets, etc.

Most of the members are unable to travel by public transport and it is necessary for the Association to provide transport for them to and from the clubs.

One of the greatest benefits provided for members is an annual holiday.

All communications to 43 Witley Court, Coram Street, WC 1.

The Society for the Aid of Thalidomide Children Ltd.

Address: Walmar House, 288–296 Regent St., London, W 1.

The Society for the Aid of Thalidomide Children Limited was formed on 12 August 1962 and is a charity registered in accordance with the National Assistance Act, 1948. At the inaugural meeting held on 20 October 1962, Lady Hoare became President of the Society and Mr. Michael Carr-Jones was elected Chairman. This Society is made up entirely of parents of thalidomide children, and is supervised by a Council of Management which meets at regular intervals.

The Society is established for charitable objects and purposes only. The principal aims are: To provide an organization for the relief of persons suffering from congenital disabilities attributable to the effects of the drug commonly known as "thalidomide", with a view to obtaining medical, educational, and other aids and advice to enable such persons and their parents to overcome their special difficulties and to live as normal a life as possible.

The Star Centre for Youth

Address: Ullenwood Manor, Cheltenham, Glos.

A specialized residential centre for 30 physically handicapped youths aged 16 to 20. The Centre does not aim to be self-sufficient but encourages students to make as much use as possible of existing facilities in the area.

CHAPTER 18

Sensory Defects

The Royal National Institute for the Blind

Address: 224 Great Portland St., London, W 1.

The work of this pioneering organization has already been indicated in Chapter 17, where there was reference to the use made by local authorities of the facilities offered by the RNIB. These facilities included pre-school, schools, higher education, vocational centres, and adult centres.

BLIND CHILDREN WITH ADDITIONAL HANDICAPS

The RNIB also provides junior schools for blind children with additional handicaps. It opened Rushton Hall in 1960 as their second such school. All pupils, in addition to being blind, are handicapped physically, mentally, or emotionally. Children who show "any particular aptitude are given every opportunity to develop it", and it is possible for a child to proceed from there to an ordinary junior or senior school for blind children.

Most of the children, however, go on to Condover Hall, the senior school for multiply handicapped blind children, at the age of 12.

CONDOVER HALL

This school, which was obtained by the RNIB in 1946, offers opportunities for learning based upon activity and experience, to blind children who would not be acceptable at other schools. Many of these pupils remain until the age of 17. On leaving some go to Hethersett or the Queen Alexandra Technical College for Vocational Guidance, prior to employment or training, some are placed in occupation centres for handicapped adults, and some go to their homes or institutional care. "Any pupil thought capable of employment will receive all possible assistance from the Youth Employment Service, the Disablement Resettlement Officer of the Ministry of Labour and the RNIB Specialist Employment Officers. The employment found suitable will normally be of a simple, mainly unskilled type, but the satisfaction of work, however simple, and of continued companionship must never be under-valued."

DEPARTMENT FOR DEAF–BLIND CHILDREN

A unit for "educable deaf–blind children" was opened in 1952 and extended to take fifteen children in 1960. "Pathways" as the department is known, is in separate premises in the grounds of the main school. The Head of the Department "has had special training and experience in the education of deaf–blind children".

SERVICES

Prints books in braille, providing a wide selection of all that is best in literature, together with periodicals such as the *Radio Times*. To meet the particular needs of the elderly the Institute also prints many of these in the more easily read Moon type.

Publishes sheet music in braille.

Supplies apparatus and equipment of all kinds for recreational and occupational use. Many of the 200 such items now available have been devised by the Institute, which constantly explores new means of lightening the handicap of blindness.

Subsidizes the cost of production of embossed publications and specialized equipment.

Provides the blind with talking books, undertaking—in conjunction with St. Dunstan's—the recording of books on long-playing discs, the maintenance of a circulating library, and the supply of the specially developed machines.

Maintains nine Sunshine Home Nursery Schools for Blind Children in England and Wales.

Educates blind children with additional handicaps at Condover Hall, Shropshire, and Rushton Hall, Northants. Since their inception, these schools have proved outstandingly successful in providing for multiply handicapped blind children scholastic and social education obtainable nowhere else.

Maintains at Chorleywood and Worcester the only two residential grammar schools for blind girls and boys respectively.

Maintains at Reigate, Surrey, the only pre-vocational training and assessment centre for blind adolescents.

Makes grants for higher education and professional training, co-operating with local agencies to provide financial help to blind people with especial need.

Trains blind men and women in physiotherapy. At its School of Physiotherapy, the only one of its kind in the British Commonwealth, blind students of both sexes qualify to become Members of the Chartered Society of Physiotherapy. Thereafter the Institute helps to establish them in professional practice.

Administers a Physiotherapy Clinic, at which qualified blind physiotherapists provide a comprehensive range of treatment.

Trains blind shorthand-typists and telephonists at its specially equipped London training college.

Secures employment for the blind in industry and commerce, and maintains a highly specialized placement department which operates in most parts of the country. It constantly explores new avenues of employment suitable for blind workers, and itself employs many blind men and women.

Is deeply concerned with every aspect of blindness—its prevention and its alleviation—and maintains a watching brief over legislation affecting the lives of those without sight.

Plays a leading part in ensuring British representation on the World Council for the Welfare of the Blind and has itself representatives on all important international committees concerned with the problems of blindness.

Is governed by a Council representing every side of blind welfare—local and national, blind and sighted, voluntary workers and official agencies. By arrangement with local agencies, it eliminates duplication of appeals and assists local organization in blind welfare work within their own areas.

PUBLICATIONS

DOCUMENTARY FILMS

Pathway into Light. 35 and 16 mm. Sound. 20 minutes. Produced by Associated British Pathé in aid of the Braille Centenary. Commentary spoken by Jean Metcalfe and Jack Hawkins. A film of general blind welfare interest, dealing mainly with the use of braille in the education of the blind, and including newsreel shots of the Braille Centenary celebrations in France.

Conquest of the Dark. 35 and 16 mm. Sound. 30 minutes. Commentary spoken by John Slater and Paul Rogers. This film tells the story of one man whose eyesight fails. Expert and sympathetic training enable him once more to find self-confidence, financial independence, and a full enjoyment of life.

Unseen Horizons. 35 and 16 mm. Sound. 40 minutes. Commentary spoken by Frank Hawkins. This film shows the opportunities available to blind boys and girls as a result of the comprehensive educational system existing in this country.

No Longer Alone. 35 and 16 mm. Sound. 30 minutes. A documentary film made for the Institute by Associated British Pathé, dealing with the education of multiply handicapped blind children.

New Lease of Life. 16 mm. Sound. 20 minutes. A documentary film produced for the Institute by Behr Photography Limited, dealing with the services provided for the elderly blind.

Talking Books. 16 mm. Sound and colour. 18 minutes. A documentary film made by the staff of our Sound Recording Studios at RNIB Headquarters and the Nuffield Talking Book Library at Alperton, Wembley, showing the whole process of the production of Talking Book Cassettes until they reach library members.

The Royal National Institute for the Deaf

Address: 105 Gower St., London, WC 1.

The Royal National Institute for the Deaf is the protective association for all deaf, deaf–blind, and hard of hearing people in the United Kingdom. It deals with all aspects of deafness. It is an independent voluntary society incorporated under the Companies Acts and registered as a charitable organization under the National Assistance Act, 1948.

It protects the deaf from exploitation and keeps their needs constantly before the public and the Government. It seeks out and follows up new avenues to improve the social, educational, and industrial conditions of all people with defective hearing.

It also strives to enlighten the general public on the problems of deafness and thus promote understanding between the deaf and the hearing world.

It has a Welfare Department skilled in communicating with the born deaf as well as the hard of hearing, and with the problems and frustrations of both.

A Technical Laboratory, in which an overall watch is kept on the development of new hearing aids, the shortcomings as well as the advantages that might attend new models. Professional apparatus such as audiometers are checked and tested and advice given on the design and equipping of sound-measurement rooms, etc. Many small devices helpful to the deaf individual are provided. Anyone with a hearing aid which is malfunctioning can have it scientifically tested and reported upon.

There is a Library where books and periodicals, current and historical, on every aspect of deafness and work connected with hearing and hearing loss can be referred to or borrowed.

The Publications Department produces not only its monthly magazine *Hearing*, but booklets, pamphlets, and reports dealing with deafness and means of alleviating or coming to terms with the handicap.

Advice is always available and freely given on schools, education, further education, careers, employment, personal problems, domestic problems, readjustment for those recently deafened, clubs, hobbies, and National Health and State welfare services.

Homes, among the most comfortable and cheerful in the country, are maintained in many centres for the care of deaf, deaf–blind, and the hard of hearing persons of all ages who require sheltered living conditions among people who can understand them. Also hostels for active young deaf people, a trade-training centre for deaf boys, and a residential school (under construction) for maladjusted deaf children.

BOOKS AND PAMPHLETS

Hearing. The official magazine of the Institute. 1*s.* Annual subscription 16*s.* or 8*s.* for 6 months. Post free.

Clinical Aspects of Hearing. A brief, simply written 12-page booklet on the causes of deafness and what can be done nowadays by medicine and surgery to alleviate it. 2*s.*

Special Aids to Hearing. 2*s.*

Conversation with the Deaf. 2*s.* 6*d.*

Homes for the Deaf. A 6-page fold-out leaflet giving details of admission, etc., to RNID homes in various parts of the country. Free.

In the Service of the Deaf. A pocket size (3¼ in. by 5½ in.) booklet giving a brief account of the problem of deafness in the British Isles and what is being done to alleviate it. Free.

Highway Code for Deaf Children. Written by a Police Sergeant and illustrated in colour, providing simple instruction in road safety for children on foot or cycling. Foreword by a Minister of Transport. Free.

Hearing Aids. A detailed account of modern hearing aids, what can be expected of them, and where they fail. Fully illustrated. 31 pages. 2*s.* 6*d.*

The RNID Library. An 8-page fold-out leaflet giving details of the library service. With pictures. Free.

Interpreting for the Deaf. A single-fold leaflet setting out the rights of deaf people to an interpreter in court, and in what other circumstances interpreting into sign language is more than usually advisable. Free.

Salary Scales for WODs. Detailing salaries and conditions of service recommended by the RNID for welfare officers to the deaf. Single-fold leaflet. Free.

Lip Reading, by J. HOUNSLOW BURCHETT. A comprehensive manual for the teacher or home-student of lip-reading. With exercises. 120 pages, stiff boards and linen bound. Inclusive of packing and postage. 10s.

Annual Reports for the current year are always available. In addition to the Institute's balance sheet, list of officials, etc., there are well-illustrated sections on the Institute's work. Free.

BBC Play Précis. Published every month in collaboration with the BBC, these contain detailed synopses of three forthcoming television plays and the Sunday serial, thus enabling the plots to be followed independent of the sound track. About 8 pages newspaper style. Free and post paid.

DEVICES

MEDRESCO PURSE

A silver-grey suede plastic pocket with soft rustle-free lining in which the Medresco hearing aid snugly fits. Removes one of the biggest drawbacks to the NHS aid—clothes rub; also acts as a protector. With nylon cord for suspending from the neck at any required height. Can be used for other body-worn aids of similar size. Price 2s. 6d.

HEARING AID HARNESS

Made of strong webbing containing two open-top pockets into which Medresco or similar aids can be fastened and strapped round the chest and shoulder. Originally designed for children at rough play, the straps are also adjustable to adult wear and have proved invaluable for manual workers, in sport, and wherever an aid must be worn under conditions of active movement. Price 7s. 6d.

BABY ALARM

An electronic device by which a child's cries, picked up by a small microphone hanging over its cot or pram are turned into a flashing light signal anywhere else in the house. Deaf parents soon learn to interpret the type of flashing produced into the kind of noise baby is making—gurgling or serious cries demanding attention. On hire at 15s. per quarter including maintenance.

HEARING AIDS

There are generally a few aids, not always of the newest or best, but very serviceable, that have been sent to our Welfare and Technical Department by users who no longer want them. These are checked over and given away to people who cannot afford to buy and who for one reason or another do not get on with the NHS instrument.

PRINTATORS

These ingenious little writing tables in which no pen or pencil is required are made in a special form for the RNID. Space is provided on the back for name and address of self, a friend, doctor, etc., and the message "I am rather deaf". The front can be written on with anything—even a pointed finger-nail, and the writing disappears as soon as the slide is withdrawn. Price 2s. 6d. including postage.

KAN-U-GO

This popular cross-word card game has been produced in a special printing with the letter shapes of the manual alphabet in place of the usual Roman capitals. Excellent for getting the uninitiated interested in the expert at finger-spelling. Per pack, with rule book, post free, 4s. 6d.

TELEVISION SETS

Sets are supplied to needy deaf people, free of all charge, from our Television for the Deaf Fund. Aerials and full maintenance are provided (by rental companies); rent is paid by the Institute for as long as the set is required.

SERVICES

PERSONAL HEARING AID TEST

AUDIOMETER CALIBRATION

For doctors, scientists, schools, and hospitals dealing with the deaf the pure-tone audiometer is the basic measuring instrument.

EXHIBITION MATERIAL

This material, in the form of literature, photographs and diagrams and, if warranted, technical devices such as visible door bells, audiometers, hearing aids, speech-trainers, baby alarms, flashing alarm clocks, radio and TV attachments, etc., can be supplied for civic and similar local exhibitions.

The National College of Teachers of the Deaf

The National College of Teachers of the Deaf is an incorporated body, and the only British association catering specifically for all teachers of the deaf, irrespective of the particular sphere of education in which they are employed.

Formed in 1918 as a result of the amalgamation of the College of Teachers of the Deaf and Dumb (est. 1885) and the National Association of Teachers of the Deaf (est. 1895), it assumed the functions of both bodies, and its field of activity has widened considerably in recent years to keep pace with the growth and diversity of deaf education.

The CTDD was formed to raise the teaching of the deaf to a recognized profession by granting certificates of competence following examination. Thus teachers of the deaf became the first body of teachers to gain for themselves the right to examine entrants into a branch of the teaching profession, and since 1909 a special qualification has been necessary to teach deaf children.

The NATD was founded to give teachers of the deaf opportunities for meeting and exchanging views, and to organize these teachers into a national association. Its journal was first published in 1903.

ELIGIBILITY FOR MEMBERSHIP

Full membership is available to teachers holding a diploma or certificate recognized by the Ministry of Education and the College, and who are actively associated with the education and/or training of the deaf or partially deaf.

Associate membership is limited to

(a) other teachers of the deaf (e.g. those awaiting training);
(b) those professionally interested and whose election is approved by the National Executive Committee.

Retired membership for former full members retired on superannuation.

Only full members have the right to vote in executive or branch elections, or to be eligible for election.

MANAGEMENT

Management of the College is vested in officers and an Executive Committee directly elected by all full members, together with ex-official representatives of the various branches.

There are no paid officials, all officers and members of committees being engaged full-time in the education of the deaf.

ORGANIZATION

Various sub-committees are formed to carry out the objects of the College. There are five standing committees:

The Examination Board
The Education Committee
The General Purposes Committee
The Publications Committee
The Research Committee

and various sub-committees and *ad hoc* committees are in existence from time to time, e.g.

The Policy-formulating Sub-committee
The Secondary Education Sub-committee, etc.

The Teacher of the Deaf, the official journal of the College, has been published without interruption since 1903. Six issues are published annually, and it continues to be in great demand in all parts of the world. Members of the College automatically receive copies of the journal free of charge as part of the service of the association.

ACTIVITIES OF THE COLLEGE

Recognized by the Ministry of Education as an Examining Body, the NCTD organizes the diploma examination, one of the approved additional qualifications needed to teach the deaf.

Publishes a journal. In addition to purely educational matters, minutes of Executive Committee meetings are published so that all members are kept informed of the activities of the association.

Courses are arranged to assist both experienced teachers and those studying for the diploma examination. The College also co-operates with other bodies arranging courses.

Conferences are held to encourage a free exchange of ideas.

Books for children, with special reference to the linguistic difficulties of deaf and partially deaf children, have been published as a result of the work of the Publications Committee, and further publications are in hand.

Travelling scholarships are awarded to allow practising teachers to investigate problems in the education of children with impaired hearing.

An essay competition is held at intervals for the Braidwood Medal, the highest award that is given by the College.

The College carries out surveys on particular aspects of deaf education. The following are examples of surveys undertaken in the past few years:

The education of the dually and multiply handicapped child
The needs of deaf children under the age of 5 years
The teaching of arithmetic
Provision for secondary education
Teacher training
Provision of hearing-aid equipment in schools
Classification of children with defective hearing
Units for deaf and partially hearing children.

Regular branch meetings are held. To serve teachers in all parts of the country, the College is divided into branches and each branch has its own committee. From time to time branches organize one-day or week-end conferences to which members of other branches are invited.

The College offers a personal service to individual members.

The College is officially represented on a number of other associations, e.g.

The Council of the Royal National Institute for the Deaf
The Children's Committee of the RNID
The Advisory Committee on the Training of Teachers of the Deaf, Manchester University
The National Foundation for Educational Research
The National Association for Mental Health
Council of the Commonwealth Society for the Deaf
Board of Governors of the Mary Hare Grammar School
Board of Governors of Burwood Park School
The Royal Medico-psychological Association's Working Party on the Psychiatric Needs of Deaf.

Co-operation with other bodies, e.g. The College has been asked to form a sub-committee to advise the BBC on TV programmes for the deaf, and to nominate an examiner to deal with sections of the College of Preceptors Examinations concerning the education of the deaf, and it is represented on various consultative committees connected with research topics. Various joint-committees exist, e.g. with Manchester University, the STD, the National Deaf Children's Society, and the Council of Welfare Officers to the Deaf.

The College represents the interest of teachers of the Deaf.

The College of Teachers of the Blind

Address: Royal School for the Blind, Westbury-on-Trym, Bristol.

Founded in 1907 as an association of professional workers, the College qualifications are recognized nationally and internationally as professional qualifications in a highly specialized field of work.

WHAT IS THE COLLEGE?

Membership comprised of school teachers, home teachers, and craft instructors of the blind, and administrative personnel directly employed in blind welfare. Teachers and instructors obtain membership through direct employment as teachers and through obtaining qualification by entering for college examinations, recognized by the Ministry of Education for school teachers and craft instructors, and by the Ministry of Health for home teachers.

The College is recognized as an experienced organization in work for the blind by all other organizations and local and national government. It has a membership of over 700.

The College is the recognized examining body for school, homes, and craft teachers of the blind.

PUBLICATIONS

From time to time literature concerning the teaching of the blind is published.

The College also issues its own magazine, *The Teacher of the Blind*.

The Deaf–Blind and Rubella Children's Association

Formerly Rubella Group for Deaf/Blind Children.

Registered in accordance with National Assistance Act, 1948.

Address: 63 Horn Lane, Woodford Green, Essex.

Begun in 1955 by a few parents of children with a combined sight and hearing handicap caused by maternal rubella (German measles) under the title Rubella Group. In May 1963 the title was changed as above and membership included some deaf–blind children from a cause other than maternal rubella. The membership in the present year is about 85 children and an equal number of professional people concerned with their welfare and education.

AIMS

1. To help parents with their deaf–blind children by sharing the difficulties and passing on helpful information based on the practical experiences of the members of the Association.
2. To press for more special educational treatment for these children.
3. As rubella is the known cause for the dual handicap in so many of the member children, to make available any information from our records that might be of assistance to research on rubella.

SERVICES

The financing of a study tour in Europe and the USA for teachers intending to work with deaf–blind children. The raising of funds for a pre-school residential training centre where children and parents can be helped and facilities can be made available for research. Organization of 5-year conference.

PUBLICATIONS

Four monthly *News-letter* to which is attached a brief report on the progress of each child. Kept over the past 10 years these progress reports now provide a unique record of the development and problems of deaf–blind children and the first 35 issues are now being published as a complete volume (price expected to be about £3).

Pamphlets for parents and professional workers, a report on the Conference held January 1961. 3s. 6d.

FILMS

Communication Limited. Shows our children at home, at play, at school, and after school days are done. 16 mm. Sound, optical colour, running for 20 minutes with a commentary by Mr. Peter Haig. Two more films are at present being made.

The Association for the Education and Welfare of the Partially Sighted

Address: George Auden School, Bell Hill, Northfield, Birmingham, 31.

This Association was founded in 1948 when the terms of the 1944 Education Act were beginning to be implemented—the blind and the partially sighted being separately educated. Since that time those in any way interested in the problems of the partially sighted have formed the basis of membership. A periodical *News-letter* keeps the members informed, whilst regional meetings allow for regular discussion of problems.

CHAPTER 19

The Socially Handicapped

Family Service Units

Address: 207 Marylebone Road, London, NW 1.

Family Service Units is a voluntary organization, formed in 1947 to continue and extend a family case-work service pioneered in Liverpool and Manchester during the war and described in *Problem Families*. The existing units in Liverpool and Manchester became the first Family Service Units and a new unit was established in Kensington and Paddington in 1948. Further units were established in Sheffield (1950), York (1950), Birmingham (1951), Leicester (1952), Bradford (1953), Bristol (1953), Islington (1953), Stepney (1954), Oldham (1958), South London (1958), Leeds (1960), and Glasgow (1965).

There have been numerous requests from local authorities and other interested bodies for the establishment of units in other parts of the country, but expansion has been restricted both by the shortage of money and the difficulty of obtaining suitable personnel.

THE FAMILIES

In almost all these families, the parents are handicapped by physical and mental disabilities, by poor intelligence or by emotional problems, arising from their own early life and family experiences. These personal disabilities are often aggravated by pressures of low income, poor housing, and the demands of several young children. Gradually everything gets on top of them; some may become depressed, apparently apathetic and resigned to failure; others try to hide their unhappiness in hostility or a "couldn't-care-less" attitude. Their difficulties become visible as school and work failure, debts and financial mismanagement, neglected homes and poorly cared for children, ill health, marital strife, and strained relationships within the family and with people outside. Such families are referred to FSU by workers in other services—by NAB or housing officials, probation officers, hospital almoners, health visitors, or general practitioners, etc., who have known them in the course of their own work and think that they would benefit from the special help given by FSU.

THE SERVICE

The FSU worker is concerned with the family's situation as a whole. Gradually she helps the parents to overcome their many difficulties and so give the children a chance of growing up in a happier home. In order to help them she must get to know the family members intimately; she must understand how they see their problems and how they appear to other people. The worker must be someone to whom they can talk frankly and easily, someone in whom they can have complete confidence. As this relationship develops, the family come to trust the worker and respond to her sympathy and concern for them. They become less hopeless and isolated, and so the worker can begin to sort out their difficulties. She discusses with them which problems can be tackled first and how best to do this, bearing in mind previous attempts, past failures, and the hopes and weaknesses within the family.

Most of the contact with the families is in their own homes, and the help given varies with the problem. Material aid (furniture, clothing, etc.) is frequently required, and the worker will obtain this for the family either from unit resources or from other agencies. Sometimes, she helps in a very practical way; thus she may baby-sit whilst the mother takes an older child to an outpatient clinic; she may help a father to carry out a household repair or decorate the house; she may accompany a frightened mother to hospital for medical attention; or a backward lad in his search for work. She may meet a father after work to ensure that the rent is paid when the money is available. She may arrange outings and holidays for the children, many of whom she may be helping individually with their own troubles of delinquency, non-school attendance, or disturbed behaviour.

Each family requires a great deal of attention, especially at first, and the worker must be able to give the time needed; hence each worker can help only a small number of families—usually ten to fifteen—at a long period, for though some families achieve improvement quickly and maintain it, there are others who have to be supported until the children grow up.

A very important aspect of the work is the establishment of good co-operation between all the social services concerned with the family. The FSU worker has to know and understand the role of the workers in the education, health, children's and other social services, statutory and voluntary, and work with them for the whole well-being of the family.

THE UNIT

FSU employs both men and women. There are at present about ninety case-workers, working in fourteen units in the large cities of England and in four areas of London. Although professional social work training is desirable, FSU personnel selection depends on the applicant's personal qualities and approach to the work rather than formal qualifications. Initiative and adaptability are needed to meet the changing needs of families. The worker must not easily be discouraged and must possess qualities of maturity, understanding, and resourcefulness if she is to be helpful to the families. Each worker joining FSU is given a period of training and orientation, usually lasting about 6 months. Each trained case-worker is responsible for work with a number of families under the general supervision of the Fieldwork Organizer or Unit Leader.

The unit operates from a centre conveniently placed in the locality it serves. The unit centre is usually an ordinary house to which parents and teenagers may come for talks with their worker and where children's play groups and activities can take place. It sometimes provides accommodation for the workers.

Each unit has a local committee responsible for the maintenance and development of the individual unit. The National Committee of FSU has responsibility for matters affecting all units, including the recruitment of personnel.

FSU was begun by donations from interested individuals, but it now receives substantial grants from the local authorities with whom it works. The Glasgow Unit receives the financial support of the City Corporation. In recent years the statutory social services have been increasingly concerned to help these families, and several local authorities have developed special family care services. The Children and Young Persons Act, 1963, gives local authorities a definite responsibility to provide help to prevent family break-up. FSUs experience and example, made known in publications and study conferences, has done much to influence such developments.

National Society for the Prevention of Cruelty to Children

The National Society for the Prevention of Cruelty to Children was founded in London in 1884 and was the pioneer in this country of welfare work amongst children in their own homes. The movement rapidly spread, and in a comparatively short time similar organizations were set up in most of the major cities in the country. The Society now covers the whole of England, Wales, and Northern Ireland.

AIMS

The Society's primary concern is the welfare of children, but since a child can only be helped in the context of the family, it has become increasingly concerned with family problems. It specializes in working on the problems and breakdowns in family life that lead to neglect and cruelty towards children—either physical, mental, or emotional.

The parents with whom the Society deals consist mainly of those who have failed to respond to other agencies or who have continually refused assistance and the welfare of whose children is endangered. It is these parents who often feel neglected and ostracized themselves by the rest of the community. Firmness often gives a form of security, since they are immature. Methods used, therefore, cannot always be entirely permissive. The Society's work could perhaps be described as case-work combined where necessary with the positive use of authority.

SERVICES

The Society employs about 275 inspectors and 45 women case-workers, who are known as Women Visitors. Each year they deal with something over 40,000 cases involving the welfare of 100,000 children. The cases are brought to notice by teachers, the police, welfare services, and ordinary citizens.

By far the largest number of cases are those represented by neglect, in fact approximately 60 per cent, and this is the sphere of activity which occupies much of the time and concern of the Society. The number of cases of physical cruelty is gradually decreasing but still amounts to approximately 10 per cent, and in about 25 per cent of the cases the parents come to the Society for help or advice.

The Society's officers live within their districts and are available at all hours of the day or night. Their addresses and telephone numbers are shown in the local telephone directories under the heading NSPCC.

THE NSPCC AND THE COURTS

Unfortunately there will always be a small number of cases for which there is no other course open than to institute legal proceedings in the child's interest. This is not a purely negative course since through court action facilities are often made available to help both parents and children which the immature parent probably would not have accepted for himself. Statistically only 1 per cent of the cases involve prosecution and a further 1 per cent juvenile court proceedings.

CO-OPERATION WITH LOCAL AUTHORITIES

The Society has always worked closely with the local authorities who value its services and a number of which contribute generously to its funds. The new powers which the Children and Young Persons Act, 1963, conferred on local authorities are greatly welcomed but do not remove the needs for the Society.

In the interests of the welfare of a child, the closest co-operation between different sources and types of help is essential. The NSPCC works closely with all the statutory and other voluntary bodies who operate in the same field. In many districts all the case-workers who might be involved have regular meetings so that each child and family can be given the type of help most suited to its needs.

PUBLICATIONS

A book on the Society's history and work was published in 1961 It was written by the Reverend Arthur Morton (Director of the Society) and Mrs. Anne Allen and is published by Routledge & Kegan Paul Ltd. It has since been reprinted in a paper-back edition.

Pamphlets on the Society's work can be obtained from the Society's Headquarters at 1 Riding House St., London, W 1.

TRAINING, LECTURES AND FILMS

The Society runs its own training school, and inspectors and women visitors undergo a 12-month social work course before taking up their duties in the field. Qualified case-work supervisors are appointed in all parts of the country to help and support inspectors and women visitors in their work. The training tutors and case-work supervisors are available to give talks on the Society's work at colleges and universities where social work courses are being held. Films illustrating the Society's work are also available.

National Association for Maternal and Child Welfare

Address: Tavistock House North, Tavistock Square, London, WC 1.

Patron: Her Majesty the Queen.

The infant welfare movement, which began at the end of the nineteenth century, sprang chiefly from growing public concern at the continuance of a high infant mortality; in 1899 the deaths of children under 1 year per 1000 births had reached the appallingly high figure of 163.

Work designed to protect infant life was already going on in France, where maternity and child welfare centres had been set up, and the French advances in child welfare attracted the attention of the Medical Officer of Health for St. Helens, Dr. F. Drew Harris, on whose advice the St. Helens Corporation in 1899 opened a similar institution; the first London centre, at Battersea, was opened in 1902.

In 1905 an international congress on infant welfare, the first of its kind, was held in Paris, and resulting from this the corporations of Huddersfield and Glasgow convened a British national conference on infant mortality in the following year. Shortly after this conference, which was held in London on 13–14 June, 1906, associations formed to promote infant welfare sprang up all over the country.

By 1911 there were approximately 100 infant welfare centres at work in the United Kingdom with others in the process of formation. To assist those wishing to start new centres and set a standard of efficient work, the Association of Infant Welfare and Maternity Centres was formed in 1911. Early in 1912 the question of forming a central permanent body, to co-ordinate the activities of the several national organizations working in the same field, was considered, and the National Association for the Prevention of Infant Mortality and for the Welfare of Infancy came into being in July of that year. This organization was amalgamated in 1938 with the Association of Infant Welfare and Maternity Centres to form the National Association of Maternity and Child Welfare Centres and for the Prevention of Infant Mortality. This name was later changed to the National Association for Maternal and Child Welfare.

AIMS AND OBJECTS

The primary objects of the Association are the furtherance of education in matters connected with maternal and child welfare and the promotion of such other charitable purposes as may be beneficial to the community.

Ancillary objects include:

(a) the study and prevention of morbidity and mortality and the promotion of good health among expectant and nursing mothers and young children;

(b) the publication and distribution of books, journals, and pamphlets promoting a sound knowledge of maternity and child welfare including the collection and publication of statistics and reports;

(c) the organization of conferences and meetings, local, national, or international;

(d) acting as a consultative body in connection with maternal and child welfare.

MEMBERSHIP OF THE ASSOCIATION

Membership of the Association is open to the following classes:

CLASS A

1. Local health, education, and children's authorities, together with such other local authorities as may exercise full delegate powers in these fields in the United Kingdom.
2. Hospital management committees.
3. Teaching hospital groups.
4. University departments of child health.

CLASS B

Any organization of national standing concerned with the welfare of mothers and children.

CLASS C

Any local organization (not being a branch of a national society) concerned with the welfare of mothers and children, and any individual maternal or child welfare centre or any federation or association of such centres, or any association of voluntary workers concerned with the welfare of mothers and children. Each body in Class C applying for membership must be proposed and seconded by members of the Council or furnish such information as the Executive Committee may require.

CLASS D

Individual members interested in the objects of the Association who are proposed and seconded by members of the Council or otherwise approved by the Council.

PUBLICATIONS

BOOKS AND BOOKLETS

To Mothers and Fathers. A comprehensive guide for all parents with advice to the expectant mother, advice on the care of infants and young children; with chapters on diet and clothing. 30th edition (revised). 1s. 10s. a dozen. £3 a 100. £28 a 1000. Postage and packing on single copy, 6d.

The Mother's Cookery Book. Notes on utensils, care of food, preparation and methods of serving, oven temperatures, etc., with over 200 recipes for suitable dishes, jams, drinks, etc., for children up to 5 years, with a special section for the sick child. 2s. 6d. £9 a 100. Postage and packing on single copy, 9d.

The Care of Babies and Young Children in the Tropics, by JOHN GIBBENS. Useful advice to those about to travel with young children. 1s. 6d. Postage and packing, 6d.

The Young Student's Book of Child Care, by LEONORA PITCAIRN. A textbook for schools and youth groups. With illustrations. 9s. 6d. net. Postage and packing, 1s.

A Guide for the Teaching of Child Care to Young Students by LEONORA PITCAIRN. 1s. 6d. Postage and packing, 6d.

Modern Baby Sitting, by LEONORA PITCAIRN. A short handbook. 3s. 6d. Postage and packing, 9d.

Quarterly Survey on Maternal and Child Welfare. Deals with vital statistics, reports, etc.; maternity and midwifery services; child care; education; books, films, etc.; and forthcoming events. 3s. Annual subscription 10s. 6d. Post free.

LEAFLETS AND CASE PAPERS

To Expectant Parents. 6d. each; 5s. a doz. £1 10s. a 100; £12 a 1000.

A Guide to Baby's Layette. 6d. each; 5s. a doz; 30s. a 100; £12 a 1000.

Breast Feeding. 6d. each; 5s. a doz.; £1 10s. a 100; £12 a 1000.

Feeding Charts for Children from Four Months to Five Years. 3d. each; 10s. a 100; £3 15s. a 1000.

Neo-natal Cold Injury. 9d. each; 7s. 6d. a doz.; £2 10s. a 100; £21 a 1000.

Cold Injury in the New Born. Practical advice for parents. 6d. each; 5s. a doz.; £1 10s. a 100; £12 a 1000.

Infant's Weight Card. 4s. a 100; 32s. a 1000.

Home Visiting Record Form. 4 pages on stiff cartridge paper. £20 a 1000 (no discount allowed).

Poliomyelitis Record Card. £4 5s. a 1000.

OTHER PUBLICATIONS STOCKED (no discount allowed)

Advice to the Expectant Mother on the Care of her Health, by PROFESSOR F. J. BROWNE. 1s. 3d. Postage and packing, 3d.

Relaxation and Exercise for Natural Childbirth, by HELEN HEARDMAN. 1s. Postage and packing, 3d.

Exercises during Pregnancy and the Puerperium. 3d. Postage and packing, 3d.

Childbirth, by W. C. NIXON. 2s. 6d. Postage and packing, 9d.

Fearless Childbirth, by M. RANDELL. 3s. 6d. Postage and packing, 9d.

Childbirth without Fear, by GRANTLY DICK READ. 15s. Postage and packing, 1s.

Introduction to Motherhood, by GRANTLY DICK READ. 7s. 6d. Postage and packing, 1s.

Good Housekeeping Baby Book. 15s. Postage and packing, 1s.

The Care of Young Babies, by JOHN GIBBENS. 6s. 6d. Postage and packing, 1s.

The Care of Children from One to Five, by JOHN GIBBENS. 6s. 6d. Postage and packing, 1s.

The Physical Health of Children, by AUDREY KELLY. 3s. 6d. Postage and packing, 9d.

Advances in Understanding the Child. 3s. 6d. Postage and packing, 6d.

Infant Feeding, by PROFESSOR ALAN MONCRIEFF. 2s. Postage and packing, 6d.

Habit Training, by RUTH THOMAS. 1s. 3d. Postage and packing, 6d.

Temper Tantrums, by RUTH THOMAS. 1s. 3d. Postage and packing, 6d.

The Nursery Years, by MRS. SUSAN ISAACS. Simple psychology. 3s. Postage and packing, 9d.

Opening Doors, by JOHN THOMPSON. Help with backward children. 6d. Postage and packing, 3d.

Hints to Mothers Travelling by Land, Sea and Air, by HON. MRS. B. R. JAMES. 1s. Postage and packing, 3d.

Play with a Purpose. Suggestions for toys and indoor and outdoor play. 2s. 6d. Postage and packing, 6d.

How a Baby is Born, by K. DE SCHWEINTZ. A book for children. 4s. Postage and packing, 9d.

What Shall I Tell my Child? 1s. Postage and packing, 3d.

The Approach to Womanhood. For adolescent girls. 1s. Postage and packing, 3d.

He and She, by KENNETH C. BARNES. 3s. 6d. Postage and packing, 9d.

15-plus Facts of Life, by KENNETH BARNES. 1s. Postage and packing, 3d.

You, too, can talk in Public. Health Visitors' Association. 2s. 6d. Postage and packing, 6d.

ABC of Cookery, published by the Ministry of Food. 5s. Postage and packing, 6d.

Good Housekeeping's 100 Fish Recipes. 2s. Postage and packing, 6d.

Good Housekeeping's 100 Cheese Recipes. 2s. Postage and packing, 6d.

The Nursery School Association of Great Britain and Northern Ireland

Address: 89 Stamford St., London, SE 1.

The Nursery School Association of Great Britain and Northern Ireland was founded in 1923 on the initiative of Miss Grace Owen under the presidency of Miss Margaret McMillan to study the needs of young children and to determine the forms of care and education that would ensure them the greatest happiness and the fullest growth of body and mind in our changing world.

The Association became an Incorporated Body in 1945.

The Association believes that the rich and harmonious development of young children can best be achieved against the background of home life, and so it seeks close and sympathetic co-operation between home and school.

It works to ensure that high standards are maintained in the staffing, building, and organization of nursery schools, nursery classes, and infant schools.

The 1944 Education Act requires local education authorities to have regard to "The need for securing that provision is made for pupils who have not attained the age of five years by the provision of nursery schools, or, where the authorities consider the provision of such schools to be inexpedient, by the provision of nursery classes in other schools".

The Association encourages local authorities to provide for nursery education and makes its contribution in the field of nursery and infant education by means of conferences, schools, and publications. A summer school is held each year and an international one alternate years. Evening lectures are arranged in London from time to time. Membership is open to all.

A quarterly *News-letter*, issued free to members, gives current news of Association activities and information of importance in the educational world, together with book reviews.

The Carnegie Library contains about 4500 volumes on child psychology, education, methods in research, children's art, music, and literature, and a collection of children's books from many countries; members can use it whilst in London.

The headquarters are open from 10 a.m. to 5 p.m. Mondays to Fridays, and visitors from home and overseas who are interested in the Association's work are welcomed. Information and advice may be obtained on a wide variety of subjects. Literature and pamphlets are on sale.

HANDICAPPED INFANTS

A recent extension to the Association's work has been to consider the whole problem of the young handicapped child in the nursery school and nursery class. Its Medical Advisory Committee is in the process of collecting information on pioneering work, for consideration which, it is hoped, will enable the Association to determine the types of handicapped children likely to benefit from nursery school education and the proportion of such children a normal nursery school can be expected to absorb.

PUBLICATIONS

The Educational Value of the Nursery School, by SUSAN ISAACS. 2s. 6d. NSA. Free leaflets.

Our Responsibility to Children, by GWEN E. CHESTERS. 1s.

Wheels for Toys. NSA. 8d.

Repairing Toys. NSA. 8d.

Improvised Toys for Nurseries. NSA. 8d.

Days without Toys, by GWEN E. CHESTERS. 9d.

Education up to Seven-plus, by LILIAN DE LISSA. 9d.

Health and the Nursery School. New edition. NSA. Medical Advisory Committee. 1s. 3d.

The Nursery School in Action. New and revised edition. 1s.

Feeding Young Children. New edition. NSA Medical Advisory Committee. 1s. 3d.

Nursery Schools Today. NSA Building Advisory Committee. 2s. 6d.

Nursery Classes in Primary Schools. NSA Building Advisory Committee. 3s. 6d.

Making Musical Apparatus and Instruments, by KATHLEEN BLOCKSIDE. 3s.

The New Nursery School. NSA Building Advisory Committee. 1962. 5s.

Starting a Community Nursery School, by A. CALVELEY. 1962. 2s. 6d.

How to use Melodic Percussion Instruments, by KATHLEEN BLOCKSIDGE. 1962. 3s. 6d.

Part-time Nursery Education, by G. M. GOLDSWORTHY. 1963. 2s. 6d.

Nursery and Playgroup Facilities for Young Children. NSA. 1964. 2s.

The Enrichment of Childhood, by W. D. WALL and ANNA FREUD. 2s. 6d.

The Under Fives in the Welfare State, by JOAN E. CASS. 1964. 2s. 6d.

Picture Books for Young Children, by JOAN E. CASS. 1964. 2s.

New Thoughts on Infant School Playgrounds. NSA Building Advisory Committee. 1964. 6s.

COLOURED FILMSTRIPS

A Day in a Nursery School.

Gaining Experience Through Play. I. Through nature discovery and building.

Gaining Experience Through Play. II. Imaginative and domestic play.

Play in the Infants' School. III. Stimulating play situations.

Play in the Infants' School. IV. Developing and practising skills.

Play—Learning to Live Together. V.

Each filmstrip is in colour. Purchase price, including descriptive notes: £2 12s. 6d. per strip. Review copies: 2s. 6d. each per week.

PHOTOGRAPHS

SETS

1–3 (24 photographs). Hiring fee for each set (24 photographs) 7s. 6d. including postage outwards.

LISTS

General Reading List. 6d.

Some Suppliers of Nursery Equipment. 4d.

Picture, Story and Poetry Books for Young Children. 6d.

Gramophone Records enjoyed by Children. 4d.

Suggestions for Music for Nursery and Infant Schools. 4d.

Books on Puppetry and Toy Making. 4d.

Books on the Subject of Reading, Teaching, Numbers and Arithmetic. 6d.

Information on Training for Nursery School Teaching. 6d.

Suggested Play Materials, by JOAN CASS. 6d.

Take Steps to Help Your Child.

1. *Starting School.* 4d.
2. *Play is the Best Homework.* 4d.
3. *Brighten their Prospects.* 4d.

ABOUT CHILDREN

Your Child's Outdoor Play. 3d.

Walks and Talks for the Town Child. 3d.

Indoor Play on a Rainy Day. 3d.

The Child in Bed. 3d.

Is Your Child Obedient. 3d.

Picnics and Journeys. 3d.

Children's Questions. 3d.

Father and the Family. 3d.

Mealtimes. 3d.

PARENTS' NEWS SHEETS—AUSTRALIAN LEAFLETS. 5d. each.

Latest editions of these informative 5d. newsheets are received from Australia. Recent titles include:

Ages and Stages—the 4–5 Year Old. No. 50.

The Child who Wont Eat. No. 80.

The Child who Steals. No. 132.

Ready for School. No. 141.

Being One's Age 2–5 Years. No. 148.

What does the Pre-school Teacher Teach? No. 151.

Freedom to Decide. No. 152.

Quiet Indoor Play. No. 157.

The Value of Make Believe. No. 158.

OTHER PUBLICATIONS

The Developmental Progress of Infants and Young Children, by MARY D. SHERIDAN. 1*s*. 9*d*.

Some Books about Children (Autobiographies and Novels) (List I & List II), selected by JOAN CASS. 1*s*. each.

Play with a Purpose. Ministry of Health. 2*s*. 6*d*.

Education under Eight, by D. E. M. GARDNER. 2*s*.

Disturbed Sleep in Infancy, by FLORA SHEPHERD. 2*s*. 6*d*.

Mathematics in the Primary School. National Froebel Foundation. 2*s*.

Some Aspects of Piaget's Work. National Froebel Foundation. 3*s*. 6*d*.

Scientific Interests in the Primary School. National Froebel Foundation. 2*s*. 6*d*.

Activity and Experience in the Infant School. National Froebel Foundation. 2*s*.

Some Play Materials for Children under Eight, by HELEN STONE. 1*s*. 6*d*.

Not Yet Five, by Ministry of Education and Ministry of Health. 1*s*.

New Playgrounds, by LADY ALLEN OF HURTWOOD. 7*s*. 6*d*.

Play Parks, 3rd impression, by LADY ALLEN OF HURTWOOD. 3*s*. 6*d*.

Design for Play, by LADY ALLEN OF HURTWOOD. 3*s*. 6*d*.

Two to Five in High Flats, by LADY ALLEN OF HURTWOOD. 2*s*. 6*d*.

CONCERNING CHILDREN SERIES

The First Two Years, No. 3, by DR. SUSAN ISAACS. 1*s*. 3*d*.

Play in the Infant School, No. 10, by E. R. BOYCE. 6*d*.

NEW EDUCATION FELLOWSHIP

Important Facts for all who deal with Children. 3*d*.

Advances in Understanding the Child. 3*s*. 6*d*.

Advances in Understanding the Adolescent. 4*s*.

CHAPTER 20

Other Relevant Bodies

The British Psychological Society

Address: Tavistock House South, Tavistock Square, London, WC 1.

The British Psychological Society (founded in 1901) has differentiated into four major sections, Medical, Educational, Social, and Occupational. It brings together those working in basic and applied psychology, ensuring that universities and practitioners are not divorced from each other.

Soon after the First World War it participated in the inquiry into mental testing. Its concern for the handicapped child was reflected in the setting up of a Standing Committee on the psychology of the handicapped shortly after the Second World War.

In 1962 its English Division of Professional Psychologists set up a working party to consider certain aspects of the 1959 Mental Health Act in relation to mental subnormality. The findings of this working party were published in a significant pamphlet *Children in Hospitals for the Subnormal*.

The Association was incorporated by Royal Charter in 1965. It has seven branches in the United Kingdom and an Overseas Branch in New Zealand. It publishes five journals:

> *The British Journal of Psychology.*
> *The British Journal of Medical Psychology.*
> *The British Journal of Educational Psychology* (published in conjunction with the Association of Teachers in Colleges and Departments of Education).
> *The British Journal of Mathematical and Statistical Psychology.*
> *The British Journal of Social and Clinical Psychology.*

Association of Educational Psychologists

Address: 51 Marlborough Park Avenue, Sidcup, Kent.

The Association of Educational Psychologists was formed originally in 1961 as a professional organization for psychologists working for local authorities in England, Wales, and Northern Ireland. It is affiliated to the National Union of Teachers and the Ulster Teachers' Union. The current membership is 221.

The initial aim of the Association was to deal with matters such as salaries, conditions of service, and so on. More widely, our interests lie in the application of psychological techniques and methods to education in general. Naturally, we are particularly interested in the school psychological service and in the education of handicapped and backward children; but we feel that there are many other educational issues towards which psychologists can make a contribution.

The Association publishes a *Bulletin* three times a year, and holds an annual conference to which representatives of all fields of education are invited.

The main services the Association provides are naturally the professional services of its members, who are always available for consultation in the areas in which they work. The Association, however, is always glad to give information and advice or to pass on problems to those best able to help.

The Advisory Centre for Education (ACE)

Address: 57 Russell St., Cambridge.

Publishers of *Where?* Annual subscription £1. ACE was founded in 1960 by Dr. Michael Young who also started *Which?* and the Institute of Community Studies. Its main aim was to give information to parents about schools. In 1962 it moved to Cambridge, and Brian Jackson (author of *Education and the Working Class, Streaming*, etc.) became Director. In addition to publishing *Where?* quarterly and two special Supplements each year, ACE set up the

National Extension College combining correspondence courses with radio and television, and also runs the Technical College Clearing House. ACE aims to spread information about education and to help parents and teachers understand each other better. By making people better informed it hopes to improve the quality of education for all children.

Where? has printed many reports on special education and articles designed to help parents whose children have special problems. These include: School Phobia, Physically Handicapped Children at School, Left-handed Children, Reading Made Easier, Rudolf Steiner Schools, Music for the Handicapped Child, Intelligence Tests, and many others. It also prints reports based on original educational research.

For an additional fee members may use the Advisory Service, which, with the confidential help of a panel of experts (university and school teachers, education officers, psychologists, and doctors) answers individual questions by private letter. This includes a parent-to-parent scheme which enables members of ACE to share information about school.

ACE publications include supplements on *Colleges of Education, Starting a New Subject at University, A Second Chance* (for those who dropped out of education early), *Streaming, the Excitement of Writing Opportunities after O-Level, Grants for Higher Education.* A full list of these may be obtained from 57 Russell Street on request.

Central Film Library of the Central Office of Information

Address: Government Buildings, Bromyard Avenue, Acton, London, W 3.

The Central Film Library holds over 2000 documentary and short films on a wide variety of subjects, both general and specialized, ranging from arts to industry.

A hire charge is made for most films. A number of films are, however, available free of charge, by courtesy of the sponsors.

A selection of filmstrips is on sale, on many different subjects, including industrial.

The Library publishes two catalogues: (1) a main catalogue at 5s. post free; (2) a special catalogue of *Films for Industry* at 4s. post free. The catalogues give full details, including the basic rate for each film. The great majority of films are with sound.

Bookings must be made not less than 2 weeks in advance of the showing date. Longer notice should be given wherever possible.

The Library does not lend films for showing in ordinary programmes at public cinemas; nor for television transmission, in whole or in part; nor to other film libraries for reloan to outside borrowers; nor for showing at political meetings for the general public.

FILMS

Phenylketonuria. MS 58. 25 minutes. Colour. Primarily for health visitors and general and mental subnormality nurses. Diagrams set out the hereditary nature of phenylketonuria, particulars of the intelligence quotients of treated and untreated sufferers, and the progressive stages of the disease. Details are given of dietetic treatment.

Health Services in Britain. UK 1865. 14 minutes. A GP describes the workings of the National Health Service through the various ways in which it has benefited a family on his list of patients. The film reviews the comprehensive care provided by family doctors, dentists, hospitals, and the local health services for mothers and babies, children, adults, old people, and the mentally sick, covering all forms of treatment— medical, surgical, dental, ophthalmic, pharmaceutical, psychiatric, geriatric, and rehabilitation.

SOCIAL FACTORS, DELINQUENCY, ETC.

Children of the City. UK 549. 32 minutes. A study of juvenile delinquency in Scotland; based on the case history of a gang of three boys who break into a pawnshop. After examining the background of each boy's life, the juvenile court sends one, a 10-year-old, to a child guidance clinic; of the other two, both about 13 years old, one is placed on probation and the other sent to an approved school. The procedure of the juvenile court is given in detail, and the methods of treatment of each boy are outlined. The film argues that much might be achieved if children living in cities were given ample and varied outlets for their energy in good playing fields and clubs.

Children on Trial. UK 776. 61 minutes. Dramatization of the problem of child delinquency in Britain. Three adolescents—a slum boy from a bad home, a boy from a comfortable middle-class home, and a slum girl who is out of her mother' control—are brought before a juvenile court for breaking the law, and sent to Home Office approved schools. The centre of the film is the career of the boy from the slum; and the climax is his return to the outside world after conversion by patience and correct handling from one of the society' liabilities to one of its potential assets.

Friend of the Family. UK 2508. 18 minutes. A school teache investigates the home background of two little girls who seem cowed and badly neglected. Shocked by the squalor of the home and by the brutal behaviour of a relative who ha taken the place of the absent father, she calls an inspecto from the National Society for the Prevention of Cruelty t Children. As a result, the parents are reunited, the hom improved, and the children cared for.

A Sense of Belonging. UK 1703. 20 minutes. The work of loca authority children's departments, including the vital role c foster parents, as seen in the story of a young boy and gi from a broken home.

Caring for Children. UK 1161. 13 minutes. One of a series er titled "Is this the Job for me?"

Probation Officer. UK 1133. A film to attract recruits and to te something about the probation system.

MENTAL DEFICIENCY AND DISORDER

The Troubled Mind. UK 1365. 22 minutes. The story of a young nurse who decides to take up mental nursing. The everyday life of patients and staff in a large mental hospital.

Activity Group Therapy. MSU 214. 54 minutes. The personality developments of a group of emotionally disturbed boys are shown through a series of treatment sessions.

"Mental Symptoms Series." MSC 101–109. These nine films demonstrate manifestations of various mental disorders (*Schizophrenia*, 1, 2, and 3; *Paranoid Conditions*, 4; *Senile*, 5; *Depressive States*, 6 and 7; *Manic State*, 8; *Folie a Deux*, 9).

Occupational and Recreational Therapy. MSU 206. 13 minutes. For physiotherapists.

Teaching Crutch Walking. MSU 207. For physiotherapists and student nurses.

A Positive Approach to the Psychiatric Patient. MSU 215. 29 minutes. A treatment study. Suitable for all concerned with psychiatric treatment.

The Feeling of Hostility. C 265. 32 minutes. A case history.

There was a Door. UK 1559. 28 minutes. How mental defectives who might otherwise spend their lives in institutions can live and work happily in the community, if proper facilities exist.

Learning Slow Motion. UK 1668. 29 minutes. A record of research into the problems of learning in the mentally subnormal. How subnormal adults can be trained to perform simple repetitive work in factories, and their placing in jobs, and how even the severely subnormal may learn to perform similar tasks at a slower pace.

Children Learning by Experience. UK 873. 32 minutes. Designed primarily for teachers in training, this is a study of children as they go about absorbed in their own affairs, learning in their own way.

Children Growing up with Other People. UK 874. 23 minutes. As with film above, intended primarily for teachers in training. Shows problems of particular age groups in relation to a continuous process of development. Deals with the early years, learning to be independent, learning to co-operate, adolescence.

THE PHYSICALLY HANDICAPPED

The Trefoil School (Undaunted). UK 1325. 21 minutes. Daily routine at the Trefoil School for physically handicapped Scouts and Guides.

Triumph Over Deafness. UK 788. 20 minutes. Advances in giving aid to the deaf. How adults are helped at the Deaf Clinic at Manchester University, and the treatment of deaf children in special schools.

The Chance of their Lives. UK 1359. 21 minutes. The difficulties faced by spastics and the work being done to help them. A special school for spastics.

We Learn to Read. UK 1744. 34 minutes. The programmed reading kit devised by Dr. D. H. Stott. The film shows how the material is used in various games, and indicates its intrinsic features of self-correction, competition, and group co operation.

From the USA: Some Relevant Films

THE EXCEPTIONAL CHILD

PURCHASE AND RENTAL INFORMATION

Prints of "The Exceptional Child" series may be purchased from the Net Film Service of the Audio-Visual Center, Indiana University, Bloomington, Indiana, 47405. Distribution in England for the NET Film Service are Gateway Educational Films Ltd. 470 Green Lanes, Palmers Green, London, N 13.

FILMS ON THE EXCEPTIONAL CHILD

This series was produced in the USA Syracuse University with the combined resources of its Radio and Television Center and its clinical and special education staff. Dramas, using children with actual problems, documentary footage, and interviews with persons experienced in handling each special problem blend to produce an interesting and informative series.

THE EXCEPTIONAL CHILD—series description

Programme I. Introductory—Individual Differences. This programme establishes the frame of reference for the programmes that follow, pointing out the individual differences of children in physical, mental, and emotional growth and development. The special and dynamic problems of the exceptional child are described and illustrated.

Programme II. The Gifted Child. Gifted children need help in directing their superior abilities toward meaningful and satisfying outlets. Also needed are proper attitudes on the part of grown-ups to help these children attain proper perspective and development. A dramatization illustrates this point and films show a day in the life of a well-adjusted child.

Programme III. Mentally Handicapped—Educable. The mentally handicapped child often lives in a confused and unrewarding world. His mental limitations make it difficult for him to cope with common situations. A prominent worker for 20 years with mentally handicapped children explains the problems of these children and the need for a society that will accept them and recognize the contributions which they can make.

Programme IV. Mentally Retarded—Trainable. Severely mentally retarded children need specialized attention to find some degree of meaning and satisfaction in life. This programme features a dramatization which illustrates the relationships of these children to their family and neighbours, then subsequently discusses the goal of training these children to live a reasonably happy life within their extremely limited capabilities.

Programme V. The Visually Handicapped Child: The Partially Sighted. The child with defective vision may appear slow and inadequate even though his mental ability is normal. The many degrees of partial sightedness and the implications of each are shown. Partially sighted children are seen in their everyday relationships with home, school, and community.

Programme VI. The Visually Handicapped Child: The Blind. The blind child lives in an environment which is difficult for those with sight to comprehend. He needs special care and understanding to develop and participate in the relationships of life. This programme explains the problems of blindness and shows how these children can be aided in living more meaningful lives.

Programme VII. The Auditorially Handicapped Child: The Deaf. The world of sound is often taken for granted. Children who are deaf face a difficult problem of adjustment because of lack of the security and stimulation which the normal sounds of life provide. That deaf children, however, can become communicating members of society is well illustrated in interviews with deaf children.

Programme VIII. The Crippled Child. "I *will* walk by myself." This is the hope of all crippled children; the film shows how satisfactory relationships in life may be achieved despite this handicap. As it points out, "A crippled leg or arm does not mean a crippled life".

Programme IX. The Cerebral Palsied Child. Cerebral palsy is one of the most complex conditions with which mankind is confronted. Psychologists, physicians, special therapists, social workers, and teachers must form a co-operative team with parents. A dramatization points out this need and shows what can be done to aid these children in finding happiness.

Programme X. Chronic Disorders. The child with a chronic disorder such as haemophilia needs special care, often away from his home and family. This programme explains the various types of chronic disorders and the attention which must be constantly given to help afflicted children adjust satisfactorily. Films illustrate the problems of these children.

Programme XI. The Epileptic Child. Most of us think of epilepsy in terms of seizures. However, there are many other problems facing the epileptic child because of misunderstanding and fears of those with whom he has contact. Through interviews with epileptic children and a dramatic vignette, the film points out the need to combat ignorance concerning epilepsy.

Programme XII. The Speech-handicapped Child—Physical Disabilities. The greatest need of modern times is the ability to communicate. Unfortunately, there are more children with speech handicaps than there are children who are blind, deaf, or crippled. This programme points out the various kinds of speech handicaps and the training which is given to help these children express themselves and find satisfaction in life.

Programme XIII. The Speech-handicapped Child—Articulation Difficulties. Stuttering is not just a "bad habit" but a problem which can seriously affect the personality development of a child unless understanding and more positive attitudes to the need for helping children overcome the handicaps of speech disorders.

Programme XIV. The Socially Maladjusted Child. This programme deals with a problem which has received much recent attention. An interview with a boy who faces serious problems in adjusting to society points up the need for channelling youth activities into constructive patterns. The causes of social maladjustment are brought out and a positive programme is proposed.

Programme XV. The Community and the Exceptional Child. This summary programme reviews the aspects of exceptionality and emphasizes that it is up to all of us—as parents, neighbours, and individual members of our total society—to do all we can to help all children achieve the maximum of their potentialities.

The Mental Health Film Council

Address: 39 Queen Anne St., London, W 1.

This Council has acted as a co-ordinating body in the production of a film:

"STRESS"—Parents with a Handicapped Child. The purpose of this film is to make people aware of the existence of the problem and to show the various ways it affects different families.

PART III

Some Inferences and Trends

CHAPTER 21

Towards a More Human Society

We modern people of the 20th century often blame those institutions where physical care was the only help given—and even this in a very modest way. Yet we should think with respect of those people who created and maintained institutions for disabled persons in countries where no legislation obliged them to do so, where no financial support from the state was available, where starvation was a common phenomenon and the life of a beggar the natural consequence of a disability.

(DR. MARIA EGG-BENES, 1962.)

General

1. Nine in ten live babies are born healthy, normally, and ready to respond fully to the stimuli of the world around them. One in ten is born *at risk* and may depend in some measure upon the humanity and skills of the society around them for their ability to respond and live happy lives.

Those of us who find it hard to identify ourselves with unfortunate children or their parents, might like to conjecture that in the history of each of our families, some children have been handicapped. Similarly, if future history emulates the past, each of us will be ancestor at some time to a handicapped child.

And if few of us can look back with particular pride to the past treatment of handicapped children, we can at least look forward, in an age of oceanography and space travel, to more effective help for the wounded or weaker of our community.

2. Prevention is young* and special education is in its infancy.

* In this connection it is interesting to note the programme on BBC television (11 August 1965) concerning "a new race of geniuses?". A new method 'of producing the infant prodigy to order in South Africa" was examined in a

The causes of handicaps are not always known, and where knowledge is lacking superstition can flourish. Today, however, we know that some children are struck at the very root of development, genetically or through some such cause as faulty arrangement of the chromosomes. By 1963 some twenty-eight different errors in body chemistry had been found to damage infants centrally or peripherally. A virus, an infection or an accident were shown capable of giving rise to different kinds of handicap or to combinations of these. If today every mother can be protected against the consequences of Rubella (German measles) which was found to damage the unborn infant, not all our mothers or sisters have been so fortunate in the past. Many newborn children have been saved from handicap by study of handicapped children. Meanwhile, the parents who formed the Deaf/Blind Rubella Children's Association help to remind us of our debt. And the following excerpt from the report for 1964/5 is worth study. Although only seventy-five children out of the entire population were known to this organization, their placement is as instructive as is the appeal in the final sentence.

At home

with no special help	11
with teacher of the deaf	10
with teacher of the blind	1
with teacher of the deaf/blind	3
attend junior training centre	2

In Sunshine Home	1
In Day Units for the Deaf/Blind	8
In "Pathways" Condover	5
In Schools for the Deaf	14
In Camphill, Rudolf Steiner Schools	4

programme on "The Exceptional Child". A decompression apparatus was used to eliminate the possibility of lack of oxygen to the unborn child. The treatment was reputed to have produced 4000 babies who later behaved like children twice their age.

In Unit for the PD	1
In Mental Homes	8
School-leavers at work	4
School-leavers at home	3

"The service set up by the LCC reported last year has now been extended by the opening in February of a Special Day Unit for six of the pre-school London children. Units of this kind have long been advocated by this Association and in wishing this venture success, we hope that the example set by the LCC will be followed in other areas."

3. In the prevention and treatment of some handicapping conditions, miracles have been performed by a few outstanding colleagues in a handful of disciplines in different parts of the world. The lives of some children who at one time would never have survived birth have been saved, though not always without some handicap. The lives of other children, already handicapped, have been prolonged and made easier. A range of aids have been invented, notably for the blind and the partially sighted, the deaf and the partially hearing, and various categories of physical handicap. New purpose-built schools have been designed, calculated to assist and enhance the education of those with physical, sensory, or intellectual handicaps. More precise forms of diagnosis have been developed, and there is a greater awareness that there is no sharp line separating the handicapped child from the non-handicapped—and that even with blindness there are degrees of disability and different kinds of resulting condition.

But for full advantage to be taken of the current situation, special education must advance to match the achievements of these related disciplines. The length and quality of training given to selected doctors, research workers, psychologists, psychiatrists, etc., must be matched by the length and quality of training given to special educators working with the severely handicapped. No intelligent society can content itself with special "education on the cheap".

4. For each category of recognized handicap today, goals vary as widely as does provision, and depend upon an interacting group of factors. Whilst these include the overall social climate, they also include individual influences, and the nature of the community (rural or urban, backward, advanced, or advancing).

Whilst exciting developments are taking place in several areas of special education, the overall impression remains one of captains without armies and of armies without captains.

In the past, teachers who had been inadequately prepared for the realities of the classroom, were an easy target for public criticism. Yet there was no section of the community upon whom more unreasonable demands were made, nor was there any discipline which could do more for a handicapped child once medicine had done its best.

Today, notable and inspiring as have been some developments in special education in England and Wales, few handicapped children can yet be offered a comprehensive range of community support, beginning before a child enters school and following him right through to successful placement in the post-school world.

Dr. Mary Sheridan, addressing a conference on "The Young Handicapped Child" organized by the Nursery School Association (November 1965), drew attention to the fact that all growing and developing creatures, including children, were subject to the interacting influences of heredity and environment. Whilst all children had certain basic physical, psychological, and emotional needs, handicapped children had seven additional needs. The community had to meet these in order to enable the children to compensate for their deficiencies (as far as this was possible) and make the best of whatever assets they possessed. The seven needs were summarized as follows:

(a) Early identification.
(b) Full assessment.
(c) Prompt medical and surgical treatment.

(d) Parent guidance.

(e) Appropriate education and training.

(f) Continuing supervision and regular, periodic reassessment.

(g) Final placement in the community or in special care.

Early identification, full assessment, training, and parent guidance depended largely upon the professional workers concerned having "a thorough knowledge of normal development so that at the earliest possible stage they may recognize and correct deviations from the normal".

5. *Special education* has not taken the form of a "natural growth", in each country, steadily improving and following a given sequence. If pre-war Germany revealed how easy it was for the work of an advance guard in special education to be destroyed by an unsympathetic or sick community, a wide range of smaller countries revealed that humanity was not necessarily proportionate to industrial strength or economic power.

If we still find in our own community people who are so inexperienced or immature as to wonder whether it is "worthwhile" to spend "public money" on handicapped children, it is more difficult to find anyone who applauds such sentiments as worthy of a humane, religious, democratic, or socially conscious citizen. If it is still necessary to point to the evidence of economic advantage in provision for some groups of handicapped children (e.g. the mentally handicapped and the ESN), it is rarely necessary to advance such arguments on behalf of invalids or the physically handicapped.

It is partly because of the curiously different approaches or attitudes towards handicaps which are socially acceptable and those which occasion fear, or even revulsion, that the separation of educationally subnormal children in particular is so controversial.

It is essential to recognize that hostility to the placement of children in special schools has not been limited to fears of stigma or to certain parents of educationally subnormal children.

K*

Segregation or Integration

Necessity, not the lack of potential in children, prompted the exclusion of some children from our crowded nineteenth-century schools, despite compulsory education. The same circumstances which gave rise to the exclusion of some, gave rise to special schools for others. This simple truth is again demonstrated with the growth of nursery school provision. Whilst nursery schools for normal children could take a proportion of handicapped (with benefit to other children as well as to the handicapped), a great deal depended upon the nature of the handicap, the behaviour of the child, the skills of the teacher, and the amount of assistance provided.

Given a tremendous shortage of trained personnel, oversize classes in ordinary schools, limited concepts of the nature of "education" and a public which narrowly sought "value for money", the needs of the majority provided the major consideration.

To oppose the trend towards separation and segregation was to be as impractical as Canute, unless the causes of the tide could be influenced. If to exclude children and ignore their existence was brutal, to care for them was at least to show compassion, whilst to separate some in special schools was in fact to begin making provision. Many children owed a great deal to voluntary organizations during the uncomfortable, if national, advance towards literacy. Those who opposed the provision of special schools (whatever their reason) were in reality reinforcing the practice of excluding children entirely, or of retaining them, rejected and miserable, within ordinary schools.

However, the point at which each handicap led to the creation of separate provision has not been constant from one local authority to another, any more than from one nation to another. More important still, the point at which any given handicap made exclusion or separate provision essential, has everywhere depended upon the community's attitude towards such children as pupils, or towards handicapped adults as workmates or employees.

The trend today is to emphasize integration with the normal community. In England and Wales, at least ten categories of handicap are today recognized as requiring special educational provision. Most colleagues recognize that the majority of these children should be, could be, or are given the special provision within ordinary schools. But those involved recognize that there is a minority of children who would be further handicapped if left within an ordinary school—and each individual case requires study.

It is increasingly recognized that some handicapped children—including some who have been left out of our school system—could be educated if given special facilities, special methods, more teacher time, and a special curriculum.

A further development is the widespread recognition that the exclusion of certain groups of handicapped children as "unsuitable for school" is unwise if not indefensible. It can only be acceptable to those who believe that (a) such children are "ineducable", and (b) that "care" has more to offer the child than has education. In practice, more and more health authorities have themselves turned to educational programmes for children in training centres—and some of the purpose-built training centres offer better physical schooling conditions than do some special school buildings.

The weakness, however, lies in (a) the totally inadequate teacher-training facilities under the health umbrella at a time when the children need highly skilled colleagues familiar with several types of handicap, and (b) the administrative barrier to the flow of educational ideas (both ways).

The dichotomy between health and education creates a serious obstruction to education advance. As one senior medical officer for mental health put it:

> Although under the new (Mental Health) Act, provided there is co-operation between the two authorities concerned with the education of children, the mentally handicapped child may have a better deal than he had in the past, the necessity in most cases to record a decision about the *suitability for school* creates a barrier between the two systems which leads to administrative difficulties and is not in the interests of the child.

The situation is more serious than is at once apparent, for "where there is a lack of co-operation and a reluctance on the part of either authority to assume responsibility, those children who are difficult to classify may well, in the future, fall between two stools" (Dr. L. M. Allen, Report of the Working Party).

Meanwhile many forms of organization invite experiment and evaluation. There might, for example, be an investigation into the value of a group of special schools for different handicaps on the same site or in the same building as a means of encouraging an interdisciplinary solution to some of the teaching problems, workshop problems, and related social difficulties. Experiments with the different kinds of nursery provision for some handicapped children also require expansion, evaluation, and encouragement. The two-stream special school (with one stream moving towards the working world and the other being prepared for a sheltered workshop) is already seen, in embryo at least, in two authorities. Special care units represent the growing awareness of potential in children who were once excluded even from training centres on the grounds of incontinence or other handicap.

It is possible, with teachers increasing their skills and with smaller classes being introduced into primary schools, that more of the children not put forward for special schools will prove capable of suitable development within the ordinary school. Equally, with increasingly skilled teachers in special schools, reductions in class size, and improvement in facilities, these schools may prove able to incorporate many of the children now excluded.

Advances and experiments in provision are likely to create a situation where special schools will more and more be responsible for multiply handicapped children rather than children with a single handicap. Even in the case of the blind and deaf, a need for special schools for children with more than one sensory handicap is recognized.

The child with multiple defects provides a particular measure of our concern. Not everyone, for example, yet recognizes that amongst children in mental deficiency hospitals there are some who are blind, or deaf, or have cerebral palsy, or are psychotic. A particular blend of disciplines is required to help these infants, including teacher diagnosticians of a special kind. As such children grow older, special kinds of regional or national provision will be essential to their progress.

Since intellectual development takes place as a result of the interaction of the growing children with a succession of environments, any restrictions upon such interaction, whether caused by physical, social, emotional, or intellectual handicaps, require treatment by skilled practitioners if the child is not to be "segregated" in some way or to some degree. That compensation is possible where the brain is unimpaired seems to be established, notably with the blind. The extent to which a society can accept its handicapped members in such intercourse depends not only upon the severity of the handicap, but upon public awareness and humanity. To summarize: it might be said that the majority of handicapped children can be educated in ordinary schools; that segregation is highly desirable if it means separate, skilled provision which would otherwise not be possible. Today not all children can be educated alongside others in the ordinary school or can work alongside others in the adult world. On the other hand, some children require separate provision in order that their health or confidence may be built up sufficiently for them to prove capable of integration with the working world at a later date.

Segregation, Streaming, and the School System

1. An advancing society makes new demands upon its members and reveals or creates new forms or shades of handicap.

2. Whilst a child's intellectual development depends in great measure upon his interaction with a succession of environments, not all handicap has its origins within the child. Awareness of socially induced "backwardness", for example, has made members of the public cautious about "streaming" in schools, a caution which occasionally extends to a suspicion about the need for

special schools for the educationally subnormal. It was abundantly apparent that a great deal of "backwardness" in the ordinary school was remediable, given treatment.

But the swing against "streaming" in ordinary schools was largely a result of social considerations. For non-streaming to be effective, particularly in socially unfavoured areas, there was a need for smaller classes, highly skilled teachers, and attitudes or philosophies in keeping with the social philosophy or objectives. Even so, it was not always recognized that the best such un-streamed school would find it impossible to contain certain handi-capped pupils, let alone attempt to educate them.

A further caution here is provided by the significant observa-tion made by *Education* (the journal of the Association of Educa-tion Committees, 10 September 1965), of the fact that the British Association had shifted its interest that year from the 11-plus examination which at one time aroused a substantial proportion of the population, to the 18-plus selection process. Even in this broad social movement, a substantial minority of the child popu-lation did not enter into the thinking of many of those parents who were passionately concerned about the 11-plus selection process.

3. Learning handicaps extend to or underline all areas of recognized handicap. Such problems invite the maximum atten-tion of any intelligent society. Traditional practice, however, has been in line with "backing the winners". As a result, inside and outside the school system (and extending to another segregated area of special education, the approved school), it is the most neglected area historically which provides the most pressing and current challenge: an area which has its base amongst those excluded from schools as "mentally defective" (although the mental defect may be an expression of other handicaps) and extends to the "school failure" who becomes a "work failure" and a "social failure". Fortunately here, too, new trends are making their impact. There is little doubt that the education of juvenile delinquents will gain considerably, when approved schools and other educational provision now under the Home Office become an integral part of special educational provision, and allows for a

simple system of suitable transfer as and when required. Meanwhile, those pioneering authorities and voluntary bodies which made the earliest provision for children suffering from neglect or from physical, emotional, or intellectual handicaps, might be excused an ironic rejoinder if they were accused of segregating such children. Whatever was originally intended by "equality of opportunity" it has come to mean for many parents, the removal of social obstacles to talented pupils wishing to enter upon certain favoured careers. What is required, however, is an equality of consideration for all our children, a real desire on our part as a nation to give each child what a wise and decent parent would seek for him.

More important then than the form which special education takes, is a study of the causes giving rise to this provision. Where the root cause lay in an insufficiently sympathetic society, the improving climate should help us evolve new forms of provision. But where the causes lay in the particular handicaps of the child; in the special needs, facilities, or methods required by the child as a result of the handicap, the changing climate should help us to maximize the value of the provision and lead the way to a healthy placement within the working world, the sheltered workshop, or the home.

Counting the Heads

How many children in fact need special educational provision? Lord Stonham in the House of Lords, underlined that we are guided by estimates, when he stated that 250,000 persons were "mentally starved" (July 1964). The numbers had "never been counted".

Some fairly broad guides to current need do, however, exist.

1. PRE-SCHOOL

Ten per cent of the children who survive the hazards of birth are estimated to be at risk. All parents of such children require guidance and special clinics which they can attend for specialist advice and assistance. Such clinics need to have close contacts with a variety of nursery school provision. At present there is only sufficient such provision for a fraction of the children who could benefit from it.

2. SCHOOLS

Not less than 0·54 children in every 1000 require training centre provision. Of the children in primary schools 20 per cent require special provision at some time, although comparatively short periods of remedial education may prove sufficient to restore more than half of these children to the normal standard.

A fraction of the school-age population (varying between 5 and 7 per cent) have handicaps of such severity as to make special "school" type provision, or a system of special classes, advisable.

Specially trained personnel are therefore required for not less than 5 per cent of the school-age population in training centres and special schools or classes, apart from a further 9 per cent, who are technically educationally subnormal within the ordinary schools. With a school population of 10 million in 1970 it could be expected that at least $1\frac{1}{4}$ million children require special education of some kind.

The very size of the problem has been one of the factors no doubt, which discouraged effort in the past—and accentuated the current problem.

The Intelligence Quotient

1. The IQ is neither constant nor ineducable. Its use in a prognosis, or as major consideration in deciding the removal of a child from the education system, is primitive if not immoral. Variations in IQ, whether due to the test, the tester, the emotional condition of the person tested, or actual growth in intelligence, condemn every inflexible administration and question any prognosis based on IQ alone. As Dr. Gunnar Dybwad expressed it: "studies both here and abroad have shown that an individual can

move from one group to another as a result of improved performance." Similarly, in their evidence to the Plowden Committee, the Association of Educational Psychologists cautioned: "William James said it long ago, and we would still agree, that no matter how well psychometry develops we will never write any individual's biography in advance."

2. Measured intelligence is nowhere considered an adequate guide to a person's ability to enter the adult world and be an acceptable and contributing member of it. The American Association on Mental Deficiency in 1959 published a *Manual on Terminology and Classification in Mental Retardation* which introduced a new behavioural or psychological classification which it added to that of measured intelligences: *adaptive behaviour*. In the same year the Department of Education and Science wrote (*Special Education Today*): "Intelligence is no longer regarded as a single factor but rather as a complex of many different abilities. . . . Teachers of backward children are therefore endeavouring to develop to the utmost the personal qualities on which their happiness and well-being as adults will largely depend."

3. The value of pre-school education for certain groups of mentally handicapped children reveals the importance of emphasizing experimental provision rather than mere measurement. As has already been emphasized, special educators have a part to play at the pre-school age.

4. Knowledge of the causes of a low IQ or of mental handicap is still limited. Descriptions of mental handicap are really descriptions of certain forms of behaviour. In 1954 the World Health Organization proposed the use of the term "mental subnormality" to describe an overall category which might then be subdivided into two major sections reflecting causative factors. (i) Where biological factors resulted in an impairment of the central nervous system, mental deficiency could be diagnosed. (ii) Where the causative factors lay in social, economic, cultural or psychological areas, mental retardation was diagnosed.

Some Americans use this terminology, but agreement on its use has not been reached everywhere. One problem arises from the different interpretations of "environmental" factors. For some these factors are viewed as being outside the growing individual, whilst for others they merely distinguish genetic factors from birth injuries or from damage to the embryo due to virus infection of the mother.

In the USSR there is a particular concentration upon the discovery of physical causes as crucial to the diagnosis. A concept of "oligophrenia" has been defined. But until there is a more effective translation system and a comprehensive study of the practice in the USSR, it will be impossible to estimate whether this kind of diagnosis and the subsequent treatment evolved for this condition is of help to us. It is necessary to note that in the USSR as elsewhere, the biological or medical sciences were at first isolated from the educational, at least as far as mentally handicapped persons were concerned.

The search for physical causes, however, is increasingly recognized as part of any diagnosis. There is growing concern today, for example, of the effects of slight sensory losses which if left undetected may lead to a false impression of dullness.

The Association of Educational Psychologists drew attention to a Special Educational Treatment Selection Test devised and used in a midland town to ensure earlier selection of children needing help. Children who scored less than 70 on a Moray House Picture Test in the autumn term were given the SETS test towards the end of the term. It was brief. The children were seen individually or in small classes by remedial teachers and the schools psychological service analysed and interpreted the result. Subsequent action was taken if necessary in conjunction with the Health Department.

Failure to select children for special education at an early age was considered to result in a complication of the child's problem and greater difficulties in the special schools.

5. Diagnosis is not yet an adequate science and the IQ has outlived its former role. Diagnosis must clearly be established as an interdisciplinary responsibility. It has little value unless it influences suitable placement and treatment. Psycholinguistic and

other psychological tests which seek to influence educational treatment may offer effective help where specific physical causes of certain conditions remain a puzzle.

6. The inadequacy educationally of the IQ and of medical classifications emphasizes the importance of a comprehensive and integrated schools psychological service or child guidance service. This has still to become a reality in many areas. Child guidance clinics and a remedial service should be available to an inter-disciplinary team responsible for diagnosing the handicapped child's needs.

7. In any reasonable prognosis today, four broad groups of disciplines have something to offer, and each needs to be aware of the others' strengths, possibilities, and limitations. The four groups might be brought respectively under the umbrellas of *medicine, education, welfare*, and *vocation*. However sketchily or inadequately, three of these affect each person from birth to old age.

Progressive authorities are finding ways to encourage forms of co-operation between these disciplines. Which specific discipline should take precedence at any given stage would matter less, if each was aware of what the others had to offer and could easily utilize such help. Administrative difficulties, however, encourage the proposal that all handicapped children up to the age of at least 19 should be an educational responsibility with specialist advice and provision readily available from health and welfare and vocational services.

Research

(a) Whilst the USA saw a need for an Institute of Research on Exceptional Children (1952), and whilst the USSR set up a considerable interdisciplinary Institute of Defectology (1924), the setting up of a distinctive British Research Centre of Special Education is only now becoming possible. There has been a distressing neglect of research and a reliance upon scattered efforts by dedicated humanists, voluntary bodies, and occasional geniuses.

Perhaps the greatest battle has been to encourage any kind of educational research, and here the activities of the National Foundation for Educational Research stand out in sharp relief. The NFER, due in part at least to its impressive leadership, was able to awaken interest in educational research in general, to point to the weaknesses of much that went by the name "research", and to seek to penetrate into the institutes and colleges of education as well as the schools by means of its journal, *Educational Research*. It is significant that articles on the blind, the deaf, the physically handicapped, the socially handicapped, the educationally subnormal, and other handicapped children were to be found in the pages of *Educational Research* and not left solely to the special journals with more limited readerships.

(b) Whilst the work of the NFER extends into the region of special education, it cannot be expected to act as a substitute for a research centre of special education, especially when the most substantial weakness in all branches of education has been the acute shortage of trained researchers. For any effective educational research, experienced researchers only with real knowledge of the classroom could be expected to ask relevant questions or see the more significant, if hidden, variables. With handicapped children, it is increasingly essential to train experienced teachers of handicapped children as researchers.

(c) A research institute will undoubtedly emerge as a result of voluntary efforts by the National Association for Mental Health, the Guild of Teachers of Backward Children, the National Society for Mentally Handicapped Children, the Spastics Society, and other . Current proposals will probably result in such an institute being embraced by an existing university and concentrating upon learning processes. Such a centre will no doubt find ways of linking up with related workers, and will gain from the new Chair of Child Development (1965) in London, the projected institute of defectology in the north of England (a medically orientated project proposed by the National Society for Mentally Handicapped Children) and with the National Foundation for Educational Research, to provide a new stimulus to educational research.

There is little doubt that the teacher-training courses for experienced teachers of handicapped children at various institutes of education and colleges of education, will eventually benefit from these developments.

The large-scale research undertakings now under way, directed by the National Foundation for Educational Research, the National Bureau for Co-operation in Child Care, and associated trusts and government departments, offer a substantial quarry for suitable research workers in special education. But research is required also into differential diagnosis, differential educational programmes, class organization, individual and group teaching, visual, manual and audio aids, time-tables, and other aspects of class and school provision and organization. The content of special education, as well as the best methods of helping children to absorb this, requires study.

Teacher Training

1. And so we come to the key issue, "the supreme essential", which has still to be confronted realistically. Mr. Percy Lord, a Director of Education, addressing a conference on "Welfare Limited and Unlimited", described amongst other things the role of the education welfare officer.

> Not only has there been a change of name. There has been a change in the character of the work. Before the war and indeed for some time afterwards, he was the School Attendance Officer. Nowadays truancy, except in the hard and almost insoluble cases, is non-existent and bad school attendance is not a common problem. The School Attendance Officer is no more. Now he is the Welfare Officer, the link between the home and school and between the child and the other social services. He is often the first to visit a troubled home; the first to put his foot on the threshold. Invariably he has no qualifications for social work except the qualifications of experience, and invariably and inevitably his salary is not commensurate with his worth. The best of them are priceless, and the mediocre are useful—but because they are unqualified they lack status and they lack social incentive.   [*Education*, 24, September, 1965.]

What Mr. Percy Lord said about education welfare officers applied in great measure to the remarkable people who worked in training centres—where only about one in five had paper qualifications of any kind some 21 years after the 1944 Act. Similarly, in special schools (other than those for the blind or the deaf) the majority of the staff had been given no opportunity for suitable specialist training—apart from their ordinary teachers qualifications and their own efforts.

2. In education, as in medicine, in welfare and in vocational guidance and training, specialists are required if advantage is to be taken of new knowledge and opportunities.

In 1954 the Ministry of Education's Advisory Committee on the Supply and Training of Teachers for the Handicapped estimated that for educationally subnormal children alone, a minimum of 10,000 teachers would require special training if one such teacher was to be available for each primary and secondary (modern) school. This modest conservative footnote has tended to be overlooked. Yet only with the provision of such specialists will ordinary schools be able to retain many of the children who are considered "educationally subnormal but suitable for special treatment in ordinary schools". Such specialists need training in more than one handicap, although educational subnormality should be a central consideration of all special training for ordinary schools. Such provision would leave the special schools free for more complex educational problems. But here, at least 5000 highly trained teachers for the ESN schools alone will be required by 1970, apart from about 3000 trained staff for training centres and allied units.

How is the immense force of teachers required in this specialized area to be provided? Who is to train the teachers? The Research Institute and the Chair of Child Development may make it easier to provide a teacher-trainer course leading to at least one specialist in educational subnormality in every college of education. But ways of overcoming current bottle-necks in teacher training are being actively sought by teachers themselves.

The Guild of Teachers of Backward Children, by setting up a College of Special Education (September 1966) sought ways of (a) providing an incentive to existing teachers to continue their interest, (b) raising the status of all who teach backward or handicapped children by offering membership and fellowship of the college, (c) evaluating short courses and other courses provided by local authorities, so that these might be included as part of a longer course leading to some qualification, and (d) various methods of recognizing experience and training, as well as providing correspondence and other courses. It aimed too, to provide an advisory and information service for all concerned with backward or mentally handicapped children.

3. But the need to reconsider the training of some student teachers as special educators from the beginning is only just being felt. The National Society for Mentally Handicapped Children is pioneering a 3-year course at a new training college (to be built in Birmingham) which may well prove the spearhead of a new development. It should be possible for such courses to be increased in number and extended in length. The practice of other countries in providing a 4-year course from scratch as "defectologists" with a status close to that of doctors, deserves experiment here. A special 3- or 4-year degree course in special education would attract the necessary recruits and make possible the planning of provision in a manner not at present feasible. Selected young people, with the right outlook, idealism, and competence, should be drawn into the work as others are drawn into medicine, with consideration for invalids as a central aim in their careers.

Special educators of this kind or with nursery school experience, will be required for a developing range of provision in different settings; in hospitals, special care units, diagnostic units, training centres, residential units, ordinary nursery schools, and even homes. Similarly: "in all senior training centres there should be facilities for education since it is known that in many of the mentally handicapped, the capacity for absorbing 3R work appears to develop in adolescence and education should continue until at least the age of 21 years." (*The Needs of Mentally Handicapped Children*, p. 70.) This requires the training of staff capable of educating older pupils with learning difficulties.

Voluntary Organizations

Pushed on by compassion, concern, philosophy, or necessity, a range of voluntary, statutory, professional, and semi-professional services evolved, sometimes isolated from or unaware of each other, but steadily weaving various patterns of co-operation and integration. It seems necessary still for voluntary organizations to pioneer the way, to demonstrate a need and the possibility of meeting that need, before the nation is ready to show some initiative in certain areas and expand upon or go beyond the experimental provision.

The National Society for Mentally Handicapped Children, for example, sees as its role the setting up of pioneering projects which prove their worth and lead to emulation. Increasingly, voluntary, professional, and statutory agencies have stimulated each other as well as reinforced each other. The challenge to the nation in this field is so considerable that a maximum pooling of energies is essential along with an encouragement of parents' initiatives.

The welfare state has been accompanied by an optimism about all human potential. Pioneers in special education, convinced of the educability of handicapped children, must be amongst the first to believe in the educability of the adult population.

CHAPTER 22

Postscript

SINCE the completion of this book there have been some notable developments in Special Education, motivating further advances. The most salient include the following.

International Co-operation

The Association for Special Education (July 1966) organized its first international conference on the theme "What is Special Education?". Amongst the 800 delegates from all parts of the world there were particularly strong contingents from both the USA and the USSR.

Wider interest in work going on outside the United Kingdom was also apparent in other ways. A one-month study tour of provision for brain-damaged children in the USA was made on behalf of her Authority by Dr. Mary Wilson, Staff Inspector for Special Education, Inner London Education Authority. Her report was subsequently published by the ILEA, and stimulated greater interest in children with *minimal cerebral dysfunction*.

The International Sonnenberg Conferences also attracted wider interest on the part of teachers. (Address, 33 Braunschweig, Bankplatz 8—Postfach 460.)

Internal Co-operation

Under the joint sponsorship of the National Association for Mental Health and the National Society for Mentally Handicapped Children, some 70 organizations joined together to promote a Mental Health Week. (The NAMH also announced that it would act as host to the 7th International Congress on Mental Health, 1968.)

Similarly, the National Bureau for Co-operation in Child Care took steps to bring together on an interdisciplinary platform all organizations concerned with children in need.

A Joint Council for the Education of Handicapped Children has also been set up, linking nine teachers' organizations concerned with different categories of handicap. (Secretary: Mr. L. J. McDonald, 19 Hamilton Road, Wallasey, Cheshire.)

New Provision for Research and Teacher Training

Some of the dreams of the past decade are now nearer to realities. The project for a Research Institute of Special Education has been embraced by Manchester University. The National Association for Mental Health accepted responsibility for the venture, and a grant of £100,000 from the Sembal Trust has encouraged all concerned to go ahead.

A parallel development has taken place with the project for a College of Special Education. The Department of Education and Science, notwithstanding the economic "freeze and squeeze" in 1966/7, saw merit in making a grant towards the Advisory and Information Centre set up by the College during its first stage. Dr. N. O'Connor, internationally known for his work with the mentally subnormal, has become the first Chairman of Governors of the College.

Results of Recent Research

The first report of the National Child Development Study (1958 cohort, see page 137) has been submitted to the Central Advisory Council for Education (the Plowden Committee) and published as *11,000 Seven-Year-Olds* (Longmans, 1967).

Eleven thousand of the 17,000 children born during a week in March 1958 have been traced and reported upon in this study. Information on the remaining children in the sample will be published at a later date. Meanwhile this extremely large sample of children reveals the problems presented to teachers, and must provoke some rethinking nationally regarding the training of *special* educators and the size of the problem with which they must cope.

Apart from the children who were already in special schools or outside the school system, 13 per cent of the sample showed behaviour indicative of "maladjustment".

Whilst the proportion of poor readers has decreased, 3 per cent of the sample were described by their teachers as "non-readers" and a further 24 per cent as "poor readers". Half the sample had not attained sufficient mastery of reading by this age to ensure success in using reading as a tool on entry into the Junior Schools. Teachers held the view that 5 per cent of their pupils would require special educational help (including special schooling) within 2 years. In all, the teachers were of the view that 13 per cent of their pupils would have benefited from special educational help were such help available.

The report stresses that these figures were likely to prove underestimates of the need, due to the influence of a number of variables which included shortage of provision.

The Plowden Report

This official report, with its determined call for "positive discrimination" in favour of children from poorer, socially handicapped areas, should provide a launching pad for special educational provision during the next two decades. A detailed study of the entire area of special educational needs (including those of children still excluded from the school system) is now seen by teachers' organizations as an urgent requirement. The pattern of educational provision is changing. The pattern of handicaps has not only changed dramatically, but with continued medical, social and educational progress will continue to change. If, notwithstanding teaching machines and programmed learning, we are still a very long way from *prescriptive* education, we are very much nearer to accepting that every handicapped child requires a *range* of services to meet individual and changing needs.

PART IV

Bibliography, References, and Index

Bibliography and References

Abbreviations

BJP	*British Journal of Psychology.*
BJS	*British Journal of Sociology.*
Brussels Congress	*International Congress on the Education and Social Integration of the Mentally Handicapped,* 1963.
ER	*Educational Research.*
FT	*Forward Trends.*
ICC	Paper read at the *International Copenhagen Conference on the Scientific Study of Mental Retardation,* 1964.
JMDR	*Journal of Mental Deficiency Research.*
London Conference	*London Conference on the Scientific Study of Mental Retardation,* 1960.
NAMH	National Association for Mental Health.
NBL	National Book League.
NSMHC	National Society for Mentally Handicapped Children.
NUT	National Union of Teachers.

Official Publications (HMSO)

1926 The Hadow Report, *The Education of the Adolescent.*

1929 Board of Education and Board of Control: Report of the Mental Deficiency Committee.

1933 Children and Young Persons Act.

1937 Board of Education: *Education of the Backward Child.*

1943 White Paper: *Educational Reconstruction.*

1944 Education Act.
       Disabled Persons (Employment) Act.
       National Health Act.

1946 *Special Education Treatment,* Pamphlet No. 5.

1948 Employment and Training Act.
       The National Assistance Act.
       Children's Act.

1950 *Reading Ability,* Pamphlet No. 18.

1954 *Training and Supply of Teachers for Handicapped Pupils,* Report of the National Advisory Committee.

1955 Report of the Committee on Maladjusted Children.
       Education of the Handicapped Pupil, Pamphlet No. 30.

1958 Disabled Persons (Employment) Act.
1959 Special Schools and Establishments (Grant) Regulations.
Medical Examinations (Subnormal Children) Regulations.
Handicapped Pupils (Boarding) Regulations.
Mental Health Act.
National Health Act, Amending Act.
1961 Handicapped Pupils (Certificate) Regulations.
1962 Report of the Standing Mental Health Advisory Committee of the
Central Health Services Council.
Handicapped Pupils and Special Schools (Amending) Regulations.
Health of the School Child, Report of the Chief Medical Officer of the
Department of Science and Education.
1963 *Half Our Future* (the Newsom Report), a report of the Central Advisory
Council for Education (England).
Children and Young Persons Act.
Special Educational Treatment for Educationally Subnormal Pupils, Circular
11/61.
1964 *Slow Learners at School*, Pamphlet No. 46.
The Education of Maladjusted Children, Pamphlet No. 47. Special Schools
and Establishments (Grant) Amending Regulations.
1965 White Paper: *The Child, the Family, and the Young Offender*.
Reports on Education No. 20.
Reports on Education No. 23, Department of Education and Science.
1967 *Children and Their Primary Schools*, and report of the Central Advisory
Council for Education (England).

Bibliography and References

ASHLEY-MILLER, M. (1964), The relationship between the development of speech and educational subnormality, *Medical Officer*, August 1964.
ASSOCIATION OF EDUCATIONAL PSYCHOLOGISTS (1965), *Evidence to the Plowden Committee*.
BARCLAY, J. L. (1960), The child permanently at home, *Community Care of the Mentally Handicapped*, NSMHC.
BATEMAN, B. D. and KIRK, S. A. (1963), *Ten Years of Research*, Univ. of Illinois.
BERNSTEIN, B. (1960), Language and social class, *BJS* **11**, 1960.
BLEACH, R. G. (1965), Transition from school to work, *FT*, Summer 1965.
BRENNAN, W. K. (1963), Preparation for leaving, *Special Education* **52** (2), 1963.
BRITISH COUNCIL FOR THE REHABILITATION OF THE DISABLED (1965), *The Handicapped School Leaver*.
BRYANT, P. (1964a), The effect of verbal instruction on transfer in normal and severely subnormal children, *JMDR* **8**, 1964.
BRYANT, P. (1964b), Verbalization and flexibility in retarded children, *ICC*, 1964.
BUCKLE, D. F. (1960), Early detection, *FT*, Summer 1960.
BURT, C. (1925), *The Delinquent Child*, ULP.
BURT, C. (1937), *The Backward Child*, ULP.

BURT, C. (1957), *The Causes and Treatment of Backwardness*, ULP.

BUTLER, N. R., PRINGLE, M. L. K., and DAVIE, R. (1967), *11,000 Seven-Year-Olds*, Longmans.

CATTELL, R. B. (1950), The fate of the national intelligence, *Edu. Rev.* **42**, 1950.

CHAZAN, M. (1963), Maladjusted children: trends in post-war theory, *ER* **6** (1), 1963.

CHILD, H. A. T. (1955), Studies in Education No. 7, Evans.

CLARKE, A. D. B. and BLACKMORE, C. B. (1961), Age and perceptual motor transfer in imbeciles, *BJP* **52**, 1961.

✗CLARKE, A. D. B. and CLARKE, A. M. (1959), Mental Deficiency: *The Changing Outlook*, Methuen.

CLARKE, A. D. B. and HERMALIN, B. F. (1955), Adult imbeciles: their abilities and trainability, *Lancet* **ii**, 357–9 (1955).

CLEUGH, M. (1957), *The Slow Learner*, Methuen.

COLLINS, J. E. (1961), *The Effects of Remedial Education*, Oliver & Boyd.

CURZON, W. M. (1960), Individual and family problems, *Community Care of the Mentally Handicapped*, NSMHC.

DANIELS, J. (1964), Research on streaming in the primary school, *Forum*, 1964.

DANIELS, J. and DIACK, H. (1956), *Progress in Reading*, Univ. of Nottingham.

DEACON, W. J. (1965), A survey of delinquency in Somerset, *ER* **7** (3), 1965.

DESCOEUDRES, A. (1928), *The Education of the Mentally Defective Children* (trans.), D. C. Heath & Co., Boston.

DIDSBURY, B. (1962), Planning a training centre, *FT* **3**, 1962.

DOLL, E. A. (1953), *The Measurement of Social Competence*, Phil. Educ. Test Bureau, Educational Publishers.

DOUGLAS, J. W. B. (1964), *The Home and the School*, McGibbon & Kee.

DOUGLAS, J. W. B. and ROSS, J. M. (1964), The later educational progress and emotional adjustment of children who went to nursery schools or classes, *ER* **7** (1), 1964.

DUNCAN, J. (1942), *The Education of the Ordinary Child*, Nelson.

DUNN, L. M. (1963), *Exceptional Children in Schools*, Holt, Reinhart & Winston.

DUNN, L. M. and CAPOBIANCO, R. J. (1959), Mental retardation: a review of research, *Rev. of Educ. Res.*, 29 December 1959, Amer. Educ. Res. Assoc.

DYBWAD, G. and DYBWAD, R. (1959), *Challenge in Mental Retardation*, Columbia.

EDWARDS, J. (1965), The pre-school child, National Conference on the Backward Child.

EWING, PROF. SIR A. (1962), Development of educational treatment for hearing impaired children, *FT*, Summer 1962.

FERGUSON, T. and KERR, A. W. (1960), *Handicapped Youth*, OUP.

FRYD, J. (1951), The place of the mentally handicapped child in society, *Mental Health* **10**, 1951.

GELLNER, L. (1959), *A Neurophysiological Concept of Mental Retardation and its Education Implications*, Julian Levinson Research Foundation.

GIBBERD, K. (1962), *No Place Like School*, Michael Joseph.

GIBBERD, K. (1965), *What Chance has your Child?*, Schoolmaster Pub. Co.

GODDARD, H. H. (1912), *The Kallikak Family: A Study in the Heredity of Feeble-mindedness*, New York, Macmillan.

GOLDBERG, I. (1963), Educational methods, *Brussels Conference*.

GOLDSTEIN, H. (1964), The efficiency of special class placement in the development of young educable mentally retarded children, *ICC*, 1964.

GOLDSTEIN, H. (1965), The effects of special class versus regular class placement on educable retarded children, *Breakthrough*, NSMHC, January 1965.

GOLDSTEIN, H. and SEIGLE, D. A. (1958), *A Curriculum Guide for Teachers of Educable Mentally Handicapped Children*, Illinois Supt. of Pub. Instr., Circular Series B3, No. 12.

GRACE, A. G. (1963), *Ten Years of Research*, Illinois, Introduction.

GUNZBURG, H. C. (1960a), The place of further education in the rehabilitation of the adult mental subnormal, *London Conference*.

GUNZBURG, H. C. (1960b), *Social Rehabilitation of the Subnormal*.

HARGROVE, A. L. (1965), *Serving the Mentally Handicapped*, NAMH.

HARRISON, S. (1953), A review of research in speech and language development of the mentally retarded child. *A. Journ. of Mental Deficiency*, **63** 236–40.

HEBB, D. O. (1949), *The Organisation of Behaviour*, Chapman & Hall, London.

HEBER, R. (1960), The concept of mental retardation: definition and classification, *London Conference*.

HERMALIN, B. and O'CONNOR, N. (1960), Reading ability of severely subnormal children, *JMDR*, 1960.

HIGHFIELD, M. E. (*née* Hill) (1951), *The Education of Backward Children*, Methuen.

HILL, M. E. (1939), *The Education of Backward Children*, Methuen.

HILLIARD, L. T. (1958), Common frontiers, *FT* **2**, 1958.

HILLIARD, L. T. (1960), A survey of the problem of mental handicap in broad outline, *Community Care of the Mentally Handicapped*, NSMHC.

HILLIARD, L. T. and KIRMAN, B. (1959), *Mental Deficiency*, Churchill.

HOPE, M. C. (1964), Prospects for ESN School Leavers, unpublished thesis.

HOXTOR, H. Z. (1965), Transition to work, *FT*, Summer 1965.

HUGHES, C. (1960), A parent's view, *Community Care for the Mentally Handicapped*, NSMHC.

HUNT, J. M. (1961), *Intelligence and Experience*, Ronal Press, New York.

IBE (1960), *Organization of Special Education for Mentally Deficient Children*. UNESCO.

ILLINGWORTH, R. S. (Editor) (1958), *Recent Advances in Cerebral Palsy*, Churchill.

INGRAM, C. P. (1924), *Education of the Slow Learning Child*, Houghton Mifflin Co. Boston.

INTERNATIONAL FEDERATION OF TEACHERS ASSOCIATION (1955) *The Adjustment of Handicapped Children to Normal Life*.

ITARD, J. M. (1932), *The Wild Boy of Aveyron* (1894), trans. Humphrey, G. M., Century Co., New York.

JENSON, R. A. (1960), The importance of differential diagnosis in mental deficiency, *London Conference*.

JERROLD, M. A. (1965), Proposed short courses for employment, *FT*, Summer 1965.

JOHNSON, G. O. (1963), *Education for Slow Learners*, Prentice Hall.

KEIR, G. (1951), *Teachers Companion* (Adventures in Reading Series), ULP.

KELLMER PRINGLE, L. M. (1962a), The long-term effects of remedial education: a follow up study, *Vita Humana* **5**, 1962.

KELLMER PRINGLE, L. M. (1962b), Backwardness and under functioning in reading during the early stages of the junior school, *Special Education* **21** (1), 1962.

KELLMER PRINGLE, L. M. (1964a), The social and emotional adjustment of blind pupils, *ER*, 1964.

KELLMER PRINGLE, L. M. (1964b), The social and emotional adjustment of physically handicapped pupils, *ER*, 1964.

KELLMER PRINGLE, L. M. and SUTCLIFFE, B. (1960), *Remedial Education: An Experiment*, Univ. of Birmingham.

KENNEDY-FRASER, D., (1932), *Education of the Backward Child*, ULP.

KERSHAW, J. D. (1962a), Medical developments bearing on the handicapped child, *FT*, Summer 1962.

KERSHAW, J. D. (1962b), Unwanted infants, *Public Health*, November 1962.

KIRK, S. A. (1962), *Educating Exceptional Children*, HM Co.

KIRK, S. A. (1963), *Ten Years of Research*, Univ. of Illinois.

KIRK, S. A. and JOHNSON, G. O. (1950), *Education of the Retarded Child*, Harrap.

KOLSTOE, O. P. (1958), Language training of low grade mongoloid children, *Amer. JMD* **3**, 17 (1958).

KRATTER, F. E. (1964), The rehabilitation and social integration of the mentally retarded trainee, *ICC*, 1964.

KUSHLICK, A. (1967), in *Foundations of Child Psychiatry*, Edited Miller, E., Pergamon, 1967.

LEE, T. (1965), Words in colour, paper read at National Conference on the Backward Child.

LEEDHAM, J. (1965), Programmed learning: revision in small groups, *ER* **7** (2), 1965.

LEITH, G. O. M. (1963), Teaching by machinery: a review of research, *ER* **5** (3), 1963.

LLOYD, F. (1953), *Educating the Subnormal Child*, Methuen.

LONDON COUNTY COUNCIL (1937), Report of a Committee of Inspectors on Backwardness in Elementary Schools.

LONDON COUNTY COUNCIL (1965), *Special Education in London*.

LUBOVSKY, V. I. (1964), Some results of physiological researches in defectology, *JMDR* **8** (1), 1964.

LURIA, A. R. (1959), Experimental study of higher nervous activity of the abnormal child, *JMDR* **3** (1), 1959.

LYLE, J. C. (1959), The effect of institution environment upon the verbal development of imbecile children, *JMDR*.

LYLE, J. C. (1960), The effect of institution environment upon the verbal development of imbecile children, *JMDR* **4**, 1960.

LYLE, J. C. (1961), Comparison of language of normal and imbecile children, *JMDR* **5**, 1961.

MARTENS, E. H. (1950), *Curriculum Adjustments for the Mentally Retarded*, US Office of Education.

McDOWELL, E. B. (1964), *Teaching Severely Subnormal*, Arnold.

McLEOD, (Editor) (1961), *The Slow Learning Child. Integration and Segregation*, Univ. of Queensland.

McNALLY, J. (1965), Delinquency and the schools, *ER* **7** (3), 1965.

MESCHERIAKOV, A. I. (1966), in *Backward Children in the USSR*, edited Segal, S. S., Arnold.

MONCRIEFF, A. (1960), Recent discoveries in the causation of some forms of mental defect, *Community Care of the Mentally Handicapped*, NSMHC.

MONTESSORI, M. (1912), *The Montessori Method*, trans. George, A. E., Heine-mann.

MORLEY, M. E. (1961), College of Speech Therapists.

MORRIS, J. M., (1967), *Standards and Progress in Reading* (NFER).

MUTTERS, T. (1960), Advances abroad, *Community Care of the Mentally Handicapped*, NSMHC.

NSMHC (1959), *Statistical Survey: The Education and Training of Handicapped Children*.

NATIONAL UNION OF TEACHERS (1961), *Conditions of Service in Residential Schools*.

NATIONAL UNION OF TEACHERS (1962a), *The Ascertainment of ESN Children*.

NATIONAL UNION OF TEACHERS (1962b), *The Education of Maladjusted Children*.

NATIONAL UNION OF TEACHERS (1963), *The State of Our Schools*.

NATIONAL UNION OF TEACHERS (1965), *Special Schools: Aims, Facilities and Amenities*.

O'CONNOR, N. (1965), How children do not learn, *FT*, Summer 1965.

O'CONNOR, N. and TIZARD, J. (1957), *The Social Problem of Mental Deficiency*, Pergamon.

OFFICE OF HEALTH ECONOMICS (1965), *The Cost of Mental Care*.

OLIVER, J. N. (1957), The effect of physical conditioning exercises on the mental characteristics of ESN boys, *JEP* **28**, 1957.

PAEDIATRIC SOCIETY SOUTH-EAST METROPOLITAN REGION (1962), *The Needs of Mentally Handicapped Children*, NSMHC.

PENROSE, L. (1949), *The Biology of Mental Defect*, Sidgwick & Jackson.

PENROSE, L. (1960), Biological Aspects, *London Conference*.

PEVZNER, M. S. (1964), The differentiation between oligophrenia and similar states, *ICC*, 1964.

PEVZNER, M. S. (1966), in *Backward Children in the USSR*, edited Segal, S. S., E. J. Arnold.

PHILLIPS, G. E. (1940), *The Constancy of the IQ in Subnormal Children*, Melbourne Univ. Press.

PIPER, A. (1965), *A Report for the Elfrida Rathbone Society*.

PRESIDENT'S PANEL ON MENTAL RETARDATION (1964), *Mission to the USSR*, US Govt. Printing Office.

PRITCHARD, D. G. (1964), *Education and the Handicapped, 1760–1960*, Routledge & Kegan Paul.

READING RESEARCH DOCUMENT 1 (1965), *Report on ITA in Remedial Reading Classes*, Institute of Education, London.

ROTHSTEIN, J. H. (1961), *Mental Retardation: Readings and Resources*, Holt, Reinhart & Winston.

SADLER, G. T. (1959), The Educationally Subnormal Boy of Secondary School Age, unpublished thesis for FCP.

SARASON, S. B. and GLADWIN, T. (1959), *Mental Subnormality*, NY Books.

SCHONELL, F. J. (1942), *Backwardness in the Basic Subjects*, Oliver & Boyd.

SCHONELL, F. J. (Editor) (1961), *Segregation and Integration. The Slow Learner*, Univ. of Queensland.

SEGAL, S. S. (1961a), Dull and backward Children: post-war theory and practice, *ER* **3** (3), 1961.

SEGAL, S. S. (1961b), Ascertainment of ESN children, *FT* **5**, 1961.

SEGAL, S. S. (1961c), *Eleven Plus Rejects?*, Schoolmaster Pub. Co.

SEGAL, S. S. (1961d), *The Teacher and the Backward Reader*, NBL.

SEGAL, S. S. (1963a), *Teaching Backward Pupils*, Evans.

SEGAL, S. S. (1963b), *Help in Reading* NBL.

SEGAL, S. S. (1964a), *Evidence to the Plowden Committee*, NSMHC.

SEGAL, S. S. (1964b), Working World Series, *Teachers Handbook*, Cassells.

SEGAL, S. S. (1965), Evidence to the Royal Commission on Penal Reform, *FT*, May 1965.

SEGAL, S. S. (Editor) (1966), *Backward Children in the USSR*, E. J. Arnold.

SEGUIN, E. (1846), *The Moral Treatment, Hygiene, and Education of Idiots and Other Backward Children*.

SEGUIN, E. (1866), *Idiocy: Its Treatment by the Physiological Method*, Wood, New York.

SIMON, B. (Editor) (1964), *Non-streaming in the Junior School*, Forum.

SIMON, B. and SIMON, J. (1963), *Educational Psychology in the USSR*, Routledge & Kegan Paul.

SONTAG, L. W. *et al.* (1958), *Mental Growth and Personality Development*, Child Development Monograph No. 23.

SOUTHGATE, V. (1965), Approaching ITA results with caution, *ER* **7** (2), 1965.

STEIN, Z. (1960), Diagnosis and prognosis by family type in the educationally subnormal, *London Conference*.

STOTT, D. H. (1960a), *The James Wykeham Experiment*, Institute of Education, Bristol.

STOTT, D. H. (1960b), Observations on retest discrepancy in mentally subnormal children, *BJEP* **30,** 1960.

STOTT, D. H. (1960c), Interaction of heredity and environment in regard to measured intelligence, *BJEP*, **30,** 1960.

STOTT, D. H. (1963), The assessment of mentally handicapped children, *Medical Officer*, October 1963.

STOTT, D. H. (1964), *Roads to Literacy*, W. & R. Holmes.

STOTT, D. H. and PASCOE, T. (1956), *Survey of Books for Backward Readers*, ULP.

SUSSER, M. W. (1960), Social selection of educationally subnormal population, *London Conference*.

TANSLEY, A. and GULLIFORD, R. (1960), *The Education of Slow Learning Children*, Routledge.

TERMAN, M. and MERRILL, M. A. (1960), *The Stanford-Binet Intelligence Scales*.

TIZARD, J. (1960a), The residential care of mentally handicapped children, *Times Educational Supplement*, 8 July 1960.

TIZARD, J. (1960b), An experiment in the residential care of mentally handicapped children, *Community Care of the Mentally Handicapped*, NSMHC.

TIZARD, J. (1963), Assessing the potentiality of mentally handicapped children, *Brussels Conference*.

TIZARD, J. and LOOS, F. M. (1954), The learning of a spatial relations test by adult imbeciles, *Amer. JMD* **59,** 1954.

✗ TRAPP, E. P. and HIMELSTEIN, P. (1962), *Readings on the Exceptional Child*, Methuen.

TUDOR DAVIES, E. R. (1965), Transition experiments, *FT*, Summer 1965.

VERNON, M. D. (1957), *Backwardness in Reading*, Cambridge Univ. Press.

VERNON, P. E. (1960), *Intelligence and Attainments Tests*, ULP.

VINCZE, ETELKE (1962), Special Education in Hungary, *FT*, Summer 1962.

VLIETSTRA, N. Y. (1963), The necessity for the scholastic training of the mentally handicapped children, *Brussels Conference*.

WALL, W. D. (1955), *Education and Mental Health*, UNESCO, Harrap.

WALL, W. D. (1958), Research into motivation, *ER* **1,** 1958.

WALL, W. D. (1960), Report in *The Times Educational Supplement*, 8 July 1960.

WALLACE, J. G. (1965), *Concept of Growth and the Education of the Child*, NFER.

WATSON, J. F. (1942), *The Child and the Magistrate*, Jonathan Cape.

WILKINS, L. T. (1963), Juvenile delinquency: a critical review of research and theory, *ER* **5** (2), 1963.

WILLIAMS, P. (1965), The ascertainment of ESN Children, *ER* **7** (2), 1965.

WOLFENSBERGER, W., MEIN, R. and O'CONNOR, N. (1963), A study of the oral vocabularies of severely subnormal patients, *JMDR*, June 1963.

WOODWARD, M. (1960), The application of Piaget's concepts to mental defectives, *FT*, Summer 1960.

ZEMTOVA, M. I. *et al.* (1965), The use of the remaining sensory channels in compensation of visual function of blindness, *International Congress on Technology and Blindness*, vol. 1.

Index

315

Text-books
  for pupils 92–93
  for teachers 90, 100, 127
Thailand 98
Theory 10, 81
  early contributions to 88–90
  and IQ 101
  pre-war 48–50
  see Research
Therapeutic atmosphere 19
Therapeutic education 124
Therapy 40
  speech 26
  see Psychotherapy
THOMAS, ELFED 33
THOMAS, R. 176, 261
THOMPSON, J. 262
TIZARD, J. 36
Trainable children 55
  see Handicapped children
Training
  appropriate 284
  commercial 20
  early 116
  pre-vocational 31
  social 31
  specialist 51, 130; *see* Teacher
  suitable for defectives 17
  technical 20
Training centres
  educational programme for 287
  for mentally handicapped 6, 8,
    64, 87, 139
  purpose-built 64, 83
Tranquillizers 40
Transfers
  to ordinary schools 22
  to special schools 64
  to training centres 64
Transition from school to work
    29, 34–37
Transport 15, 28
Treatment
  differential xi
  electric 40
  medical 118
  orthodontic 26
  see Special education

Truants 67, 68
  see Juvenile delinquency
Tuberculous 32
TUDOR-DAVIES, E. R. 36, 37
Tuition group (hospital) 26
Typewriting 19

UNESCO 153
University entrance 20
University of London Institute of
    Education 58
"Unsuitable for school" 6
  see Excluded
USA 54, 111, 113, 114, 116, 118,
    127
  and Child Guidance Clinics 51
  films **273–277**
  and incidence of handicap 54
  research in 129, 131, 133, 141,
    151, 154, 156, 157, 158
  schools 36, 43
USSR 98, 99, 100, 101, 103, 109,
    111, 113, 114
  research in 127, 131, 136, 151,
    294, 295

VALENTINE, C. W. 171
Verbal instructions 115
  see Research
Verbal reinforcement 110
VERNON, M. D. 60, 90
VINCENT, MRS. J. 230
VINZE, ETELKE 101
Visitors, Health 26
Visits 17, 144
  by parents; *see* School
  by psychiatric social workers 19
  by social workers 28
Visual aids 93
  telescopic 21
  see Audio-visual aids
Visually handicapped 148
  see Blind; Subnormal
Visuo-spatial disorders 109
VLIESTRA, N.Y. 96
Vocational counselling 31, 35